'A new kind of football writing developed — passionate, disrespectful, self-mocking yet steeped in personal bias. In book form, young writers such as Nick Hornby and Pete Davies became to the New Football Writing what Tom Wolfe and Hunter S. Thompson had been to the New Journalism'

Terence Blacker, *The Sunday Times*

My
FAVOURITE
YEAR

A COLLECTION OF NEW FOOTBALL WRITING
EDITED BY NICK HORNBY

GOLLANCZ/WITHERBY

LONDON

First published in Great Britain 1993
as a paperback original
by H. F. & G. Witherby
Reprinted four times

This Gollancz/Witherby paperback edition
first published 1994

Victor Gollancz is a Division of the Cassell Group
Villiers House, 41/47 Strand, London WC2N 5JE

Page 72: verse from *I Can't Help Falling in Love With You*
composed by George Weiss, Hugo Peretti and Luigi Creatore.
Lyrics reproduction by kind permission of Carlin Music Corp.,
Iron Bridge House, 3 Bridge Approach, London NW1 8BD.

A catalogue record for this book is
available from the British Library.

ISBN 0 575 05841 2

Typeset at The Spartan Press Ltd, Lymington, Hants
Printed in Great Britain by Cox & Wyman Ltd, Reading, Berks

CONTENTS

Roddy Doyle

Republic Is a Beautiful Word

REPUBLIC OF IRELAND 1990

1990 started on 4 June 1989. Ayatollah Khomeini died and Ireland beat Hungary in a World Cup qualifying game at Lansdowne Road in Dublin. We went to Toner's on Baggot Street after the match. It was well packed, hard to get near the bar. We didn't say much; we grinned a lot. The news came on. We pushed up to the corner, to the telly. I got into a position that allowed me to see most of the screen between shoulders and heads and inflated bananas and waited for the sports news, to see if Paul McGrath's goal had been as good as it had looked in the flesh and maybe, if there was loads of hush, to hear Jack Charlton at the post-match press conference – and just to cheer with everyone else. I clutched my pint into my shoulder – where babies fit when they're being winded or walked – and watched.

First the picture of Khomeini.

We cheered.

Then thousands of people grieving in Tehran.

–They must've lost their match.

–Ah, God love them.

Then Salman Rushdie.

We cheered again.

–ONE SALMAN RUSHDIE –

  THERE'S ONLY ONE SALMAN RUSHDIE –

We had already beaten Spain and Malta at home, and now Hungary.

–ONE SALMAN RUSH-DIEEE –

That left just Northern Ireland at Lansdowne.

–No sweat.

And Malta, in Malta.

–Easy.

Beating Spain at Lansdowne had been a brilliant agony. I'd spent most of the match watching the clock after Michel's own goal in the first half. It had felt good after that game but this was better. I was becoming brave enough to let the thought take shape: we were going to qualify. After years of close things, bad football, rain, short-sighted refs and fascist bastard linesmen, we were going to do it. I could tell: everyone else was thinking the same thing. And Paul McGrath's goal was as good as it had looked.

We beat Northern Ireland in October, three–nil, after a hairy first half.

Now for Malta.

The fog at Dublin Airport became the main news story in the days before the Malta match. The fans were stuck. Half of the country's journalists and RTE's cameras were at the airport, watching the fans. It was Ireland's boy-trapped-down-a-well story. The camera caught a woman in tears.

–I want to go to Malta, she cried.

Behind her, in the crowd somewhere, a male voice.

—Where's the national airline representative?

There was a travel agency rep standing up on a table, looking like a man getting ready for his crucifixion. There was a cameraman up there with him. A man on the ground spoke up to them and tried hard to remain reasonable.

—We paid our money, he said. —Three hundred and seventy pound cash it cost me, and we haven't even got off the island!

—Where's the national airline representative?

It was dreadful to watch. These were the Ireland fans, the loudest and best humoured in the world. Many of these people had followed Ireland all over the place; they'd seen them being beaten by Trinidad and Tobago and they'd watched example after example of the poxy refereeing that had made playing anywhere more than ten miles away from Dublin an inevitable misery. All that had been in the bad old days and now, when their loyalty was about to be rewarded, they couldn't get out of the country, and there wasn't even anyone they could blame properly.

The fog cleared on Wednesday morning. Most of the fans made it on time to see Ireland beat Malta two—nil. We watched the match in a pub on Dame Street. We cheered in all the right places and stood up and punched the air above us at the end of the game but it wasn't a great afternoon. We'd had that last June, after Hungary.

—WE'RE GOING TO ITAL-EEE—

QUE SERA SERA—

In June 1970 I was just twelve, in fifth class in primary school. The World Cup was on and I was full of it.

Chelsea had won the FA Cup. Two of the Chelsea team, Peter Bonetti and Peter Osgood, were in the England squad. They were the two Texaco medals I wanted most. I got them. My parents fed my habit. My father, I suspect now, filled his Volkswagen with Texaco petrol, siphoned it, dumped it and went back for more. By the end of the Mexico World Cup I had the full squad. I had seven Alan Mullerys and four Bobby Moores. My mother bought me a World Cup kit, containing a wall chart fixture list and dossiers on all the teams. I knew all about El Salvador's short war with Honduras over a disputed match result, crazy now but it made perfect sense then. In the second round of the Community Games Cup my team, Kilbarrack, got trounced nine—nil, I think, by a team from Finglas wearing brand-new El Salvador jerseys; I recognized them, three weeks before the World Cup started. My sisters got me 'Back Home' by the England World Cup Squad, my first record. I was allowed to stay up till all hours to watch the matches. I pretended I was knackered the next morning in school.

—I didn't go to bed till midnight.

—Huh, that's nothin'; I didn't go till after midnight.

I read and watched and never shut my mouth for the whole month.

—Uwe Seeler's balder than Charlton.

—He is not.

—He is so.

I never, not even once, wondered why Ireland weren't in Mexico, why there wasn't a dossier on Ireland, why there weren't any Ireland Texaco medals. I didn't miss them in 1974 either. In 1978 I watched a qualifying match in the student bar in UCD; I can't remember the opposition. The day was not Ireland's; neither was the ref. The bar was quiet. Then RTE's commentator, Jimmy McGee, spoke.

—And it looks like a case of Don't Cry for Me Argentina.

A stool rose out of the crowd and hit the wall beside the television.

In 1982 I watched Northern Ireland milling everything around them in Spain and I cheered them and hated them. I remember nothing about the '86 qualifying games even though I went to all the home ones.

In 1990 there were Ireland Texaco medals.

—I'm going. Are you?

—Yeah; definitely.

I said one or other of those things virtually every day in the second half of 1989.

—I'm definitely going.

Italy was no distance away; it was only down the road.

—Definitely.

Then came the draw on 16 December; England again, Holland again – the same as the European Championship – and Egypt. It was very disappointing – no Brazil, no Argentina, not even Colombia.

—I'm still going; are you?

—Probably; yeah. I'll have to talk to the wife.

It's-very-dear-in-Italy rumours pinged off the walls of every pub in the last weeks of '89.

—Seven quid a pint, I'm tellin' yis.

—Sixteen pound for a burger and chips, and he said it was shite.

Sardinia was miles from the mainland; it wasn't really a part of Italy at all. Getting from Sardinia to Sicily would cost a packet. Sicily wasn't really part of Italy either; it was nearly Africa. It was Mafia country; they'd knife you if you looked crooked at them; they weren't like the real Italians at all. Fun was illegal down there.

—It'll be as good on the telly.

I stayed at home. I was always going to. I was ashamed of myself. I'd never gone further than five stops south on the DART to Lansdowne Road to watch Ireland. The match and a few pints after, that had been the limit of my loyalty. Here was my chance now to really follow the team and I wasn't taking it. I'd been to Italy before; I loved it. But I wouldn't go. I looked around for a good excuse, and found one: I bought a house.

—Are you going?

—No, I can't; we're just after buying a house.

—Ah, no —

—I'd love to — but —

I'd shrug here. It was out of my hands.

June came. School closed. The opening match, Cameroon beat Argentina. The next day Arnotts on Henry Street sold all their Cameroon jerseys and the dry cleaners on Kilbarrack Road started a World Cup special offer — all your curtains cleaned for thirty-five pounds. It was looking good.

The Bayside Inn was packed but not loud on the night of the Ireland–England game. There were people in green but not that many. There were a few tricolours but they weren't being waved. There was no one singing. I was excited, but I always was when Ireland were playing. I was nervous, but I was always that as well. I'd expected more. Maybe I was too old. We got a table, one of those tall round ones, parked our pints and waited, and tried not to let our anxiety suck up too much Guinness. The national anthems; a few booed theirs, no one sang ours.

We heard George Hamilton, RTE's commentator.

—The moment of truth is almost upon us.

The game started; Lineker kicked off.

—Yeow!

We watched. We ooohed, aaahed, clapped but it wasn't much of a game till England scored. It looked like a dreadful goal then; the ball went over Mick McCarthy's head and Lineker seemed to whack it in with his gooter and crawl after it into the net. The pub went quiet.

—Fuck.

The replays showed Waddle's work and Lineker's triumph, a good beginning and end, but the goal in the middle still looked stupid.

Then a shout.

—Come on, Ireland!

And more shouts.

—Come on, lads!

No one condemned Mick McCarthy. It was early days yet. This was what we really loved, being one down with plenty of time to get back. It was kind of relaxing. We began to enjoy ourselves. The noise went up and people began to sweat. We shouted at the television.

—Good man, Steve Staunton!

The second half was more worrying. Time was running out. There was no sign of the equalizer. Paul McGrath gave it a ging; the ball shaved the bar on its way over. The pub groaned. The time had come to intervene.

—I'm going to the jacks, I said.

We'd discovered this years ago. When one of us went to the toilet a goal was scored; not always, but it was frightening how often it happened. There was a risk: the goal might not be for the right side. I didn't need to visit the toilet. I was the only one in there. It was pleasant; cool. The shouts from outside sounded less desperate. I suddenly felt lonely. I stayed, though. I unbuttoned my fly.

—Ah, lads; for fuck sake! — Come on!

I was pressing my forehead against the tiles and trying to remember the second half of the Hail Mary when it happened: the rush of human noise pushed open the Gents door. Either we'd scored or Lineker had run into the goalpost. My vigil was over. I didn't wash my hands.

I ran back into a sea of jumping and dancing people. They were up on tables, under tables, going wild. It was like I'd come out the wrong door. Kissing, hugging, skipping, there were men virtually having sex with each other in front of their wives and girlfriends. I got over to my friends. They queued up to hug me. I'd done my bit.

—Great goal.

—Thanks.

I watched the replay. A great goal, a wonderful goal; Kevin Sheedy, the man with the mammy's boy haircut. And the first of the great World Cup images, Packie Bonner gritting his teeth.

—ONE KEVIN SHEEDY —

—Go for another one, lads!

I remember nothing else about the match. I sang, hissed, laughed, groaned but I can't remember why. The crowd never quite settled down after the Sheedy goal. Nobody cared about the commentary. Our noise was blocking the Irish goal; we were there. Suddenly the pub was full of flags.

—Get your flag out of the fuckin' way!

Then the final whistle, and the place went madder. The roof stayed on but the foundations were definitely damaged. We jumped, dived, skidded, waltzed. I hugged people I hadn't seen in years. I hugged people I hated. I hugged the table.

—YOU'LL NEVER BEAT THE IRISH—
  YOU'LL NEVER BEAT THE IRISH—

When I got my breath back I realized that I was drunk.

—LA LA LA LA
  LA LA LA LA—

I walked through Donaghmede in north Dublin on Sunday morning, before our second match, against Egypt. There were tricolours hanging from bedroom windows, a teddy bear in an Ireland jersey, sitting on a tricycle, on top of a porch. I was going to Paul's house. We were going on to the airport to collect his brother, Eugene, who was flying up from Cork for the day because he wanted to see the match live in a Dublin pub. It was an all-ticket affair; the pub, apparently, had been dangerously full for the England game. On the way to the airport Paul's three-year-old son, Ian, sat in the back of the car and sang 'Give It a Lash, Jack' over and over. The whole country was waiting for the match.

It was dreadful. I don't want to write about it; nil—all,

the worst competitive game the Republic had played in years. Half-time wasn't too bad; it was only a matter of time before we scored. Frustration really got stuck in during the second half and by the final whistle I felt bruised and depressed. No cheers, no flags, no singing.

—The beautiful game, me bollix.

True, Egypt had drawn nil—all with the Dutch as well; maybe the result wasn't all that woeful. Still, it was disappointing, very annoying. Before the game we'd been about to qualify for the last sixteen of the World Cup, now we were on the verge of getting knocked out. The lovely spirit and atmosphere of the past week, the excitement that had been growing for two years, were gone; it was terrible – such a poxy game.

Then Eamon Dunphy said something. Dunphy and John Giles were RTE's panellists. They wiped the floor with the BBC and ITV opposition. They were brilliant, often funny; Giles wise, Dunphy passionate. I didn't see or hear what Dunphy said after the Egypt match. I read about it and was told about it the day after, and the days after that. Dunphy had said that he was ashamed to be Irish; he'd thrown his pen across the studio. He hadn't said that at all; what he'd said was that if Ireland were going to play like that all the time then he'd be ashamed to be Irish; he'd only thrown his pen on to the desk, hadn't really thrown it. I never found out what had really happened. It depended on who you were listening to; it depended on whether they liked Dunphy or not. Dunphy went to Palermo. Jack Charlton refused to be interviewed with Dunphy in the room. I read that Dunphy had warned English journalists to be there, that something like this was going to happen. Dunphy's presence was defended by some other Irish journalists; a fight broke out. Again, I never really found out what exactly happened in Palermo. I didn't like Dunphy much but he was entitled to be at the press conference. Charlton had always said that the way to play was to stop the other team from playing, and Egypt had done exactly that against us and now he seemed to be whingeing.

It was simple but ugly: you were either pro-Charlton and anti-Dunphy, or the other way round. Neutrality wasn't acceptable; no interest in football wasn't an excuse. The football didn't matter; you had to be for one or the other, him versus him. I was a Charlton man. I liked him; I loved the team – McGrath, Houghton, Bonner – they were all marvellous. They'd been dreadful on Sunday against Egypt, but so what? They'd been great many times before that and they'd be great again, possibly on Thursday against Holland. If they lost on Thursday it would all be ruined. There was always a gang of miserable little fuckers waiting for things to go wrong.

–None of them are really Irish, that's the problem.

–He's only in it for the money.

–Any nigger with an Irish granny can get on to that team.

For me, Dunphy represented those miserable little fuckers. That wasn't fair on Dunphy, but tough. I'd waited all my life to see Ireland in the World Cup. As far as I was concerned Jack Charlton had got them there. He had style, humour; he was honest. Dunphy hated Charlton; Dunphy hated lots of things.

–He's right.

—He's only a bollix.

Thursday night, the Bayside Inn again.

We needed a win; we needed a draw; we could still get through if we lost two—one. We needed England to beat Egypt; they'd be doing us a favour.

—When did that shower ever do us a favour?

The atmosphere was wonderful. Everybody was determined to go down screaming. Eugene had gone back to Cork and Paul had gone to Palermo, so there was just myself and Frank. It didn't matter; it was like being on a packed terrace, the only place I've ever felt at home with total strangers. A packed terrace with a bar running down the middle of it.

I'd been worried but not now; the game hadn't started yet but the result didn't matter that much any more. The memory would be safe.

Again, we went one—nil down in the first half. Gullit's goal was a good one, a one—two and a great shot; again, the Irish defence was snared.

—Come on, Ireland!

I spent the rest of the game roaring encouragement at the television, urging, pushing the team on to the equalizer. I wasn't just watching the game; I was on the sideline – fuck it, I was playing. I screamed and oohed and clapped. I bawled my approval when Ronnie Whelan came on in the second half; I clapped Kevin Sheedy as he came off. I was helping. I believed that then and I don't think I was the only one.

I didn't go to the jacks this time. I didn't have to. Packie Bonner gritted his teeth instead. He gave the ball an almighty boot up the field. Van Something sent a bad pass

back to the keeper, Van Breukelen. He made a mess of it
(– Serves the cunt right for looking like Howard Jones)
and Niall Quinn was in like – eh, Flynn. Quick, clumsy
and deadly; it was everything a good equalizer should be.
I watched it again. A slide along the ground; even better.

I saw a past pupil of the school I worked in. We
grabbed each other in mid-air. I hadn't seen him in years.

–Brilliant.

–Yeah; brilliant.

We let go; we had other men to hug.

–EAMON DUNPHY –

  IS A WANKER –

  IS A WANKER –

We got back to the match but it had stopped. They
were still kicking the ball around but that was all; they
were just messing. The players had heard that England
were beating Egypt. Mick McCarthy and Gullit had got
together and decided to take it easy. It was all over; we'd
qualified, into the last sixteen.

–EAMON DUNPHY –

  IS A WANKER –

  IS A WANKER –

More flags than had ever been seen in a pub before,
noise that condensated when it hit the windows, a
woman with her hair dyed green, a guy on a table leading
his pals through 'Ghost Riders In The Sky'; these are the
things I remember about that night, and a feeling of utter,
utter happiness.

A middle-aged man roared it twice.

–I love Ireland!

So did I. I was glad I was Irish, proud of it. I'd never felt that way before; I'd have been embarrassed to. Not now, though. I was Irish and it was a fuckin' wonderful thing to be. I can't remember how I got home.

The fans headed for Genoa. All sorts of stories went around: weddings and funerals postponed till after the next match; phonecalls home begging for more money; second mortgages; mammies posting tin-foiled ham sandwiches and flasks of soup to Italy. Men and women who were supposed to be back at work on Monday morning were walking to Genoa. Ireland were playing Romania on Monday. The real World Cup; the last sixteen.

It was the best Monday of my life.

The country closed and squashed into the pubs. I went to the Bayside Inn again. There were as many women now as men. The clothes were getting more and more lively; Ireland was becoming Brazil. Dyed hair, painted faces, flags, flags, flags. We watched the Romanian names on the screen.

—Are any of them orphans?

—That's not nice.

The stadium looked magnificent. Ireland's home games were played at Lansdowne Road, a rugby pitch, a bumpy disgrace, or at Dalymount, where they had to cut the grass on the roof of the stand at the start of every season. This was something else: pillars and cables, beautiful green grass.

We had a table near the telly. We had enough drink to get us through the first half. We were ready.

—Here goes.

Romania flew at us for the first twenty minutes but it

was always going to be a draw; I had a feeling about it. Sheedy came close twice, Quinn, Cascarino; Hagi for them — Bonner made two or three good saves. I remember one thing about extra-time, cheering when David O'Leary came on. We all liked David O'Leary, a great player and a nice man, a link between the old team and the new, the same age as ourselves. We waited for extra-time to end; nothing was going to happen. The penalty shoot-out was certain.

It seemed to take for ever to get going. The players sat and stood in the centre circle and tried to look like they weren't terrified. Jack Charlton walked among them, smiling. Then, there was Packie in the goal. Hagi placed the ball.

—He'll score.

He did. So did Kevin Sheedy right after him, walloped it straight in. They scored again, and Ray Houghton scored his, into the right corner. They scored again, and Andy Townsend. They scored again. I have to admit, I was surprised when I saw Tony Cascarino going up to take our fourth one.

—Jesus; he'll take it with his head.

—Give him a chance, give him a chance.

He buried it.

I was standing on my toes now; I couldn't stay still. I scratched my neck, I pulled my hair. Packie Bonner dived to the left and saved Romania's last penalty. He dived to the left and parried the ball and got up quickly and jumped into the air, his arms up, one leg slightly lifted. I was in the air too. It was unbelievable.

—He's saved it!

Packie's grin; I could count the teeth from where I was standing. It was marvellous.

We had to score our last one.

David O'Leary.

No one spoke.

He placed the ball. It took him ages. The tension; I was going to have to groan or roar; something was going to snap. He sent the ball up and right and it hit the net in a way that was gorgeous. The Irish squad started running towards him. He stood up, raised his arms and gathered them into him. He disappeared.

I cried. It wasn't the winning; it was the sight of the squad charging towards David O'Leary; it was David O'Leary standing waiting for them; it was Packie Bonner with his hand covering his eyes, almost afraid to smile; it was the physio Mick Byrne's tracksuit top flapping as he ran up to David O'Leary; it was the sight of the Irish crowd in Genoa; it was the crowd here in the pub; it was being Irish.

My wife, Belinda, had watched the match in town. She got a taxi out to the Bayside and found me drunk and crying. I ran over and hugged her. We went home. I cried again, watching the penalties again on the news. I tried to explain to Belinda.

—I had all the Texaco medals —

It was hopeless.

—Texaco medals, she said; she was trying to help.

—You don't understand, I said. —Texaco medals.

It was hopeless. I was too drunk. My tongue wouldn't work.

—Texaco medals.

She put her arm around me.

—I understand.

We went down to O'Connell Street. Every car horn in the city was being leaned on. We went to Beshoff's, got cod and chips, sat at a window seat and watched. The pool around the Anna Livia statue was full; people were queueing up to climb in and get drenched. Every car and van that went by had people hanging off it and sitting on it. Lads stood on the street, waiting to grab a car and cling on to it. Every tree and monument along the street was occupied. One guy sat by himself in a tree wearing only tricolour shorts; he seemed to be lost.

The food and the insanity outside sobered me up. Belinda saw this. She knew that all this was important to me.

—What about Texaco medals? she said.

—Ah nothing, I answered.

I'd never have been able to explain about the medals and 1970 and me when I was twelve and me now when I was thirty-two. I'd have started crying again. We looked out at the madness. The cod was good but the chips were shite.

(The day after, on the RTE news, I saw David O'Leary's wife — I think her name is Joy — being interviewed. She'd gone into the garden during the penalties. Their son had run out to tell her. She wouldn't believe him. Then she'd believed. I envied her and David and their son. I'd never have anything like that.

—Mammy, Mammy; Da's after finishing another novel!

—Don't be ridiculous, love.

—He has, he has.

—Oh my God!)

Italy next, the quarter final in Rome. The Republic squad met the Pope. I am an atheist and I think that the current pope is a bit of a bollix – I don't like the man at all – but I couldn't fight down the lump in my throat as the lads in their tracksuits lined up to meet him. They were all Catholics, the reporter told us. Great, I thought; and I wasn't messing. It was strange.

I didn't think we'd win. The Italians were brilliant; Schillaci, Baggio, Maldini, and we had Mick McCarthy to stop them. Slaughter was on the cards. Reasonable defeat was what I hoped for but I didn't tell anyone. It was Saturday night; the same pub, the same friends, Belinda. The game started. My left hand was in my hair, pulling away. McGrath got a great cross over to Niall Quinn and Zenga had to jump and stretch to save the header. I whooped and clapped. I relaxed a bit. We were good. Schillaci came close. But we were good. We weren't going to be destroyed.

Their goal looked great the first time. Something fell through my stomach as I watched Schillaci aim the ball towards the right side of the net. McGrath's foot almost got there but the ball kept going.

–Good goal.

–Yep.

We watched it again. Donadoni's shot, the power of it, Packie's save, the ball bouncing off his fists, Packie falling to the left, Schillaci, the side of his boot, in.

–Great goal.

Again. Schillaci running before Donadoni's shot, to be in the right place if the save wasn't perfect, Donadoni's shot, the save, Schillaci.

It hurt.

—Come on, Ireland!

I was glad that Schillaci had scored it.

—Come on, Ireland!

They tried. They rattled the Italians. They hounded them and bit their arses. They ran and slid after them and got in their way. They never let us think that it was all over. They charged and ran back, and charged again. The second half. Schillaci hit the bar. Schillaci scored but he was offside. But the Irish kept at it, kept running and bullying. They were great and I loved them.

Then it was over.

We said nothing.

The fans in Rome were still waving the flags, still singing. People in the pub were doing the same. I told Belinda I loved her.

It was over.

It was one of the great times of my life, when I loved being from Dublin and I loved being Irish. Three years later, it still fills me. The joy and the fun and the pride. Adults behaving like children. Packie gritting his teeth. Being able to cry in public. Getting drunk in daylight. The T-shirts, the colour. Mick McCarthy's long throw. The songs. The players. Paul McGrath. The excitement and madness and love. It's all still in me and I'm starting to cry again.

They came home the next day. Nelson Mandela was in town as well, picking up his freedom of the city.

—OOH AH PAUL McGRATH'S DA—

 OOH AH PAUL McGRATH'S DA.

The city was packed. Half a million people waited. We

got a spot on O'Connell Bridge. O'Connell Street was
smothered in people, every tree, pole and window. The
wonderful news zipped through the crowd: Cameroon
were beating England.

   –ONE ROGER MILLA –

   THERE'S ONLY ONE ROGER MILLA –

We waited. We saw the open-topped buses coming off
Frederick Street, on to O'Connell Street. From our distance, it looked like they were being carried over the
crowd. The road had disappeared. Slowly, slowly the
buses came towards us. I could see Jack Charlton, Chris
Morris, David Kelly, Frank Stapleton. Then they were
passing. I raised my hands over my head and clapped.

   –Thank you.

Then we went home.

Harry Pearson

A Season of Mellow Fruitlessness

MIDDLESBROUGH 1990/91

Someone once said that the true living drama of human existence lies not in success, but in failure. Whoever it was (Jean Anouilh? Archie McPherson?) obviously never visited Ayresome Park in the late sixties. Over a period of some five seasons Middlesbrough managed to fail in a way that was neither tragic, mysterious, nor even vaguely farcical. Presided over by Stan Anderson — a smoothie whose teddy was so precisely chipped it must have been the inspiration behind the Brylcreem 'bounce' ad — Boro simply cruised along without shock, scare or belly laugh; the post-war drawing-room comedy of British football. These were my formative years. They coloured my judgement.

Boro finished sixth.

Alas, such times couldn't last. Anderson departed. His replacement, that angular angry young man, Jack Charlton — the John Osborne of Ashington. The pitch at Ayresome (the finest turf in England — and that's official!) became the stage for gritty realism, passion and commitment; bestrode by anti-heroes with names that sounded like they'd been plucked at random from a textbook on Viking farm management – Boam, Spraggon, Woof, Craggs. It was stimulating, it was provocative, it was thrilling. It was all a bit much, really. To be frank, it was frightful.

Saturday afternoons of genteel amusement and polite laughter were a thing of the past. Now I spent each visit to Ayresome Park in agony. Every game was serious; each was significant. If we went one up in the first minute I spent the next 109 praying for the game to end; for the ref to make some horrendous horological error and blow for time ten, fifteen, forty minutes early.

And then we got promoted.

I just wasn't prepared for it. Of course I'd thought about promotion in the past, but in the half-hearted, it'll-never-happen kind of way you plan holidays in Papua New Guinea on freezing February nights when there's nothing on telly and you've just put your last 10p in the gas meter.

I knew the First Division existed. I'd seen it on TV. But it seemed as far removed from my bi-weekly experience of football as those primitive jungle tribes who periodically appeared in documentaries did from my family. Here they were, though, the faces that launched a thousand sticker collections – Willie Carr, Glyn Pardoe, Kevin Keelan – live, in the flesh. I couldn't have been more disorientated if the aboriginals had suddenly pushed past the camera crew, stepped out of the screen and begun inserting our crockery into their lower lips. I didn't expect to look out of the kitchen window and see a man in a loin cloth, lurking in the lupins, bringing down our spaniel with a skilfully aimed blow-pipe dart; and I didn't expect to see Emlyn Hughes at Ayresome Park either. It was an aberration.

Disgusted, I took off for Europe where I divided my time between the ski slopes of Gstaad and the gaming tables of Monte Carlo, sparing ne'er a thought for Middlesbrough Football Club.

Some ten years later, I had given up the life of a jet-setting playboy in favour of a job in a Soho off-licence. One summer morning when I came into work the manager, Roy, a Wolves fan, handed me a newspaper and said, 'Looks like your lot are going the same way as mine.' There was a headline about Boro going into liquidation. I said, 'Well, about time too. Bloody useless buggers. Best thing that could happen to them. Never won anything. Hopeless. Good riddance . . . '

And Roy said, 'D'you want to borrow a hankie . . . ?'

I started going again the next season whenever I had a Saturday off. Which as I only got four weekends off a year was none too often. However, providence was on my side. I got made redundant.

Because I was broke and living in London, I only went to away games. I travelled on my own. This made me a prime target for Lone Lunatics (Teesside Branch). In America a Lone Lunatic would probably come armed with a 9mm automatic and a celebrity's address. In England he is armed with either: a) a pair of tattooed forearms and a garish necklace of lovebites, or b) a copy of *The Big Boy's Book of Every Football Fact in the World. Ever* which he has memorized from cover to cover, and a carrier bag.

Lone Lunatic A stalks his prey on station platforms. He

relies on his intimidating appearance to cow you into becoming his companion for the day. As you watch him lurching towards you, you will yourself to escape, but you are powerless to move – mesmerized by the rhythmic swish of his knuckles scraping on the tarmac.

Loonie B prefers to strike when you are cornered in a railway carriage, or window seat. He slips in beside you, sniffing and giving off an odour of burgers and Biactol. He has cut off your line of retreat. You are trapped. Shoving him out of the way is impossible – he is wearing so much man-made fibre the static he produces could power an arc-welder; touching him would be like shoving your finger in a socket. He rummages in his carrier bag and pulls out his packed lunch. This consists of Wonderloaf and meatpaste sandwiches. Meatpaste is made from the off-cuts rejected by dog food manufacturers because they smell too bad.

Once at your destination Lone Lunatic A drags you into the roughest pub he can find within 100 yards of the home end. 'Lot of Portsmouth fans in here,' you whisper nervously.

'Aye,' the Loonie booms, 'I had a fucking good barney when I come in last year.'

Lone Lunatic B on the other hand leads you on a five-mile detour so that he can drink cask-conditioned ale so authentic it has splinters in it. Why do you go with him? Why don't you bolt? Because he has broken your spirit. He has subjected you to the merciless mental torture of interrupting everything you say in order to correct it: actually it was seventeen and a half minutes; actually it was John Mahoney; actually it was St Andrew's.

The situation was beginning to grate. Then in December 1989 I was at a *WSC* book launch in Terry Mancini's pub in Fulham when I was accosted by two blokes in suits who looked like extras from *Get Carter*. They said, 'You're Harry Pearson. You wrote the stuff about Boro.'

I thought, 'Oh Christ.' Because some years before someone had told me that one day my big mouth would get me into serious trouble and, though I had dismissed it at the time with a witty cry of 'Bollocks', somehow the seed of the idea had taken root in the fertile dung-heap of my imagination and grown and grown like a prize leek. Now it seemed like it might be showtime.

Luckily it wasn't. It turned out they had liked what I had written. This news came as such a relief to me that I forgot every code of North Riding conduct I'd been inculcated with since childhood. I broke down completely. I got a round of drinks in. (I didn't, really – that's just poetic licence.) The blokes were Mike Millet and Geoff Vickers of Middlesbrough Supporters South – an independent supporters club with discounted rail travel, a ticket allocation and a strict no lunatic ruling. It sounded ideal.

Often people who were brought up during the austerity years of the fifties cannot tolerate rich food. Cream is just too much for them. So it is with me and football. Excitement, euphoria, despair, agony; if I wanted that I could stay at home. No, when I go to football I do so for something bland and reassuring – a sort of sporting milk-pudding. And Boro hadn't dished that up for ages. In the previous five years they had: avoided relegation to

the Third on the last day of the season (1985); been
relegated to the Third on the last day of the season and
gone bankrupt ('86); been promoted to the Second ('87);
been promoted to the First via the play-offs ('88); been
relegated to the Second and got to Wembley for the first
time (ZDS, sadly) ('89); and avoided relegation to the
Third on the last day of the season again ('90). Things
had got out of hand.

However, I remained hopeful. I felt that the '90/91
season could see a return to normality. The turbulence
couldn't continue indefinitely and all the signs seemed
propitious: Colin Todd, a man renowned for his serenity
on the field, was now in charge; the close season had seen
the acquisition of perennial nearly-man John Hendrie, the
ancient John Wark, and a midfielder from Oxford,
Robbie Mustoe, who looked unlikely ever to become the
new Ray Houghton. Peter Davenport, £700,000's worth
of well-oiled goal-scoring machine (hem, hem), had been
flogged to the Roker scrapyard, and an MSS newsletter
report that described Mark Brennan as being reminiscent
of Graeme Souness had obviously set the boot room
alarm bells ringing – he was off-loaded to Man City
before he could seriously undermine team morale.

Things started promisingly enough too. A 0–0 draw at
home to West Ham was followed by a pleasant 1–1
away at Plymouth. Even successive victories over Notts
County (home) and Swindon (away) were counter-
pointed nicely by a 3–1 drubbing at Port Vale and a
home defeat at the hands of Oldham. Six goals against
Leicester and none against Newcastle seemed to suggest
that Boro were finding the requisite inconsistency for

mid-table comfort, and so it was with happy heart that I set off for Watford.

Because of its proximity to London, Watford was not an organized MSS trip. This meant I had to travel alone. (Actually, I wasn't alone. I had my mate Steve with me, but, as a Newcastle fan, he offers only limited protection.) Sure enough, ten minutes out of Euston I saw, swaggering towards us, a youth – red curly hair worn in a savage marine crew, phosphorescent skin and a love-bite so raw and immense the person who administered it could have found gainful employment as a ship's pump. After brief preliminaries his mission became clear. 'Give us your train ticket,' he grunted. I ventured to ask him why. He explained that he had not originally deemed it necessary to purchase one but had since become aware that travelling without a valid ticket was against the law and might result in a £200 fine and a criminal record. He was, therefore, entirely reliant on a fraternal gesture from a fellow fan to save himself and his family from disgrace.

I said, 'No.'

He said, 'Well, give us the return half, then. I can hand that in.'

'And how will I get home?' I asked.

'Bunk the fucker,' he replied logically.

Having reached a temporary impasse in his travel arrangements, the loonie turned to football matters. He'd been to see Hartlepool play Spurs. He thought Joe Allon might be worth a few quid. 'He scored about twenty goals last season and he – '

'Actually,' I said, 'it was eighteen.'

The loonie went so pale his lovebite stood out like strawberry jam in semolina.

'Er, right, lads,' he stammered. 'I'm off to mingle.'

The same bloke turned up ticketless on the train to Cambridge some months later. Funnily enough, I couldn't seem to catch his eye.

For some reason we had trouble finding Vicarage Road. This wasn't helped by my decision to get there by following a group of people I saw in the street who were wearing Watford scarves. After a brief tour round Boots and ten minutes standing by the continental meat counter in Safeway's, Steve suggested it might be best simply to ask them where the ground was. He was probably right, though I was kind of hoping that Beattie's Model Shop might have been next on their agenda.

The approach to the Watford away end is something of a footballing legend. Like one of those optical puzzles that used to appear in kids' comics, the more you advance towards it the further away you seem to be. You wander through allotments, past balding men in cardigans with spray-guns of phosphrogen cradled in their arms like Uzis, through acres of creosoted larch-lap fencing and tongue-and-grooved pitch-pine sheds, between cabbage patches and rhubarb beds, you lose sight of the ground completely and then, suddenly, there it is, back in front of you again. Unfortunately by that stage the bearers have panicked and run off with all your baggage.

When we finally got inside it was pouring down. We sheltered by the snack bar, amidst a fog of fried onion smells and grumbling: 'These burgers? Man, they wring the bastards out before they put them in the bun.'

Personally I never eat or drink anything that's been made in a football ground. Whenever I'm tempted I always remember the words of David Bowie after a visit to the Brunton Park tea hutch: 'This isn't sausage roll, this is suicide.'

Watford had survived the season so far without a win. As the game went on it was easy to see why – they were totally unlucky. Every time Rod Thomas got the ball they seemed certain to score, while Paul Wilkinson, sporting a Daryl Oates haircut, was rampant (albeit in the knock-kneed manner that was later to become familiar to us all).

Throughout a torrid first quarter (when you've followed football for as long as I have you just pick these clichés up) the only thing that stood between Boro and humiliation was Stephen Pears. Though he lacks the half-man-half-fish physiognomy of Willie Wigham and the dazed detachment of Jim Platt, Pears is far and away the best goalkeeper I've seen at Ayresome. Even a zapata moustache and a propensity for falling over whenever anyone in a Newcastle shirt shouts at him can't alter my opinion of him. Against Watford he produced a string of stunning saves. Then, with just about their only attack of the half, Boro won a corner. Hendrie floated it in, Baird flicked it on and Mowbray steamed in to score.

The second half followed much the same pattern. Watford attacked, Boro scored. First Paul Kerr (nicknamed 'Nookie' for reasons that have thus far escaped me) broke down the left and crossed for Ian Baird (who probably would have been nicknamed 'Nookie' if the sobriquet had still been available) to score with a diving, glancing header. Barrel-chested and with a face that permanently looked as if it had been on the wrong end of a pummelling, Baird had been a bit of a crowd-displeaser at most of his other clubs, but he seemed to have settled in well at Ayresome. He'd scored important goals towards the end of the previous season, including two in the final-game thrashing of Newcastle.

Baird demonstrated his greed for goals a few minutes later when he snatched another from the plate of Watford defender Gary Porter. Porter clearly booted the ball into his own net. But Baird was not deterred, claiming the goal; presumably on the grounds that his presence on the same pitch had been decisive. A 3–0 win.

Outside the ground, standing on a street corner in the rain swaying, a fat lad in a red and white cap wore a t-shirt emblazoned with the words 'Birds, Booze & Boro'. His kite was hanging so far over his trousers you couldn't see the bit underneath saying 'But not necessarily in that order'.

Brighton was next on the agenda. Before that Boro paid a visit to Newcastle in the Rumbelow's Cup, which gave Pears a chance to show that he always goes down well at St James'. This time on the end of a Mick Quinn slap.

A home win over Millwall followed to which John Hendrie contributed one of those brilliant goals you'll some day re-create in the garden for your grandchildren. Picking the ball up in his own half, slaloming through the opposition marigolds and crashing the ball into the back of the cucumber frame. Not that I actually saw it, you understand. But as Joseph Heller observed – some events in human history are so great that even those who were not there can remember them.

Happily this stirring run of success was ended by defeats at the hands of Bristol Rovers and Wolves.

The run-up to the game at the Goldstone Ground had not been a happy one for Bernie Slaven. Boro's top scorer for the previous three seasons had gone six games without a goal, a rare barren spell for him, and the fans were beginning to mutter. The thing with Slaven was that he only ever did two things in a game: score and get caught offside. When the goals weren't going in, the only reason you knew he was there was because the linesman's flag kept waving. And Slaven's offsides didn't come, as other forwards' might, from mis-timed runs, or as a result of well-drilled defending, but because he was loitering about like some playground goal-hanger. To see him twenty yards offside was not uncommon. With Bernie when the opposition had a corner you half expected to look down the field and see him leaning against the post sharing a fag with their keeper and arguing with him over the respective merits of various makes of moped.

The inevitable pay-off to this preamble would of course have been for Slaven to go out against Brighton and score a hat-trick. And who am I to argue with inevitability? Baird got the other in a 4–2 win.

By the time my next trip came around Boro had managed to slip into the top four courtesy of victories over Barnsley and West Brom, and back out of it again thanks to a home defeat against Charlton.

On the train down to Portsmouth, Andy Smith and I talked about Cliff Mitchell, the old *Middlesbrough Evening Gazette* football writer, who invariably began his match reports with a comment on the weather:

'Middlesbrough kicked off into a steady easterly breeze on a bright, sunny afternoon. Showers are expected later and these may turn wintry on higher ground. And now a gale warning to all shipping in sea areas Tyne, Dogger and Fisher . . . ' And always spelt Boro 'Borough' — setting it in inverted commas to show he was brainy and knew it wasn't a proper word.

Andy had been brought up near Ayresome Park and on Saturdays he would sometimes hang around outside the ground to see the players arriving or leaving. When he told me this I was lip-shrinkingly envious. I grew up in a village about ten miles outside Middlesbrough and never saw the players except on the pitch, which hardly seemed to count. Never, that is, save on one memorable occasion. My mum and I had been shopping in town. On the way home we pulled up at some traffic lights and I looked across to see, sitting behind the wheel of the vehicle next to ours, Johnny Crossan! By the time we pulled up outside our house, I was fit to pop. I ran straight up the road to see my best friend, Martin Dean. 'Deano. Deano,' I jabbered when he opened the door, 'I've just seen Johnny Crossan. *And he was in a car!*'

It was in the Red, White & Blue pub, Portsmouth, that I first became aware of a strange phenomenon — I was always the last person at the bar to get served. In the past, I had considered that being six feet five and having a nose the size of a small Commonwealth country was enough to catch a barman's eye (or, indeed, take it out). This was because I had never before entered a pub simultaneously with twenty or so hungry, thirsty Teessiders. In the Red, White & Blue I watched as a great pyramid of rolls was gradually eroded away until, by the time it was my turn, all that was left was a doily and a parsley sprig (just add mayonnaise for a tasty snack all the family will enjoy). This happened time and again throughout the season. By the end of it, in a bid to get served before the sandwiches ran out, I was wearing a luminous baseball cap, a revolving bow-tie and a t-shirt bearing the slogan 'Me Next, Or Your Wife Dies'. And they still only ever had meatpaste left.

At Fratton Park Boro produced perhaps their most commanding display of the season. It wasn't so much the fact they won 3–0, but the manner of the victory – they just strolled through it. Portsmouth didn't even manage to win a corner until well into the second half, by which time Boro were two up thanks to a typical Slaven six-yarder and a cracking goal from Baird who cut in from the left and whacked a low shot just inside the right post.

My celebration of former England 'star' Gary Stevens' own goal was somewhat muted. By that stage I'd visited the Fratton Park away end gents and was lost in reflection on one of life's great mysteries: why is it you never notice your shoe laces are undone *before* you wade through ankle-deep urine?

The following Saturday Boro were away again, this time at Oxford. That weekend my girlfriend, Catherine, and I were going to stay with her step-grandmother in Malvern. We were driving over on the Friday night and I planned to get the train to Oxford the following lunchtime. All of which would have been simple enough had it not been for the fact that our car needed servicing. At that time we were living in the Old Kent Road. With a degree of naïvety which readers who know the area will doubtless find touching, we decided to get the job done locally. We took it in on the Thursday morning. Those of you who own a car can insert your own 'My Hell in the Garage of Doom' story here. Those of you who don't might like to construct an all-purpose scenario using the following list of handy words and phrases: 'Faulty', 'Order up the parts', 'We'll have it ready', 'This morning', 'This afternoon', 'Tea-time, I swear', 'Can you come back Tuesday?', 'Incompetent', 'Bastards', 'Plus VAT'.

The upshot of all this was that we found ourselves driving along the M40 at 8 o'clock on a freezing November night in a car which, thanks to forty-eight hours of expert maintenance, had no heating, fading lights and a battery that was good for about half a dozen starts. Car mechanics, don't you just love 'em?

In a bid to conserve the battery we had concocted a cunning plan. We would only stop to refuel at a place we could also get food. That way we'd only have to start the car once instead of twice. Despite chattering teeth and rumbling stomachs, we stuck to this brilliant strategy with such grim determination that when we did finally halt it was not because we had arrived at Le Manoire des Quatre Etoile Pompes, but because we had run out of petrol. This was in Burford. There actually was a filling station in the main street, but in an attempt to preserve the atmosphere of historic Oxfordshire this kept pre-war opening hours. Unfortunately, as it didn't happen to be harvest time, 10 p.m. wasn't one of them. Left with little choice we checked into a hotel. There is no wonder tourists flock to this part of Britain from all around the globe. I mean, where else in the world could you get a double room, complete with candlewick bedspread, chipboard fitted units and a communal bathroom just forty yards down the corridor, all for a mere £50 a night? Yes, when it comes to value for money you just can't beat the Cotswolds.

The next morning we set off for Malvern and arrived in perfect time for me to get on the train back to Oxford.

I walked into the pub chosen as the MSS meeting place a tired, penniless and embittered man. 'What a bloody trip I've had,' I announced. 'The car broke down and I had to spend the night in a hotel with my girlfriend.'

'Sounds champion to me, like,' someone shouted.

Which only goes to show . . .

The game that followed almost made up for the journey. Boro, by now boasting the best away record in the League, took the lead through Baird after two minutes. Slaven added the second fifteen minutes later, following an inept display of ball-juggling from Kee in the Oxford goal. At this point, perhaps overwhelmed by the ease of it all, the Boro players nodded off, allowing Stein and Nogan to level the score.

By this stage the school children in Oxford's junior enclosure were going into a frenzy. 'We love you, Oxford, we do!' they shrilled, threatening greenhouses for miles around with destruction. 'You're back to school on Monday,' the Boro fans taunted, but to no effect.

The second period began with Oxford on top, Pears producing a blinding save to deny Foster. The juniors, wired up on half-time E numbers, went into overdrive: 'United! United!' they shrieked at roughly the same pitch as that reached by dragging a thumb-nail across a blackboard. 'Fuck off, munchkins. Fuck off, munchkins,' the away end chanted through teeth set on edge. At which point, probably fearing for their eardrums, the Middlesbrough players decided to do something to stop the racket. Wark slotted a long pass through to Baird who was brought down just inside the penalty area. He got up and scored from the spot. From then on Boro dominated. Baird crossed for Mustoe to score against his old club, then completed his hat-trick with another penalty after a foul on Slaven.

None of which seemed to dampen the enthusiasm of the Oxford mouseketeers, but at 5–2 nobody gave a toss any more.

By the time we got to Upton Park, Boro had moved to third in the table. West Ham were top. It was ten days before Christmas and the ground was packed. In the away end, the low roof of the stand reverberated with the noise, the air was chill with the sharp crackle of frost and anticipation; the pitch glistened under the floodlights. It's at moments like these that you know for certain why you come to football. Then the game starts and ruins everything.

Only joking.

West Ham dominated the match, but neither team ever looked particularly like scoring. Pears played well yet again and his opposite number, Miklosko, seemed so big as to be practically impassable without the aid of scaling equipment. A 0–0 draw.

It was mid-way through the season and Boro had begun to look unnervingly likely to drag me into yet another promotion nail-biter. They had become invincible away and suddenly their home form seemed to be perking up too. The festive season looked like being a crucial period for those of us looking for an easier life. We were not to be disappointed. The lads timed their slump to perfection. Between 22 December and New Year's Day they played four games and lost three of them. A 0–0 draw at home to Plymouth followed and Boro dropped to fifth.

Which seemed as bad a time as any to take on Notts County, fourth and unbeaten since November, at Meadow Lane. And so it proved.

Things started off well enough, Baird getting his gnarled cranium to a Wark cross to put us in the lead after ten minutes. Unfortunately County then equalized with an indirect free kick reminiscent of the one Pearce had produced against Holland the previous summer. The difference being that Pears did better than van Breukelen and got a hand to it.

Boro nosed in front again when Stuart Ripley shot into an unguarded net after Cherry had saved from Hendrie. It was the first decent moment of the season for Ripley. Troubled by injury, he'd had a wretched time of it. His form had dipped alarmingly. Ripley had always had big feet; nowadays it looked as if they'd taken on an independent life of their own and were locked in bitter dispute over which direction to go in.

County got their second just before half-time, Tommy Johnson wandering through a Boro defence that was apparently too busy pondering the question of why the Meadow Lane floodlights point at one another and not at the pitch. Regis scored from his cross.

Johnson put his team 3–2 in front shortly after the

break. Boro, obviously aware that I had not yet seen them
lose all season, strove manfully for an equalizer. With
eight minutes left, Baird flopped over in the area (a sight
which was becoming increasingly familiar). The ref,
evidently as keen to preserve an unbeaten streak as
anyone, decided this warranted a penalty. Baird (fresh
from his two-effort triumph at Oxford) and Parkinson
(never missed from the spot for the club) opted to decide
who should take the kick by engaging in a wrestling
match for the ball. Baird won and blasted it into the
crowd. So much for my days as lucky mascot.

There now followed a short intermission in the main
feature which allowed Boro to complete their Cup run.
Having knocked out Plymouth we were drawn away
against Cambridge United. Middlesbrough's record in the
FA Cup is a source of considerable irritation to me. I
know we've never really had a team good enough to win
the League, but the Cup? Everybody seems to have won
it. Wimbledon, for Christ's sake.

The sixth round, that's as far as we get. If we're lucky.

Not that I actually want to live through a Boro Cup
Final victory, you understand. Far too nerve-jangling.
No, I want it to have happened in the late 1920s, so I can
enjoy it vicariously. So when I was little my grandad
could have told me about it and exaggerated all the good
bits till they were heroic and comical simultaneously.

The trip to the Abbey Stadium had always looked like
being a tough one. A view that was reinforced by the
news that Pears was injured. His replacement, Kevin
Poole, was one of those keepers with the unnerving
ability to make the goal seem larger.

Nor was the sight of Cambridge's playing surface likely to allay our fears. It seemed to consist of two strips of ploughed field with a beach down the middle. 'If you think it's bad now, lads,' someone muttered, 'just wait till the tide comes in.'

The effect the pitch was to have on the game quickly became apparent. John Hendrie burst through on goal and looked certain to score, when suddenly the ball began to hop about as if it was being used for target practice by a Mexican gunfighter. Ping! Ping! Ping! Ahahaha! Dance, gringo dog! Hendrie eventually got it under control again only to be violently assaulted by a returning Cambridge defender. The referee was apparently using the 'two falls, or a knock-out' method of determining whether to give a penalty, and so waved play on. Towards the end of the first half Mustoe had a similar run in on the keeper. Again the ball bobbled erratically – this time off his shin.

In the second half Boro were simply brushed aside. The defence looked plodding and Poole was so reluctant to leave the safety of his goal I began to wonder if he was agoraphobic. John Taylor scored twice as a result and in the end we were lucky only to lose 2–0.

At the station I bumped into Phil Douglas. I asked him what he'd thought of it. He said: 'The ground was awful; the pitch was awful; the game was awful; and I wish I'd never come.'

Which pretty much summed it up, really.

Boro bounced back from this disaster with home wins over West Brom and Swindon.

Some people might consider that the best place to spend your thirtieth birthday would be in a jacuzzi full of warm custard with En Vogue. Me, I plumped for Selhurst Park with Charlton Athletic. I can't remember much about this game at all. This is not because I was rip-roaringly drunk, but because it was so dull I'd rather have spent my afternoon being lectured by a leading authority on the history of carpet tiles. Slaven scored the only goal.

Boro's mini revival was ended in the next game with a home defeat by Portsmouth. Consecutive 0–0 draws against Oxford and Hull followed. Then Newcastle arrived at Ayresome for their customary defeat and duly got it, 3–0.

Which brought us to Filbert Street. I could go on about Leicester for hours, but when I was a kid my mother always used to tell me: 'If you can't say something nice, then don't say anything.' So I won't. We lost 4–3.

The following Wednesday we played Millwall at the Den. Say what you like about the Lions, they certainly commanded regional loyalty. In most towns or areas in Britain you'd expect to see the kids wearing a mixture of team shirts and colours with the local club's predominating. In Bermondsey and the Old Kent Road you never saw anything other than Millwall's. Positive proof of the effectiveness of the club's football in the community scheme. And the power of fear.

When we'd first moved to SE1 I'd been walking along Leathermarket Street. There was a boy sitting on a wall. He was about eight and he was wearing a Millwall sweatshirt. When I came level with him he said, 'Oi, mister. What team you support?' 'Middlesbrough,' I replied, bold as brass (he was only little – I was certain I could outrun him).

I walked on and when I got a few yards past him I suddenly heard the kid singing, 'Sign on, sign on. Cos you'll never get a job, you'll never get a job.' Astonished, I turned round. When he saw me looking at him the kid fished in his pocket and pulled out a coin. 'Here's 10p,' he shouted. 'Buy yourself a house.'

A storming Boro victory seemed the most fitting form of revenge to inflict on this urchin (though a persistent, irritating skin disease would have done almost as well).

In the first half this didn't seem likely to come. Boro's problems between the sticks continued. Pears had suffered a long-term injury, Poole had, unsurprisingly, lost favour and Andy Dibble had been brought in on loan. Dibble was a good shot-stopper, but when he came out to claim a cross he looked more like Wayne Sleep flagging a taxi than a goalkeeper. The problem was compounded by the absence of Simon Coleman which left a distinct lack of height at the back. Millwall discovered these faults for themselves after five minutes, when a corner was headed home unchallenged. Fifteen minutes later, a second lofted ball into the box and they were two up. Somehow Boro survived the rest of the first half and the first fifteen minutes of the second without conceding another, at which point Colin Todd introduced his secret weapon. This came in the unlikely guise of 'Nookie' Kerr, who had recently been dropped from the first team after displaying an appetite for the game that had left him in severe danger of being diagnosed anorexic. Now, however, he raced on and single-handedly transformed the match (cynics might conclude that this miraculous change in Kerr's attitude was not unconnected with rumours that

Millwall's boss, former Boro manager Bruce Rioch, had expressed an interest in signing him. If so, 'Nookie's' ploy worked – he was at the Den before the season was out). Within two minutes of coming on, Kerr had pulled a goal back. He seemed to be everywhere, a regular whirling dervish. Millwall were so bamboozled by this performance that when Wark hit a speculative shot from so far out he was almost stepping on the toes of the bouncers at the Frog & Nightgown, they simply watched it trickle into the net. For the final ten minutes Boro battered away at the Millwall goal, but couldn't quite manage a winner.

The remainder of March and all of April saw Boro continue on their inconsistent path. By now it seemed odds-on that Wednesday, West Ham and Oldham were destined for automatic promotion. Boro would have to content themselves with a place in the play-offs. Despite form that was at best indifferent, they never seemed likely to miss out on one. Eventually they finished seventh, by avoiding a four-goal defeat away at Barnsley in the final League game. Of the other play-off contenders only Notts County had recorded a victory over Boro that season. Which was a tad unfortunate as it was them we had to play.

The first leg of the semi-final, at Ayresome, ended in a 1–1 draw. It was an intensely physical game. Neil Warnock, the County manager, seemed to have picked up plenty of plaudits from the media that season, but watching his team play it was hard to see why. They were robust to the point of brutality and, despite skilful individuals like Johnson and Bartlett, never seemed likely to entertain.

After Boro's previous display at Meadow Lane and the débâcle at Cambridge, that other arch long-ball results-machine, I didn't travel with much hope. Ripley who had recently come back into form, was injured, Slaven, who had been throwing paddies off and on all season, was sulking again and Pears was still out.

It was a warm, sunny evening in Nottingham and virtually every pub in the place was shut. Simon Chapman and I sat by the canal eating chips. There was the musty smell of approaching summer in the air; a mood of lethargy.

The game, which should have been the most exciting of the season, was pitiful; about as enjoyable as being trapped in a lift with a Jehovah's Witness. A bloke standing near me kept shouting, 'Get a goal, lads, and we'll sing you home.' But Boro never seemed likely to score, while the tedium numbed the whole crowd into silence. It was a match neither side deserved to win. Though County did, with a goal in the seventy-fifth minute. When the final whistle blew I watched Tony Mowbray sink to his knees, his head bowed. If anyone deserved better it was him. All season he'd thrown his battered body about the place with the same disregard a builder shows for a firm's Transit. If there's ever anyone who embodies the town of Middlesbrough more than Tony Mowbray, then I certainly wouldn't like to meet him.

Afterwards we drove back to London. No one said much. Ian Magor was reading Jose Torres' book about Muhammad Ali. A phone-in about pit-bull terriers was on the radio. We got in just before midnight. And that was that.

Not much of a season, you might think. Little lost, and certainly nothing won. If you were a Man United or Liverpool fan you'd probably have found it rather dull. Me, I enjoyed it. But then, when it comes to Middlesbrough FC, I'd seen enough in previous years to recognize the deep truth of that old Chinese blessing: 'May you never live in interesting times.'

And the following season we got promoted.

Harry Ritchie

Take My Whole Life Too

RAITH ROVERS 1992/3

The bloke at the next table finished his Sunday brunch (glass of red wine, mushrooms in tomato sauce, a bowl of what may well have been squid), bantered incomprehensibly with a passing chum and swaggered off down to the beach. Among the debris on his table was a scrunched-up newspaper.

It was a long shot but you never knew . . . Promisingly, the front page carried a big colour photo of Linford Christie unbelievingly breasting the tape. There was more Olympic stuff in the news pages – local heroes winning wrestling bouts or triumphing in heats of the egg-and-spoon race – but God alone knew where the proper sports pages where hidden. Some frantic rustling later, I made out a headline which indicated that Maradona may or may not have said or done something in, at or concerning Seville. I scanned the page, then its neighbour, until I spotted the small type of the results. Olympic matches, native pre-season friendlies, then – way hay! – Escocia. And not just the Premier League but the First and Second Divisions as well. Presumably this was not because the locals were passionate supporters of Clydebank or Arbroath, but because there are few countries in the northern hemisphere in which the football season starts on the fresh, cool, blustery date of 1 August.

With a heart grown heavy from decades of coping with failure, misery and angst, I followed the alphabet down the column. We were playing St Mirren, hot favourites to cream the division and return to the Premier League, whence they had just been surprisingly relegated. It was only a few years back that I'd watched them against Dundee United in the Cup Final. Never mind that the game was atrocious and the result a travesty, St Mirren had won the damned thing. If not a sleeping giant, St Mirren were certainly quite a big lad having a nap. A draw at home would do me fine. I braced myself. Well, I thought, there are other things in life. A few deep breaths and I forced myself to read the score.

Rath Rover 7 St Miren 0.

Seven. It was the best misprint I'd ever seen. Maybe it was supposed to be a 1. But the fact that we had some kind of number and St Miren had 0 meant we'd won. Unless of course, they'd really scored 10.

The British Sunday newspapers arrived the next day, to ruin what had been a pretty good holiday. Dalziel (3), Brewster (2), Dair and Coyle had been Raith's scorers. So what the hell was I doing on the Costa del Sol? Why hadn't I spent this fortnight back in Kirkcaldy? *And* we were at home for the next match as well, *and* we were playing Stirling Albion. Christ, if we could stuff St Mirren 7–0, how many would we get against that bunch?

Next Sunday morning, I invested in my own copy of a

Spanish newspaper – puzzling the woman in the shop who couldn't understand the fact that I didn't understand a word of her jabbering – found myself a café, ordered a celebratory beer and flicked through the meaningless paper to the results. Stirling Albion? Easy peasy. They were fall-guys, no-hopers, rabbits.

Rait Rovers 0 Stirling Ablio 0.

Well, another 27 points from the remaining 42 matches and we might avoid relegation.

My rueful reflections on our achievement on holding the might of Stirling to a draw were interrupted by someone gabbling at me. A swarthy type who seemed to want to borrow the paper and had, not unreasonably, assumed I was, or at least spoke, Spanish. And who turned out to be more than keen to practise his English.

Spotting an article about Barcelona's summer transfers, he embarked on a stumbling but enthusiastic account of how he had celebrated a couple of months back when they nicked the title from Real Madrid on the last day of the season. Maybe he didn't know how to say 'spectacular bout of heavy drinking' or 'stoned out of my skull', but his celebrations seemed to consist of three days' constant driving around town waving a flag out of his sun roof.

I smiled encouragingly and nodded, feeling only the faintest ache of envy. I could cope with this. I had three decades of practice in accepting the fact that I'd never drive around Kirkcaldy waving a Rovers flag in celebration. I think I'd known that even three decades ago, when it dawned on me that they weren't really near the top of the League if they played at Airdrie or Ayr. So I'm quite happy to listen to friends telling me what it was like when Dundee United won the League, just exactly how they felt when Thomas scored at Anfield. Really. It's fine. It requires a bit of self-control, but only that of a lifelong eunuch listening to Rod Stewart chat about his sex life.

Not that Raith hadn't given me weeks of pride. Not so long ago, we'd held Rangers to a draw at home to them in the Cup. In 1967, when I was nine, I'd been one of thousands in Stark's Park to watch the Rovers beat Queen of the South 7–2, thereby winning promotion. Along with a place in media folklore, when someone on 'Grandstand' – could it have been Coleman? – avowed, 'They'll be dancing in the streets of Raith.'

The imaginary streets of Raith, alas, had seen no dancing in my lifetime. Nor would they. You supported Raith because you came from Kirkcaldy, and you supported them in the hope not that they would win anything but that they would avoid shame and catastrophe. To expect anything more you'd have to be as mad as a bucket. As well plan a romance with Cindy Crawford.

My father had consoling tales to tell me of our heyday in the fifties, when teams could still be recited, and the names he intoned – 'Young, McNaught and Leigh, what a trio!' – had brought us neither cups nor medals but heroic exploits. I'd been brought up on stories of these greats – how Willie Penman was so fast he'd once crossed a ball to himself, how McNaught was the best left foot in Scotland, how, in a semi-final goalmouth scramble, a prone Penman had tried to blow the ball into the net. My Dad had a special affection for Penman, our record goalscorer and a 'character'. According to my father, Penman had once fallen asleep in the post-match bath, avoiding death by drowning only when a team-mate noticed amid the steamy fug that Willie was missing. Another favourite story described how Penman had once been knocked unconscious and revived with the trainer's smelling salts, which Raith's record goalscorer promptly swallowed. Just how faithful these stories were to reality I don't know, for my Dad has a certain gift for . . . anecdotal exaggeration. But even he couldn't make up their fourth-place finish in 1957's First Division, and their semi-finals against Celtic and Falkirk.

We had a few other claims to fame. It was Raith that introduced to Scotland in the twenties a revolutionary training method – ball practice. Alex James started out with us. So did Jim Baxter. As a child I'd seen Ian Porterfield score two for us at a frighteningly dark and massive Ibrox. A game we lost 10–2, but win some, lose some . . .

That's not quite accurate. Draw some, lose a lot more was Raith's formula after 1967 and, therefore, the one I had grown up knowing. For three years we flirted outrageously with relegation to the Second Division, and then in 1970 relegation finally got us drunk, dragged us to bed and stole our honour. Despoiled, abandoned, we'd had a few empty flings with the likes of Stenhousemuir and Berwick, then reconciled ourselves, after League reconstruction in 1975, to the ruination of life in what was effectively the Third Division.

I had left home by that time to spend four years in an Edinburgh made especially enticing by Hibs, with whom

I'd cultivated a mildly desperate infatuation. An adolescent thing, a phase I had to go through, and I'm not proud of it.

The phase passed quickly enough, but then I moved abroad, to England, and started following Raith from exile. It was a painful time. I rarely made it home to see them, my support being confined to toilet graffiti and a campaign to force English chums to recognize that Raith Rovers was not the creation of the *Beano* or *Hotspur*, and not pronounced with two Ws. And on the infrequent occasions that I did make it home to see them, the Rovers proved themselves to be resolutely crap. With the exception of the '80/81 season when, for a time, we were rather good. Feeling no trace of my pubescent folly, I saw the Rovers slaughter Hibs, then top of the First, 2–0. Raith were three points behind them with three games in hand. A swish new seating area was built to replace the crumbling Railway Stand, in preparation for our entry to the Premier League. But of course we blew it. The Premier was an absurd prospect. Our rightful place was the one we occupied for a dozen years after '75 – either struggling for promotion from the Second (i.e., Third) or avoiding relegation from the First (i.e., Second). We aspired to mediocrity.

In the past six years we seemed to have found a better level – fifth or sixth in the First, so seventeenth or eighteenth in Scotland. Fair enough. With a population of 50,000 and a local economy based no longer on coal and linoleum but apparently centred on a large Asda on the outskirts, Kirkcaldy couldn't finance a big club. It couldn't even finance the biggest team in Fife – that, it must be admitted, is Dunfermline Athletic, blessed by a good stadium, recent memories of Cup and even European glory, and a bigger catchment area. Along with St Mirren and Kilmarnock, Dunfermline would be likely to dominate the '92/3 promotion race. Our ambitions would have to be modest. As long as we could hold our own against similar clubs – Morton, say, or Hamilton – we'd be OK.

The arrival of Jimmy Nicholl as our player-manager had given me the rare certainty that we would be OK. I'd made it home for the last match of the '91/2 season when we drew 1–1 against Kilmarnock, a fluent, skilful side of Old Firm oldsters. Both sides had earned an ovation at the end, and I found tears itching my eyes as I clapped the Rovers off.

The third game of '92/3 was another 1–1 draw against Kilmarnock, made all the more satisfying for the fact that we had been playing away. Four days later we went to Edinburgh for a Skol Cup tie against Hibs, the lowest scorers in the Premier over a decade. My mate Alan phoned to tell me that we had played attractive, open football. And that we'd scored one goal and they'd scored four. Ho hum.

Back to the League, where Raith won their next seven matches. Now there's a sentence. Raith won their next seven matches. Seven matches. Raith won them. Seven. In a row. All wins. There's an even better sentence coming up. That run included a 1–0 victory away to Dunfermline.

Down in London I cut out a league table to stick on my kitchen board as a souvenir. Raith were top. Played 10, won 8, drawn 2, lost 0. Goals for, 21. Goals against, 4. Tee hee.

Five games later we had become one of the last unbeaten teams in Britain. OK, OK, so we'd drawn four in the league and once in the B&Q against the normally generous Meadowbank, who did then allegedly beat us on penalties, but, quibbling aside, the fact was that we'd somehow made it to the end of October undefeated in the league.

We'd even appeared on the telly. My Dad sent down a video of a 2–0 thumping of Meadowbank in Edinburgh. The STV highlights occupied the screen for a length of time a subliminal advertiser would have considered short, but slo-mo replays and freeze-frames eked it out. I was too busy pushing my mouth closed to record the short feature 'Football Focus' did on us, but I'm quite glad about that in a way. It was one of those head-patting exercises 'Football Focus' indulges in with small clubs who make it through to the fourth round of the Cup or are discovered to have a pet rabbit mascot. The cutesie aspect was played up back in the studio by Gary Lineker, who joked about not understanding a word of the interview with our perfectly intelligible groundsman, Andy Leigh – he of the legendary fifties midfield. Gary who?

Starved of match reports even in the Scottish papers I hunted for in London, I had been relying on phone summaries from my Dad. 'They're steady, you see,' he explained. 'They don't make mistakes at the back. Dalziel's in great form up front. And Nicholl's got them playing the ball on the ground.'

This was all too much. The next match was Dumbarton at home. It was probably the kiss of death to our unbeaten run, and I didn't have a car, and it was going to clean me out, but I had to do it. I flew home.

A handful of nerve-settling whiskies at the splendid Novar Bar with Alan set us up for the game. It was a perfect autumn day. Please, Raith, I silently prayed, please, please don't screw up. Alan, however, was confident that nothing could go wrong. Not with this team. Encouraged and squiffy, I rashly predicted a 4–1 victory.

We arrived just in time to see Gordon Dalziel flick in his fourteenth of the season. Dumbarton, a typical west-of-Scotland team, big bruisers at the back and wee ginger guys dribbling like crazy up front, somehow equalized, but our right-back, Jock McStay, cousin of the more famous Paul, stole in at a free-kick to make it 2–1 after a quarter of an hour. Six minutes afterwards, another free kick was headed back out to Jimmy Nicholl. He raced in to meet the ball as it bounced a foot or so off the ground all of thirty-five yards out – all right, twenty-five but at a bit of an angle to the goal – and caught it perfectly. A nanosecond later the ball was stretching the corner of the net, and Nicholl kept on sprinting to the crowd, both arms punching the air in astonished joy.

The competition, admittedly, is not fierce, but it was by some way the best goal I'd ever seen us score. We are supposed to score through dodgily awarded penalties, daft own goals, scrambled toe-pokes trundling through mud. This, though, was a screamer, and immortalized on my father's video of STV's round-up. Extensive slow-motion study of the video shows one particular brown smudge in the by-now-volcanic crowd disappear for a moment. It is me, sinking to my knees.

Dumbarton came back at us for a while, but we were — hah! — too good for them. Dalziel collected his fifteenth of the season late in the game. We had indeed won 4–1. What the hell was going on?

Two words help a great deal in explaining just why Raith were not only unbeaten and top of the League but playing fine football, and they are 'Jimmy' and 'Nicholl'. Having served an apprenticeship with countless teams, including, of course, Man United and Rangers, Nicholl had reached the pinnacle of his career as our player-manager. In addition to the fact that he was still playing a class game himself, though now in midfield, he had contributed two innovations to the Raith set-up. One was the daring experiment of having the team go full-time. Another was persuading them to play a patient passing game, one that often involved a sweeper system. Miraculously, the players had learned to adapt to the demands of giving the ball to a colleague instead of hoofing it up the park in the usual First Division kick-and-panic style.

And by luck as well as by cunning, we had acquired players who were, strange to tell, both good and not about to be transferred to bigger clubs. Peter Hetherston, our captain, and Gordon Dalziel, as well as Nicholl, had already been to bigger clubs. Coming up to thirty, Dalziel was in his sixth season with Raith, having almost given up the game after playing for Rangers and then, disastrously, with Manchester City. Why Hetherston hadn't made it at Watford, Sheffield United and Falkirk was, I can joyfully report, a mystery. Dalziel's goal-scoring exploits helped camouflage the talent of his partner up front, Craig Brewster. Shaun Dennis, a young colossus of a centre-back, had played for Scotland's Under-21 side but, somehow, hadn't been sold for the usual derisory fee. The defenders Ian McLeod, Ronnie Coyle and George McGeachie were just a bit too old to attract Hearts or Newcastle, the bastards who usually stole our favourites. We also had really promising YTS lads, and, even more incredibly, not one but two good goalkeepers, Carson and Arthur.

Nicholl's boys played another seven games before I saw them again, when they drew 1–1 on Boxing Day against Ayr, a big, brawny bunch and exactly the kind of nasty, awkward side we usually lose to. There were over three thousand at the game – double the attendance Raith used to get. One of that three thousand shouted the most remarkable comment I have heard at Stark's Park. It was at a time when we were playing down the hill, pressing for an equalizer, and I heard the following anxious yell: 'Slow it down, Raith!' Amazing.

The intervening seven matches had included another 1–0 win over Dunfermline (young Stevie Crawford scoring his debut goal) and a 4–3 win away at Morton, when Dalziel, with a preposterously skilful flying header, scored his 145th goal for us, beating Willie Penman's record which had stood for forty-odd years. But we all knew it couldn't last. Three days later, away to Clydebank, we lost. There was a preamble-free message on my ansafone that night.

'Maybe you've already seen it on Ceefax, but they beat

us three—nil. Not as bad as it sounds. I've heard that the coach broke down or got held up on the motorway or something, and they just made it to the ground in time for kick-off. A shame, but it had to end some time. Not a disaster, though. Talk to you soon. It's Dad, by the way.'

No, it wasn't a disaster but the run had ended and I knew we'd be struggling now. Kilmarnock, St Mirren, Dunfermline, even Hamilton, they were all good teams and they'd catch us up. It was only a matter of time.

I had to go back down to London because I was working over New Year — thanks, God — so I missed out on the big derby at Dunfermline. 'Nil—nil,' announced the voice on my ansafone abruptly. 'Nicholl was kicked off the park early on, and we struggled a bit after that. Young Crawford was through on the keeper but missed it. Big crowd. Nearly eleven thousand, apparently. Oh, and compliments of the season. It's your father.'

It was the ansafone that kept me sane a week later. We were away to Kilmarnock in the Cup. A draw there, bring them back to Kirkcaldy, stuff them, that was my plan.

'Oh dear. I've just got back from Ayrshire. Terrible journey, as you can imagine. But it's not as bad as it sounds. Carson was taken off early on and Sinclair had to go in goal. And then McGeachie got himself sent off. Dear, dear, dear. They did their best. And maybe it's good that we won't have the Cup to distract us. But there it is. Five—nil. Dad.'

Two games later, to prove the idiocy of my father's sunny optimism, Kilmarnock did us again, 3—0 this time, for our second League defeat. In the next four games we won two and drew two. We were still top, but every point was valuable now. We were almost in March, the month when the '80/81 team had pissed on their chips, and the month this time round when we would be up against Morton, St Mirren, Kilmarnock, Dunfermline and Ayr. The month, in other words, when we would collapse. There was one game left in February, one game left when I felt confident that we could bask in glory. We were away to Cowdenbeath. From their thirty games so far, Cowdenbeath had amassed seven points. And conceded seventy-nine goals. I flew up.

Now don't get me wrong. Kirkcaldy is not a prosperous place. But Cowdenbeath, only a few miles up the road, makes it look like Cheltenham. My Dad nobly drove me and his buddies Ron, Jim and Roger into streets that would disgrace Gdansk. Central Park looked like it had been abandoned a decade before. My father and his mates insisted on a seat in the stand, a small and ancient fire hazard beside which the Portakabins that served as changing rooms looked rather flash. There was, astonishingly, a minute of unbroken silence in memory of Bobby Moore, then we resumed our seats on what could well have been railway sleepers to watch Raith fight against a blustery wind, an appalling pitch and a team devoted to inept but zealous defence. The young boy Cameron scored in the first half, Dalziel in the second, and Cowdenbeath had one shot on goal, a fifty-yarder direct from the kick-off that barely reached our penalty spot. Cowdenbeath's nickname, incidentally, is 'Blue Brazil'. They have blue strips.

I thought we played quite well, considering, but a mark of how good we could now be was the restless

dissatisfaction of my father and his cronies. I would gasp
in awe as Hetherston would lob the ball forty yards into
the path of Brewster, who'd lay it off to McLeod, who'd
just fail to complete a one-two with Dalziel, and my four
companions would be shaking their heads in dismay.
Even worse was the incessant moaning of an old biddy
behind us, who complained even when we scored. I
wanted to shake her, to tell her that we were good, that
this was the best we'd ever be, that she'd soon have
reason enough to get really depressed. March loomed.

I spent even more hours than usual the following week
watching page 168 on Teletext. The League table showed
that we'd played thirty-two games of the forty-four and
were seven points ahead of Dunfermline. Say Killie and
Dunfermline both won all their remaining twelve games,
and we somehow gained twelve from ours, then, then . . .
they'd both go up. We needed fifteen points. Maybe our
goal difference would do it. I knew deep down it
wouldn't come to that. I stared at the League table on
page 168, at the outrageous lead we'd created – and knew
we wouldn't make it. We deserved to go up, after all, for
we were a great wee team, but that, I had to
acknowledge, was only going to make what would
happen in March all the more poignant. To hell with
poignant. Heartbreaking. Why hadn't I been born to a
family of Orange bigots in Govan?

In London, I spent the next Saturday afternoon
monitoring the Morton match on Ceefax. Despite
Lineker's wisecrack about this being the best way to
watch Wimbledon, there can be no worse method of
following a game. How reliable is the information? How

out of touch is it? What is really going on? And if the teleprinter misses out your result, the classifieds on 'Grandstand' are just plain excruciating. Particularly if your team is in the division dealt with seventh. I had grown to hate that bloke who does the classified results. I loathed the way his voice goes all chipper for the first part of a home victory, fading to a more-in-sorrow-than-in-anger note of disappointment for the away team's pathetic one or nil. Even worse, the matter-of-fact announcement of a home team's score rising to chuffed delight for the away team's victorious result. And how had he acquired a fixation this year about a team he kept on calling 'Bromsgrove Warriors'? Why, in the name, bother with the Vauxhall bloody Conference at all, far less *before* the Scottish results? Eventually, Bromsgrove Warriors and their ilk had been dealt with, the Premier came and went, and the man's voice rose to say 'Raith Rovers two' and sauntered downhill for 'Morton nil'. The Teletext hadn't been lying.

When I came back in again that night, there was a message waiting for me on the ansafone: 'We played really well. Dalziel and Brewster again. I'll get your news from Mum tomorrow.'

Midweek we managed a draw with St Mirren, and then we had to face Kilmarnock at home. With ten games still to play and Raith still seven points ahead of Dunfermline, the safety net was looking more secure, but Killie had hammered us twice already, and another defeat could only mean that our safety net would begin to fray, a little at first, and within weeks disintegrate.

It was match of the day in Scotland. The BBC 'Sportscene'

cameras had come to Kirkcaldy for the first time since 1969. Whatever happened now, at least we'd made it on to 'Sportscene'. My Dad recorded it for me. I watched the video, stunned. Raith really had been given the telly treatment — our team sheet filling the screen, our players described as though the commentator Jock Brown had been following their fortunes for years. After three or four screenings of the video, I had to accept that all this had been part of a real broadcast. I also had to force myself to accept that the result couldn't be changed, that it had happened, that what had happened had irretrievably happened. Over and over, I watched Brewster pounce on a deflected Nicholl shot to open the scoring, then Arthur make a brilliant and crucial near-post save early in the second half, then Dalziel fight his way through to shove in our second. Gubbed them 2–0.

Nine games to go, seven points needed for promotion.

And now it was time to cope with a home match against Dunfermline, chasing us in second place. It was billed, quite justifiably, as Fife's most important league game. Ever. My father made no mistake about getting me a ticket. A ticket, for crying out loud. Mine was numbered 134, a tribute to paternal love. Disdaining the imminent wrath of my bank manager, I booked yet another flight home.

Saturday lunchtime I met Alan for a pre-match drink in a Novar so full we were fighting for oxygen as well as space. Somehow, we managed to buy two much-needed and very large whiskies. These did nothing to reduce the tension. It may seem odd that supporters of a club seven points clear at the top were praying for a draw, but

Raith's record in messing things up has been paralleled in Scotland only by the national team.

Apprehension increased as soon as the match started in front of a 6500 crowd. Raith were playing downhill towards us, the favoured end for the first half, but Dunfermline were soon on top. They were fast, they were harassing us out of our passing game, and their left-winger looked like he had the measure of Jock McStay. We had a few chances, they seemed to have more. We held on. Just. No score at half-time.

The second half provided only more of the same. I have an atrociously vivid memory of one Dunfermline attack down their right, the ball hurtling across our goalmouth, their forwards rushing in and McStay unwittingly knee-ing the ball just past the post. Sweet Jesus.

Our own expeditions in their half offered welcome relief rather than any promise of a goal. We won a corner. Another minute of respite. Nicholl swung it in from the left, and there was a commotion in their six-yard box. From this end, I could gather only that Raith players were shouting. Appealing for a handball? No. It was a goal. Nicholl's corner had gone in direct. Silence at the Dunfermline end, pandemonium down at ours.

I'm not sure about this, but I think that happened after an hour. I had no doubt that they would equalize, but a draw might do. We were holding on to possession now, stroking passes around, but they were still stretching us at the back every time they heaved the ball forward and played bagatelle around our penalty area. There was just so much of this I could physically stand.

Another break, another little respite. Far up the

ground, someone – Brewster – was holding on to the ball.
Shoot, man, for the love of Christ, have a go, balloon it
out the park and waste a few more seconds. But he held
on to it, then casually slid it to the left, and right into the
path of someone haring up outside him. It was Jimmy
Nicholl. Who placed his shot. And scored.

I stopped leaping around only to hug Alan, and then
we were jumping up and down in tandem. Around us was
delirious mayhem. I had experienced a variety of emotions with Raith over the years – boredom, exasperation,
shame, fear, despair. This was new. This was profound
and complete bliss. This was ecstasy.

There were eight games left, and there would be two
games to play before we finally clinched the championship by beating Dumbarton 2–0 at home, yet another
game I had to watch on Ceefax, until the phone rang and
a voice sang, from 400 miles away, 'We are the
champions, *we* are the champions,' and I replied, slightly
dazed, 'Mum?'; a game whose match report, in the *Fife
Free Press* that my father sent down, was accompanied by
pages of photos of the 4893-strong crowd going crazy,
with a big flag and everything. That would be followed by
another hammering of Cowdenbeath, when my Dad
described how half the Blue Brazil support celebrated
their goal (a deflected free kick) by dancing a conga round
the wide open spaces of the visitors' end (and went on to
explain that the celebrants were, in fact, the twenty-five
members of the North London Cowdenbeath Supporters
Club, inspired to follow the team by their name and
hilarious goals-against tally). That match would, in turn,
be followed by a scraped win over Meadowbank, the last

home game of the season and one I just had to attend, and two daft defeats against Stirling and Clydebank, thus doubling our number of losses in the league but what do you expect when you win the championship with five games to spare? We had been the last undefeated team in Britain that season and the third last undefeated team in Europe (I suspect AC Milan were one of the other two), and we had gained the most points (65) in any 44-fixtured Scottish first division, and had equalled the biggest winning margin (11 points), remaining unbeaten at home where we scored 54 of our 85 league goals, of which 33 had been netted by Gordon Dalziel, the division's player of the year and top scorer, and 20 by Craig Brewster, the division's third top scorer.

There's more . . . As the season came to an end, Jimmy Nicholl would spurn an approach to manage a bigger club, preferring to sign a two-year contract with 'his own wee team', and then, in a meeting to decide on league reconstruction, a Raith director would put his decisive vote for a reduced Premier League, thus condemning us to certain relegation the next year, because, he said, he had voted 'for the betterment of Scottish football'. What a club.

But all this was to come. Swaying with joy after Jimmy's second goal against Dunfermline, I knew, we all knew, that we had really done it this time. Next year, we'd be playing Celtic, Hearts, Aberdeen. Rangers, for God's sake. And now . . . and now, we were, for once, wonderful. A few yards to my right the Rovers choir was singing a song I recalled having first heard drifting faintly over the soundtrack of my Kilmarnock video, a song, I think, unique to us, and one that dared to express just what this improbably requited passion felt like. By the second verse, more and more scarves were being held aloft as the song spread and gathered us in.

> Take my hand.
> Take my whole life too.
> For I can't help
> Falling in love with you.

Ed Horton

Going Down?

OXFORD UNITED 1991/2

There is a paradox in football's literature: the closer you get to the game itself, the less compelling your narrative becomes. Take Eamon Dunphy's biography of Busby. The dominance of his personality, the personal accounts, the crumbling of the Old Trafford dreamworld: all hold the reader with power and fascination. But describing the passage of each season drags a bit, and as for the accounts of the matches themselves: well, we've heard it all before.

One reason for this is that one melodrama is very much like another. No one-day cricket match is ever worth more than the next morning's newsprint: and not even the finest of Wembley finals lives long in the memory except as a fragment or two of the most dramatic moments. Unless you were there, or it meant something to you beyond the mere content of the game and the occasion. And there we have our second problem: how to describe something so completely personal with any hope of a reader's empathy? It's not a novel, dealing in the universalities of human character: we're talking about the part of your life you share uniquely with your football team.

It's hard enough to explain to the outsider: even between one fan and another the emotions can hardly be shared. If it doesn't concern you, it's no more than a story overheard: and the same tale every time at that, where only the names have been changed.

So why should you cherish the memory of this particular season? Because it's not about the games I saw or the friends I made. Nothing could be more mundane. But because it was a *different* season: one not about achievement, but pride and principle. You can understand what happened to Oxford United in 1991/2 as a parable about wealth and its corrosive effect. And for its universal theme, the man who dominates the tale was famous right across the world. Nineteen ninety-one/two is also the story of Robert Maxwell – though not the way he, or Joe Haines, would have written it.

The tale of Maxwell's involvement with football is well understood by many within the game. Outside our circle, the opposite is true. Even in his critical biography, *Maxwell: The Outsider*, Tom Bower writes of his takeover of United: 'there can be no doubt that he was solely motivated by philanthropy'.

When Maxwell shelled out £128,000 on 6 January 1982 to clear the debts of a struggling club he may have had no thought whatever for himself. But even at its most noble, it is hard to disentangle philanthropy from the ego and whim of the benefactor: all the more so where Maxwell is concerned. In truth, the takeover resembled his ventures into different parts of the publishing world.

Come into my parlour, said the spider to the fly. When Maxwell bought Oxford United he was getting the same sort of deal he got at the *New York Daily News*. For a relatively small amount he got, through gratitude and fear, a free hand to do as he pleased; and, crucially, a new arena into which his empire could spread. Whether this was his original intention, we can't know: Bower states that right back in 1949, Maxwell had expressed the desire to own a football club. Most likely it was an instinctive deal. A low price, little risk, potential opportunities when he wished to take advantage. Take advantage he certainly did.

In fact it was a remarkably small investment. United's playing fortunes had revived: it was simply a question of a debt that called for immediate payment. The sale of Kevin Brock would probably have raised sufficient funds to avoid the begging trip to Maxwell.

Much of what happened over the next few years was a prime example of how to make a success of a football club. It was not a personal spree in the manner of Walker or Berlusconi. Vast sums were not expended, nor the finest players engaged. Profits were made – indeed, the personal cost to Maxwell was minimal. But Jim Smith had two advantages not permitted to other managers. First, he didn't have to sell: he could keep the players he desired. Second, he could offer the wages he required to get these players in the first place. The rest was down to inspirational management and the players he believed in. A Third Division title was followed, to our disbelief, by the Second Division Championship. Maxwell's name was chanted from the terraces.

Even then, there were signs of the monstrous egotism and ignorance that always mangled his achievements. In

March 1983 he announced the merger of the club with
Reading under a flag of convenience: 'Thames Valley
Royals'. The plan was, he told us, utterly irreversible.
Within two months it was buried under a welter of
protest. Managers and journalists like to say that football
fans are fickle. The truth is, we're not remotely fickle
enough. Many of those who called for the blood of the
Great Innovator were invading the pitch two years later
in the hope of touching his side, in the manner of peasants
attending to their scrofula. But some fans at least learned
to see Maxwell as the enemy within, even at the time of
his greatest triumphs.

They were embittered further by his persistent bullying
of the local council in the cause of a new stadium. Most
of those on the terraces knew it was needed: they'd
known for fifteen years already. But the same people had
a second loyalty, to their community: and a third, to the
Labour Council that represented them. They viewed
Maxwell's antics with distaste, and despised his threats to
close the club. The hearts and minds campaign was lost
when Jim Smith resigned in June 1985, shortly following
promotion. Here was a man who two years earlier had
claimed: 'My chairman, Robert Maxwell – they ought to
let him run football.' Now, after Maxwell had abused the
celebration party to attack the council and threaten
closure once more, he decided he'd had enough. There
was another, more material cause: Maxwell refused to
pay him the wages appropriate to a First Division manager. Not for the only time, a man who spoke in billions
was exposed as a cheapskate when it really mattered.

Now his greed and self-regard came to the fore, and

United suffered for it. Certainly, the League Cup was won, and three years of First Division football enjoyed at the Manor. But they were missed by many disillusioned fans who abandoned the Manor after grotesque fences appeared on all sides of the ground. These exemplified, perfectly, Maxwellian bombast: they represented the sweeping solution, the love of authority, carelessness for the rights of others. They were backed up with a membership scheme that prevented the casual fan from gaining access to the least affected areas of the ground. Maxwell responded by publishing a book called *Rags to Riches, The Rise and Rise of Oxford United* – a hymn to his own glory written by an abject local hack who now writes for the *Telegraph*. The photos of Maxwell were copious, the text so glutinous the pages stuck together.

United had risen as far as was possible: so Maxwell threw them overboard. Acquiring stakes in other clubs in contravention of League regulations, but stymied in his ambition to take over at Old Trafford, he resigned as chairman in May 1987 to go to Derby. His son replaced him.

Had the Select Committee questioned Kevin Maxwell on his knowledge of football rather than pensions, he could have responded with silence in perfect faith. Memorably, he once referred to a crowd figure of 4000 as 'four grand'. His preference for business matters was more real than symbolic. It became traditional for the Shareholders' AGM to be held on a Monday lunchtime, to make it as hard as possible for anyone to attend: Kevin himself was a 'victim' of his own tactics, as shareholders would arrive to be told he was unavoidably abroad.

Normally he worked through the Managing Director Pat McGeough, who looked after day-to-day affairs like failing to reply to requests for a meeting and denying irregularities in the books. He was an accountant from the Headington heart of Maxwell's empire, the publishers Pergamon. He was a gofer.

Never mind, the press would say — hadn't Kevin's father saved United? Kevin was at the Baseball Ground in September, where our victory won him a crate of champagne off his father. I don't know how many games he saw after 7 November, when a Dean Saunders penalty beat Coventry; I do know there were twenty-six of them, none of them were won, and we were relegated in bottom place. Unruffled, he claimed: 'There will be at least a million pounds available for Mark Lawrenson to bring in new players . . . we've been well managed and prudently run.'

What actually happened was a shock that nearly killed United. In September, with Oxford in the top half and reasonable optimism among the fans, Saunders was suddenly sold by Kevin — to Derby. Lawrenson, who'd just persuaded Saunders to sign a three-year contract, knew nothing of the sale, and was sacked for objecting. 'What are we now but Derby reserves?' asked one of the players. Four thousand fans signed a petition demanding that the Maxwells get out of football. This was prefaced by an angry post-match sit-in and a march of 200 fans down to Headington Hall.

No one was in, and no one resigned. Eventually the anger subsided, and although the local press had to reflect the public mood for a few days, eventually they toed the line. The *Oxford Mail* reported a meeting of fifty people as 'Fans shun protest meeting'. If the press was unwilling to speak, many fans did so with their feet. Attendances plummeted.

Those who remained wondered why Kevin stayed in a post for which he didn't care. We presumed that it was all to do with the campaign for a new ground: that he was after the income from the attendant leisure facilities. This was probably not the case: but it was another three years before we understood what was happening. In the meantime we knew that he took his orders from elsewhere; Robert Maxwell still pulled the strings at the Manor.

You could get in trouble for saying this. The fanzine discovered that despite Maxwell's claims of non-involvement in United, complimentary tickets were on offer to employees at Pergamon (where a long-running strike was also in progress). On printing this information we were treated to letters from a firm of solicitors – 'we act for Mr Robert Maxwell'. It informed us that not only was it untrue about the tickets, but that any implication that Maxwell retained any involvement in the club 'is also wholly untrue'. It was a small taster of the man's technique. We were not worthy of a full-scale writ but were warned that 'there will soon come a stage when action will have to be taken to limit your excesses'. It was intimidation enough to people whose savings and property were worth a weekend's work to a libel lawyer. It later emerged that in the very month he had his solicitors send that letter, Maxwell was involved enough to be at the Manor interviewing a candidate for a directorship.

Boardroom disinterest nearly killed the club for ever.

We may have been the only fans in the country who wanted their board to spend less rather than more. It became the club's habit to publish their accounts months after the maximum period prescribed in the Companies Act. This relaxed attitude seemed scarcely justified by losses that went from half a million a season, then up to a million and more until it appeared the club would still owe money if they sold their stadium and everything in it, and the club played games with coats down in a park. 'Well managed and prudently run' was not the way the supporters put it: we used to contrast the tiny debt which Maxwell had paid off, and the enormous one which he had left. The press, however, noting that Maxwell had saved United, refrained from calling for a halt to the financial helter-skelter. They blamed it all on the fans for not turning up. If United closed, it would be *our* fault.

While waiting for Armageddon we checked the accounts ourselves. We added up the transfer fee figures that the club had given to the press – and got a different total from the one in the accounts. This was particularly so for 1988/9, when several transactions had occurred between Oxford and Derby County. Almost £400,000 appeared to be unaccounted for. We pointed this out, in as detailed and, remembering the solicitors, as non-accusatory a form as we could. The club denied that anything was wrong. When we asked for a full break-down of the figures we were told that this would con-travene League regulations. As the club did precisely this every time they announced a transfer to the press, the excuse rang hollow.

Private Eye did not reply. An article for *When Saturday*

Comes failed to halt the rotation of the Earth. And then, a few months into the 1991/2 season, the lid came off in the most spectacular way.

It's hard to describe the atmosphere at the club by the time that season was two months old. If you work, like I do, at the bottom of a huge bureaucracy, you might recognize the flavour. A lack of interest at the top feeds right through the organization: morale at the bottom is completely missing. That was United. It had been clear since Saunders went to Derby that the club had no ambition: the chairman's habitual absence served as proof. And from the spiralling of the debt and the dwindling of the crowd, a mood of disillusionment and foreboding permeated every crevice of the club. Sometimes, there were moments of passion, victories to savour. The previous season culminated in a fifteen-game unbeaten run that had taken us from bottom almost to the play-offs. But the chickens came home to roost in 1991/2: we lost our first five league games on the trot.

It was a threadbare team we were watching. Even the crowd's favourite son, Johnny Durnin, was popular less for his goalscoring than for performing the three-card trick of speeding while disqualified in an untaxed car. A succession of incidents earned him the soubriquet 'Johnny Lager'. He was the man most often left out, for attitude problems. At the other end, the keeper Paul Kee was throwing them in at about one every match before he fortunately broke his finger. In front of him Steve Foster was being paid six figures for performances at walking pace. The crowd were starting to hate his guts. He was the captain.

The man in nominal charge was Brian Horton, a classic frightened man of football, with the hangdog expression to match. He looked like a man on the fast track to ulcers and the country pub. In a club with ambition he would have been removed long since and most of the crowd wanted to see him go – but a vocal minority, perhaps won over by his obdurate refusal to give way, supported him with the blind, courageous loyalty of Great War soldiers.

There was still a lot of loyalty to be had. Hundreds of people were prepared to miss the last train home to watch a ZDS tie go to penalties at Swindon. The passion and commitment of these people was wasted: wasted on the team, utterly wasted by club owners who cared not a fig for them or for the club to which they gave their all. Wasted too by a local media that scarcely bothered to report the matches. This hadn't always been the case, but there was an air of poisoned decline about the city, whose famous Cowley car works was on its way to closure. The city was losing much of its pride and its sense of community; the football club reflected this depression. An apathetic media did the same. This disillusion was dramatically expressed at the start of September in a spate of joyriding displays and some subsequent rioting. A city built on cars was stealing them and wrecking them at the dead of night.

It was not until a fortnight later that we actually won a match, swapping chants with Derby fans of 'We hate Maxwell more than you.' The following month we even won an away game and were briefly out of the bottom three. Brian Horton celebrated by claiming 'the chairman has been great'. On the second of November we lost at home to Barnsley on a Saturday morning with barely 3000 home supporters present.

We were going down with barely a whimper. What followed was a bang heard all the way round the world.

Come the early hours of 5 November, Oxford United were desperate on the field and doomed on the balance sheet. I doubt that their fate caused the slightest flicker in the consciousness of the man who held their future in his hands. The *Lady Ghislane* was cruising from Tenerife to Gran Canaria. Maxwell wandered out on deck. It was after midday before anyone in Britain heard the news.

The next day great statesmen expressed their sorrow at the death of their criminal acquaintance. Neil Kinnock was 'deeply saddened', John Major considered him 'a great character'. I retain with pride my copy of the *Mirror*. 'The Man Who Saved the Mirror – A Great Big Extraordinary Man'. At the sharp end of the prong, reactions were different. Tom Bower recalls the *Mirror*'s editor having to warn his staff of their behaviour. An employee recalled 'he didn't want them in the boozer telling Maxwell jokes'.

This is precisely what had occurred on the evening of the fifth in the Fir Tree Tavern on Iffley Road. The body was identified at 20.29 and at 20-not-much-more the celebrations were under way. We made no concessions to taste that night: Maxwell had shown no pity to his victims, our football club among them, so we reciprocated. It was a great day.

It was a great day, but those that followed were desperate and chaotic. Not only the Maxwell empire, but the football club at its most distant fringe, imploded.

On the sixth of November United lost at Watford. The *Oxford Mail* informed us that 'Oxford United owes an enormous debt of gratitude to Robert Maxwell'. I fortunately arrived too late for the minute of silence. Next day trading resumed in Maxwell company shares. The Maxwell Communications Corporation had a nightmare, but Mirror Group Newspapers surged ahead on the assumption that it would soon be out of family hands. On the eighth of November Maxwell was buried on the Mount of Olives. On the ninth Oxford lost at Portsmouth. 'Down with the Maxwell,' we chanted. 'When the Rob, Rob, Robert goes Bob, Bob, Bobbing along.' On the sixteenth we drew with Bristol City in a fog as impenetrable as the Maxwell finances, and sank to the bottom of the division.

The plunge of MCC continued and rumours were rife of a Fraud Squad interest. On the twenty-third we beat Brighton and on the Monday more than ninety top bankers met in the City, desperate to recover their loans. The debt was estimated at £850 million. On the Saturday, an excellent result: we drew at Cambridge, who were top.

On the second of December share dealings in MCC and MGN were suspended. Next day Kevin and Ian Maxwell resigned from the board of MCC. Rumours were 'quashed', as the *Oxford Mail* put it, that Kevin might resign from United too. MGN announced that a 'significant' part of its pension fund was loaned or transferred to private Maxwell companies 'without due authority'. This was about 300 million quid. The Serious Fraud Office was to investigate. Betty Maxwell announced she was leaving for France. The *Mirror* changed its tune.

'Millions Missing from *Mirror*,' it complained. On the sixth, the *Financial Times* claimed that the brothers authorized the transfers from the funds. On the seventh, United lost to Blackburn and went bottom again.

On Monday, pandemonium. It emerged that in the previous week, four out of five directors had resigned. One was the eponymous 'Lady' Ghislane. My friends woke up next morning, turned on the 'Today' programme and were surprised to hear my voice denouncing the quitters as 'rats leaving the sinking ship'. The resigners rejected the criticism. They had accepted Maxwell's assurances – and after all, he had saved the club – and now they were simply protecting themselves from liability. What more could they have done?

For the fan, to have a position at a club is a privilege; it brings responsibilities. What is a director for, if not to over-see the club's finances? But the ex-directors were like the JP and the councillor who go on about their 'service to the community'. Just being there appeared to be service enough for them. Who were we to question their performance?

All our professionals went up for sale. The club was 'actively looking for a white knight'. The *Oxford Mail* announced a campaign to help save the club – details were yet to be announced. Next day, Lee Nogan was sold to Watford: Johnny Lager was back in the side. The Football Supporters' Association demanded an open meeting, immediate publication of accounts and the resignation of Kevin Maxwell. Next day, workers at Nuffield Press in Oxford were told that millions were missing from their pension fund.

It was also announced that week that United's debts

were largely repayable to Kevin Maxwell himself. A £1.8 million loan had apparently been made to the club by a mysterious organization called PH (US) Inc. Its function was described in the press as 'paying Kevin Maxwell's wages'. The loan was repayable at once and with interest. *Now* we understood why he had remained at the club. A no-risk deal: get out when you want with a profit in your pocket. This appeared to fans to be a remarkable piece of parasitism.

On the sixteenth, McGeough promised United's accounts would be published by the end of the month. On the seventeenth the brothers failed to show up at the Select Committee. United announced they were so hard up that no Christmas cards would be sent that year. I crossed Kevin Maxwell off my list. At Christmas, staff of the *European* were sacked without compensation.

On Boxing Day we lost at home to a last-minute goal from Brett Angell of Southend. We were adrift, six points below the nearest team. At the game, thousands of leaflets were distributed. They bore a simple headline:

'NO MORE BULLSHIT.'

Our credentials established, we asked, 'What's all this about a £2 million loan . . . ? What kind of "support" is that?' We wondered why Kevin, having his debts rescheduled, couldn't wait for *our* debt to him in the same way. 'Who's going to take responsibility . . . when will the club hold an open meeting?' The ex-directors were described as the 'gutless four'. We urged everybody to write to the club and demand a meeting. In the following days we persuaded supporters individually to do so.

The mainstream press had nothing to say. Our leaflet was reported, but as for support – forget it. BBC motorcycling reporter and veteran Oxford fan Nick Harris described the leafletting as a 'personal vendetta . . . this was not the time to be handing out leaflets'. Presumably we could hand them out after Oxford won the European Cup. 'It's a case of everybody pulling together,' Nick went on. It was clear that pulling together consisted of supporters not poking their noses in where they weren't wanted, and paying for someone else's mistakes. The *Oxford Mail* was little better. Their plan to save United emerged – everybody was to buy yellow ribbons so the money could go to the club. Coincidentally, the ribbons happened to advertise the *Mail* as well as United. Butter wouldn't melt. We calculated the debt could probably be paid off if sufficient ribbons were bought to stretch all the way to Bulgaria. After a few weeks they'd got as far as the ring road.

We were hanging off the table like a broken tree-branch. Millions were owed, all the players were for sale, the directors had run away, the press was engaged in a smokescreen and the club was in weekly danger of closure. And yet, in the crisis, *something changed*.

Paul Foot once wrote about the *Mirror* in the days that followed the Maxwell plunge. He observed that once encouraged to criticize, once freed from fear of the boss, people regained their self-respect. They wanted to tell the truth and they wanted to write well. They worked harder. It became a newspaper again. Oxford United became a football club again.

Most of the fences came down, just in time for

Christmas. Suddenly it was like a football ground again. The membership scheme was suspended. The word began to spread and the crowds increased. On 28 December Sunderland were ripped apart 3–0, their manager, Denis Smith, sacked in shame. On 4 January, Tranmere were beaten in the Cup.

It was refreshing to hear the crowd in voice again. Nine days later the brothers were not so vocal when they sat in silence in front of the Select Committee. On the Saturday, a last-minute fluke stole a point against Port Vale. We were still six points below the rest and the goal was dismissed as an irrelevance. Pat McGeough informed us on the twenty-third that new owners were 'likely to be announced next week'. The press speculated that Frank Warren might be bidding for the club. There was still no sign of the accounts. On Monday, it was announced that the AGB Group pension fund would be wound up. This meant poverty for recent employees of Nuffield Press. Another person pleading poverty was McGeough, who announced he had lost a lot of money in the MCC pension fund. This cheered us up no end.

On 1 February we beat Newcastle 5–2 and Ossie Ardiles went the way of Denis Smith – was it really such a stigma to lose to United? Foster had been out through illness and returned, to score twice from centre-back. He was booed and heckled for his pains. His gesture to the crowd suggested his contempt for their opinion. He got injured in the next game and we never saw him play again. When Brighton were beaten a fortnight later, we were off the bottom.

The enthusiasm was back. A fifteen-year-old wrote to

the club suggesting he do the PA. They could have laughed at him. He got the job. One of his first moves was to play Gary Glitter as the teams ran out. A fanzine writer had proposed the glam rock classics of the Banbury boy as suitable pre-match entertainment. It was silly, tacky and it worked quite perfectly. Come on come on, come on come on, come on come on come on, Oxford! It was a big psychological boost. (Foster's replacement Ceri Evans said the same of the win at Brighton. With a PhD in psychology he was presumably qualified to know.)

On the way back from the Goldstone, United fans were imprisoned in a railway carriage that was locked, and the windows sealed, all the way back to Victoria. They had done nothing, but a fire would have killed them. It was a criminal act by the police. We told *Liberty* about it but there was nothing they could do. It was a dark reminder of the real world in football.

Back in the real world, eleven United officials lost their free company cars. These had apparently been exchanged for free advertising space, by a club supposedly desperate for cash. *Daily Mirror* hoardings were removed from the ground, supposedly because payments had not been renewed. Cynics wondered if they'd ever been made. And December ended in the middle of February. Put another way, the accounts were actually published. They recorded not only the loan from PH (US) Inc., but a loss for the year of nearly a million pounds. The accountants, who had happily signed the books for years, were finally moved into adding a comment that they were unable to ascertain the terms of the loan.

February ended with a 1–1 draw at Blackburn. In the

days preceding, the contents of Maxwell's Holborn
Circus penthouse apartment had been auctioned and a
report by the insurance companies suggested suicide as
his likely cause of death. If true this would save them £20
million. The vultures were feeding on the vulture's own
meat. The Pergamon strike reached its 1000th day.

Oxford United were offered for sale in the *Financial
Times*. Kevin rowed with McGeough over whether any
bids had been received. The interesting thing was the
subtext – the lapdog McGeough had realized his master
wouldn't fend for him any more. He was fighting for his
life. All over the world, former acolytes of Maxwell were
similarly scrapping it out between themselves.

One sale did happen – Paul Simpson went to Derby for
half a million. The previous summer United had wanted a
million for Simmo – an unorthodox winger with the
subtlest touch and the quickest wit with the ball I've seen
at the Manor, and a dead-ball ability rivalled by few in
the League. The wages had to be paid and the sale had to
be made. But to *Derby*? I was depressed. I knew we were
relegated. I skipped the Blackburn match to watch Be-
veren play Antwerp instead. United won Performance of
the Week, a curious outcome for a draw.

Although the jewel in the crown was gone, the spirit of
the team had somehow been transformed with triers and
fighters where the deadbeats used to be. Foster's injury
had been one stroke of luck; Kee's another. The sale of
Nogan, as well as bringing Durnin off the bench, had
helped create a regular place for a young local winger
called Joey Beauchamp. Simpson's departure did the
same for another, Chrissy Allen, a lad from Blackbird

Leys. This served as a footnote to the joyriding saga of the autumn: the Leys was where most of the 'hotting' took place. From despair to local pride. On 7 March, Swindon, the local enemy, at home. We were 1–0 down in about thirty seconds.

The local boys refused to put up with it. Five–three it finished, Beauchamp scoring twice, Allen winning us a penalty and laying on the fourth before trotting quietly off, apparently too shy to acknowledge his ovation. All around me was disbelief and joy. 'I'm an Oxford lad,' said Joey Beauchamp. 'I was desperate to put one over Swindon.'

The joy was not confined, apparently, to the Manor – later that month the local press carried a heartwarming story from Kevin's local boozer, the William IV. It appeared that he liked to treat the locals to a 36-pint barrel at his own expense. The locals found him a charming and generous man, one of them claiming, 'all I know about his involvement with Oxford United is that he is always happy when they win'. He reinforced this unlikely impression at the AGM in March, telling us, 'My parting will be extremely sad.' Not so sad as the employees of Maxwell Aviation in Oxford, who were to lose both jobs and pension. Two-thirds of the Nuffield Press pension fund was missing. We were informed that United could expect new owners 'by the end of the month'.

The ribbons campaign, for all its cynicism, had caught the public imagination, and there were sightings of the yellow threads in Nepal, and in Australia. The team was beginning to creak with injury and two of the squad were

players on loan. It made little difference. We played the
Pompey side that was to come within a penalty shoot-out
of the Cup Final, went 1–0 down with an injured keeper,
and the crowd, who prior to Christmas would have
dropped their heads, gained in fervour instead. United
poured down the slope and scored two goals in reply. The
following Saturday Bristol City got a late equalizer but
despite that, we were out of the bottom three. Our heads
were above water.

An anxious transfer deadline day passed without
further sales and we breathed again. We paused for
thought when Aldershot expired, well aware that we
could take the same path. The AGM had been adjourned
and when it met again Kevin Maxwell's re-appointment
to the board was defeated by fifteen votes to four. For the
shareholders to make such a move was akin to a revolution in the streets of Esher. The receiver showed his
respect for their democracy. He cast his vote, 89.5 per
cent of the shares, in Kevin's favour. In an echo of the
past, club sponsors Unipart were to derecognize trade
unions in April. There had also been disputes about their
pension fund.

The revival stuttered, although Wolves were beaten at
home: a last-minute goal from outside the box by David
Penney, the first goal by an Oxford right-back for more
than three years. It was our only win in April: four times
we led away games for the gain of only two draws. On
the ninth, we had a foretaste of the sickening feeling.
Labour lost the General Election, in a long, long night of
smug Tory faces and socialist recriminations. Only Colin
Moynihan's defeat could make me smile. Next day I

couldn't go to work, smothered in depression. It lifted in the morning. Saturday was football, Derby away, and football must go on. United were to have new owners 'by the end of next week'.

At Middlesbrough, it snowed. Penney was sent off and it was a long way home after a 2–1 loss. Worst of all was a six-pointer at Plymouth on a Bank Holiday Monday where this time it was Magilton ordered off. We lost 3–1 and played, for the first time in weeks, like a lower division side: so did Plymouth. On the Saturday, a two-goal lead was squandered against Bristol Rovers: the final fortnight was down to nerves and watching the scores come up on Ceefax. A late Charlton equalizer at Port Vale threw us a lifeline. Brighton couldn't win at home to Portsmouth. The receivers had 'no news yet of the sale timetable'.

As April closed we were held to an easy draw by an impressive Ipswich side whose point won them the Championship. The game ended in bitterness: as we fell back into the bottom three, the Ipswich fans ran all over the pitch in celebration. It was also the day the fanzine published the results of a supporters' poll. These might have startled an outsider. Ninety-nine per cent didn't believe the club had been honest over finance, 99 per cent didn't think Kevin Maxwell had done a good job. (The other 1 per cent was believed to be a joke.) Ninety-seven per cent wanted a supporters' rep on the board and 98 per cent wanted open meetings. Not one respondent wanted an all-seater stadium for United and two out of three wanted to remove the manager. The results were instructive – more so, the reaction to them. The press had always criticized us for 'continual criticism', they wanted us to be 'constructive'. Presented with a poll that did exactly what they'd asked us to, there was only one thing they could do – they ignored it. Except for the local television station, who reported only that Mickey Lewis was the 'player of the season'. It was an insult by omission: there were a dozen more important questions in the poll. They thought of us as ignorant outsiders, fit to cheer but little else. We knew of them as gutless hypocrites.

In midweek, as the LA riots began, we were told that new owners would be announced the following week. (They weren't.) And we prepared for Tranmere, the bottom line. We were third from bottom, a defeat was relegation. Even a win might not be enough. Six teams were in danger but none of them was doomed. It was a situation full of drama, and yet, as I began this piece by pointing out, not one that in detail can be shared: it happens every year to millions of fans across the globe. It means little except what it means to those who underwent the trial, and it wasn't what made that season such an exhausting and a passionate year. Still, for those who were there (and to those who weren't, pacing round the radio, driven into the garden by nerves and fear) the day was unforgettable: it deserves some effort at description.

Let me give you some images. Three thousand fans, squeezed shoulder-to-shoulder on a sunny, open terrace, wind all around them, 200 miles from home. Two lads who'd chosen that day to complete their set, all League grounds visited in the season: one of them locked in a cell below the ground, too drunk to watch his final match.

Joey Beauchamp through four times before half-time and missing every chance, despair as the radio told us all the other sides were winning – and then, as soon as the second half began, eruptions of noise as Blackburn scored at Plymouth twice within a minute. A draw might be enough! and then a backpass put Johnny Lager through, 1–0, only for a goal from Aldridge to pull us back to earth. Then Beauchamp gets away, it's through the keeper's legs for a winner, while in Devon, Speedie gets his hat-trick. For the final minutes I can scarcely breathe. A last-minute Leicester equalizer puts Newcastle below us! The whistle goes, the team go in then come out to join the celebration, and bending down to catch my radio above the noise, I hear that Newcastle have won with a goal five minutes into injury time. Plymouth are running late, and, surrounded by delirious faces and almost deafened by singing, I scurry back to the car but the Plymouth result is still not in, almost half an hour late. I seem to be the only one refusing to celebrate until finally it comes through, Plymouth 1 Blackburn 3, and we're away home to Oxford to toast our success, twenty-first place and a miracle escape, down the motorway, down the pub.

And that was it, so far as anything in football is ever really 'it'. The following season Oxford once more toyed with relegation, without half the fight they showed in throwing off the shackles of the Maxwells. Football carries on – even though, for months in 1992, we nearly didn't carry on at all.

The pensioners have yet to see their money and the case against the Maxwells remains unproven pending further

action in the courts. The Pergamon strikers lost their fight
after their union ended its support. McGeough became
chairman for five months, then resigned. The Serious
Fraud Office was reported to be investigating transactions made with Derby. New owners were finally
announced. The fans, of course, remained.

And the lessons went unlearned. Still we're told to be
thankful to the owners of our clubs, for their enormous
contribution. In return, they show none of the prudence
or responsibility urged by them, and their willing captive
journalists, on the working people who take their weekly
ease upon the football terrace. Football always runs at a
loss; provided there are new Agnellis, Tapies, Walkers,
Maxwells and their smaller equivalents prepared to spend
their money in the search for greater glory, then their
rivals must compete. They could always pack it in, forgo
their privileges and spend their money elsewhere. The real
problem is that most of us who follow football have so
little cash ourselves that we need the crumbs that fall
from the rich man's table. Our *gratitude*, for *that*?

United survived because Robert Maxwell did not. That
is the long and short of it. We made it through, not
because of a saviour, but thanks to the lack of one.
Without the events of 5 November 1991, the fences
would have stayed up, the fans would have stayed away.
The players who were sold might have gone in any case —
we scarcely missed them anyway.

It gave us a desperate opportunity — our backs were
against the wall, but *it was up to us*. We could expect no
help from anybody, so we did it for ourselves. The fans
and players were transformed. As the dead weight of the

Maxwells was lifted from the Manor, and as we were threatened with the loss of our football club, we learned anew, not what it was to care, but what it was to know you made a difference. *We took back what was ours*, if only for a matter of months.

I said that this was a *different* season. So it was: it's not the results that made it, but the reasons. And when we celebrated, late that lovely evening in May, in our oddly quiet city so full of people unconcerned with football, yet with so many to whom it matters so much, there was one thing I felt that I do not normally associate with football. I felt joyful, certainly. Elated, proud, relieved, ecstatic, pumped up and exhausted all at the same time. Sure, I felt all of these. But also, I felt, well – *vindicated*.

Olly Wicken

Delusions of Grandeur

WATFORD 1974/5

Small boys are easily seduced by glamour. In May 1974 my twin gods of soccer and pop music were at their most glamorous: Bowles and Worthington had both just played for England in the 1–0 Home International win over Northern Ireland, while Slade had just scored their eighth consecutive Top Three hit ('Everyday'). The way I saw it, soccer and pop shared the same glitz. By way of proof I had sequinned my initials on to my shin pads.

Small boys also easily become obsessed. Now eleven years old, I had been preoccupied by soccer's heroic allure for six years already. I played, watched, talked, read and dreamed football. The era embraced the technique of Beckenbauer, the grace of Pelé, and the guile of Cruyff. But there was only one team whose name I was writing in cow gum and glitter. Watford.

*

May 1974. No. 1 for 4 weeks:
'Sugar Baby Love' — the Rubettes

In May 1974 I was starry-eyed. Spotty-faced and starry-eyed. I was a Hornet groupie whose only aspiration was to mingle with the glitterati gathered behind the club's imposing portals in fashionable Occupation Road. I dearly wanted to be as close as possible to my heroes. I dearly wanted to be part of the club.

So I applied to be a ballboy for the 1974/5 season.

The attraction was immense. It was clear, even to an eleven-year-old, that Watford was a club going places. They had finished seventh in Division Three in 1973/4, were developing the stadium, and were the bookies' favourites for the championship in the coming season. Plus they had Billy Jennings.

Billy Jennings typified the flamboyantly gifted striker of the mid-seventies. The perfect set of pearl-white teeth. The spring-heeled headers. The snap-strikes from twelve yards. And, most of all, the abundance of petulance, and the ability to maintain disinterest for eighty-five of every ninety minutes. I had a serious crush.

Billy was golden-haired, sun-kissed and good-looking. In 1973/4 he had scored twenty-nine goals for the Hornets. Most of these were, as I recall, sixty-yard headers. And all of them were re-enacted by me in the lounge at home with a rolled-up sock or balloon. But it wasn't what he did, it was the way he did it. Billy had an indolence which made his goalscoring hateful to opponents and totally aspirational to local eleven-year-olds. Every time an opposing boss complained that

Jennings had done nothing all game except score the winning goal, it only made me goal-hang in the play-ground even worse.

Becoming a ballboy would get me close to my hero. I'd have a claim to fame. I'd be able to blurt an unintroduced 'Hi, Billy!' to him before a game and then boast at school that I had chatted to the great Billy Jennings. *I* would become glamorous. Me. Olly Wicken.

So, hopelessly besotted with all things Watford, I penned my letter to Ron Rollitt, the Club Secretary. I could have worn down my Platignum's italic nib with everything I wanted to say about how much I supported the club. But instead I wrote a short, formal letter addressed 'To whom it may concern'. It was a brilliant gambit – I knew that I would come across as responsible and grown-up by bunging an 'm' on the end of 'who'. And Mr Rollitt fell for it. He gave the job to a starstruck young fool.

It was as easy as that to receive my Vicarage Road groundpass. My passport. My dream ticket. This was undeniable evidence that I was friend to the stars. This was showbiz.

I knew I was destined for a season of trailblazing success. Unlike friends of mine who chose to associate with the Rubettes and wound up with a white beret on their heads and egg on their faces, I knew I was backing the right horse. Somehow I knew that Billy Jennings would again finish club top scorer and, just to round things off, would also set up the clinching goal in the FA Cup Final, surpassing all Hornet fans' hopes and dreams. Somehow I knew that we weren't going to hang around in Division Three for long. The glamorous set-up — of which I was now part — certainly wasn't Third Division material.

August 1974. No. 1 for 2 weeks:
'When Will I See You Again?' — the Three Degrees

Hey, everyone! I was chatting to Billy Jennings at the weekend! And Bobby Charlton said hello to me!

My first duties as ballboy were at the first home game of the season — against Preston. It was mind-blowing. Not only did I that day become an insider at Vicarage Road, but the visitors' playing staff that sunny afternoon included such household names as Bobby Charlton and Nobby Stiles. Not forgetting a couple more former United players in David Sadler and Franny Burns. Too much. I'm not sure I've ever really recovered.

I vividly remember the moment I first stepped through the main entrance of the club in Occupation Road. For the week before, I had had sweat-soaked nightmares about losing my pass or the pass not being valid, but in the event I was respectfully nodded through the door by the man in the Club Blazer. As I passed the doorman, I eyed the blazer covetously. I instantly pictured the scene of Dad dropping me off by the allotments, and me stepping out of the car proudly sporting a Club Blazer underneath my parka.

Then suddenly I was in. Inside the Inner Sanctum of Vicarage Road. Wide-eyed, I found myself at the top of the long steep staircase that led down to the changing rooms. Was this Hollywood or what? It seemed like one of those glitzy, sweeping, showbiz staircases. And it seemed to be inviting me to inhale the adulation as I descended in regal fashion – all the way down the concrete steps to the window in the brick wall at the bottom.

Asking at the window, I was directed towards the changing rooms. The changing rooms! Through my mind ran all kinds of images: coat hooks each with a numbered teamshirt hung (in order) carefully on a hanger; plunge baths large enough for an entire World Cup squad to pass the carbolic; a treatment room full of *chaise-longues* and physiotherapists massaging liniment into the lower backs of ballboys. Nirvana. I followed the corridor round and arrived at the top of the tunnel. My ears seemed to ring with the hubbub and acclaim that greets the entry of the gladiators at Vicarage Road: sporadic foot-stamping in the Shrodells Stand and the distorted blaring of the tannoy. The headiness was quite overwhelming.

To the left were swing doors leading to smart, modern, Home and Away changing rooms, and on the right was the groundsman's toolshed. 'In you go, son,' I heard someone say. Stepping towards the swing doors, I turned to say thanks, only to see Ron Rollitt holding open the door to the toolshed.

I consoled myself, as I clambered past a couple of lawnmowers, that I shouldn't be expecting too much star-treatment straight away. Not when the club clearly needed to focus their spending on the season's promotion push. What did it matter to me (I post-rationalized as a rake-handle leapt up to meet my nose) where I changed into my ballboy uniform? As far as my public were concerned, what mattered was what went on out on the park.

And what did occur out on the park that afternoon was, for me, a blur of excitement and wonderment. OK, so I threw the ball back a few times to the most famous English footballer of all time, but Billy Jennings was sharp, Stewart Scullion was inspired, and Watford were 3–0 up within forty minutes. Watford played football of such scintillating quality that later coverage in the programme and local press speculated that it was the finest performance in the club's history.

In truth, Watford wins had always felt like a personal victory for Olly Wicken (and still do to a certain degree). But this ballboy wheeze made the emotional tie as tight as it could possibly be. On 23 August 1974, I was suddenly a star. Promotion and Cup Finals were already inevitable. What's more – to compound the celebrity status I felt – even the Number One of that week understood me, capturing the closeness I felt with my beloved club: 'When will I see you again?/When will we share precious moments?'

The answer to these questions, of course, was, at home to league-leaders Southend United. Every which way I turned lay glamour.

September 1974. No. 1 for 3 weeks:
'Kung Fu Fighting' – Carl Douglas

We comfortably and professionally beat the league leaders. Two–nil, with Ross Jenkins getting his fifth goal in six games. Star quality. Even in September, surely there were now just the details to be ironed out before we were up.

While the other ballboys excitably celebrated in our changing room with a few boisterous Kung Fu kicks aimed at motor-mowers and upturned edging shears, I basked quietly in the glory that the lads and I had earned for ourselves out on the park. This had been amply demonstrated when our star midfielder Dennis Bond had come and put his arm round my shoulders while he waited to take a throw-in which was being delayed by an injury. He didn't put his arm round anyone else. Just me. Me and Dennis — buddies for life. Six thousand nine hundred and fifty-five people had seen it and knew it.

Indeed, mixing with the players was the high spot of most home games. Although the rota dictated that I was ballboy only every other game, my groundpass let me in through the main entrance for every match. So, in the event, I was down by the changing rooms at 1.30 p.m. for all games (whether on duty or not), clutching my bulging autograph book and always ready with an over-familiar 'Hi!' Against Hereford, this qualified as a 'chat' with Terry Paine, holder of the record for Football League appearances. (I only had time for the true celebs.)

Celebs visiting Watford in 1974/5 surprisingly included a referee. This was Gordon Hill, who was that rarity of a referee whom players liked and respected. He was therefore termed, in fashionable parlance, 'the players' ref'. It was Mr Hill from Leicester who was in charge for Watford's game against Hereford in October.

I had already heard of Hill's reputation as a referee who talked back to dissenting players in their own language. But, as a ballboy standing only a yard from the touchline, I was given a close-up of what this actually meant. After a goalmouth mêlée, a Hereford player ended up sitting on the ground with his legs either side of the standing leg of a Watford player who was thudding his boot into the grounded player's groin. 'Bloody hell, ref!' screamed the understandably peeved Hereford man. 'Get up and bloody well get on with it!' roared Mr Hill in reply. Looking on from only a few yards away, I was impressed. I felt I now understood how to command liking and respect in the adult world. Puzzlingly, though, when I tried out a similar riposte with Mr Wise at my new secondary school the following week, I found myself in detention. For some reason I didn't become 'the teachers' pupil'.

Undeterred by how my football world didn't quite relate to real life, I continued to feast upon the glamour of my association with illustrious Third Division athletes. Indeed, just before the next game, I felt chuffed, nay honoured, to have my scarf playfully nicked by Bury's cocky blond-haired centre-forward – Derek Spence – who later on in the season would play for Northern Ireland in the Home Internationals. And when, in that same game, Watford's seventeen-year-old débutant Keith Mercer scored the winner, my astuteness in having personally unearthed 'the new Billy Jennings' was something I was able to use to try and impress my new classmates at school. Needless to say, it proved about as impressive as my gambit with Mr Wise.

October 1974. No. 1 for 1 week:

'Sad Sweet Dreamer' – Sweet Sensation

The title of Sweet Sensation's chart-topper was only two-thirds appropriate. I wasn't sweet when I was eleven.

But there were no signs of any end to my dreaming on 19 October, at home to Bournemouth. Watford won again. After the game, I sneaked up to the empty Directors' Box so that I'd be familiar with the view at the final home game of the season, when the frenzied crowd would inevitably salute the promotion-winning players and ballboys. I stood there for several minutes, imagining the acclaim and waving triumphantly across the pitch, pretending I knew how to get the corks out of champagne bottles.

I had spent that afternoon throwing the ball back to Les Parodi, the Cherries' left-back. Immediately I had worshipped him. His appeal was to my twin weaknesses of soccer and pop: not only could he hoof the ball up the touchline like a good 'un, but more importantly he was a dead ringer for the guitarist out of Mud. This was particularly cool for two reasons: first, Mud were at the peak of their popularity, having had a monster Number One with 'Tiger Feet' in January; and second, I knew that Mud's guitarist was so technically proficient that he had not only got to Grade Three on the guitar, but had also once played his instrument *behind his head* on 'Top of the Pops'. So Les Parodi was my man – the rocking and rolling full-back who knew how to rebel: I particularly admired the way he not only wore a bead necklace while playing, but had worn it outside his shirt in that season's team photo. Predictably, I suppose, I straightaway mimicked Les at school the following Monday by wearing one of those necklaces of Refresher-type sweets you used to be able to get for 2p; and equally predictably I failed to develop a rebellious reputation among my peers: hunger got the better of me by breaktime — with the school photo still six months away.

By this time in October, Watford's stadium had under-gone considerable development since the previous season. In keeping with the club's ambitions, the development had transformed Vicarage Road from just a football ground into a venue of wider sporting significance, a more spectacular stage. It was a big step. The club was undeniably going places, and was now proving this by regularly playing host to other major sporting events that added stature to the stadium in a way that not even the San Siro or Bernabeu could claim. There was now a dog track surrounding the pitch.

From a ballboy's perspective, this was to be welcomed: there was now an extra set of railings we could athletic-ally leap over (if we were tall enough) in order to show off. OK, so we had to keep an eye open for dog-poo as we landed, but that was a small price to pay for progress.

All the time I basked in the growing kudos attaching itself to my spiritual home. Vicarage Road was fast becoming 'The Second Wembley'.

October 1974. No. 1 for 3 weeks:
'Everything I Own' – Ken Boothe

It's surely the key ingredient of a successful pop song that millions of listeners each find personal meaning in the lyrics. Certainly, when Ken Boothe sang of giving up everything he owned to have someone back again, the lyrics exactly mirrored the way I was feeling this October: my golden-haired hero Billy Jennings was now out of the side.

Without Billy, I sensed that the team risked lacking that touch of greatness that would make 1974/5 not only my own favourite year but one to be revered throughout Hertfordshire for years to come. I wanted that touch of glamour back as soon as possible to keep us shining brightly through the coming winter months. As a sacrifice, I was indeed prepared to give up everything I owned — or at least a week's supply of Spangles and Texan bars with a go on my Raleigh Hustler thrown in.

But even without Billy we scored four goals away to Chesterfield.

November 1974. No. 1 for 3 weeks:
'Gonna Make You a Star' — David Essex

Billy's absence continued. But no worries — because in mid-November Watford announced a new signing who instantly captured my imagination. This was the up-and-coming Alan Mayes — a free-scoring and handsome twenty-year-old talent snapped up from QPR where he had been making waves in the reserve side.

In the local press, Mike Keen, the manager, was keen to emphasize that Mayes wasn't intended to *replace* Jennings. On the contrary, he was one for the future: 'A little bit for now, and more for later,' as the boss said. We were going to make him a star.

Of course, this kind of talk was almost indecently provocative to a young lad in my state. (If hero worship had been on the school curriculum, the amount of time and effort I was putting into it would have earned me an A++ at the very least.) And what made Mayes such an immediate hero for me personally was his *potential*. As a young striker myself, for Northwood Rovers Under-12s, I identified. Alan Mayes was clearly me in a few years' time: the new rising star at Vicarage Road. When Alan agreed to sign my autograph book before his home debut against Port Vale, this was an undeniable sign that we understood each other.

And, against Vale, when Mayes hit his debut goal at the Rookery End, I was beside myself. So much so that I remember shouting 'What a lad!' – which was high praise indeed.

December 1974. No. 1 for 4 weeks:
'Lonely This Christmas' – Mud

Lonely? Not likely – not when I could pop down to the club on Boxing Day to catch up with the players again before they took on Brighton.

One important feature of my feeling 'in' at the club was that all the ballboys used to receive a free programme. The buzzword was 'complimentary' – with all its con-notations derived from the ultimate status symbol of complimentary tickets in the stand. The club wouldn't dream of making a VIP like you fork out for a publication that would otherwise set you back half your week's pocket money. I vividly remember the feeling of collecting my programme at each game: there was the juvenile excitement of getting something for free, mixed with the panic-stricken fear of missing out if the programmes ran out. Collecting the programme always meant putting on an act. I'd desperately be trying to appear nonchalant in order to accept the complimentary item, whereas in fact I used to arrive at the ground at one o'clock with a look of manic greed in my eye before sprinting to the boot room to grab myself my freebie. (Two if I got there early.)

Up until Boxing Day, the Watford programme had always included League Football — the second incarnation of the Football League Review. Looking back now, I feel a nostalgic affection for these supplements: they're evocative period pieces, and I remember their style and content fondly. But at the time I felt very different about them. I used to read them reluctantly, finding them mildly irritating because they sullied the purity of my all-Hornet communiqué with unwanted tidbits about players who meant little to me. Peripheral bit-players like Osgood, Bell and Keegan. Players who couldn't hope to make an impression on me to the extent that my Watford 'colleagues' had. What need did I have of a Top Ten of good-looking players from *other* clubs, when I hung around with the likes of Billy Jennings or Alan Mayes? Why on earth would I need insights into the abilities of First Division stars when my own programme would, the following week, diagrammatically reveal how Roger Joslyn 'forms a penetrative triangle in the middle of the park to break up oncoming attacks, occasionally thrusting out to either flank'? My cup was already brimming over. I was suffering from cliquishness. Consequently I wasn't upset to read in the Brighton programme that this was the last appearance of League Football.

The only players from other clubs who interested me were those centre-forwards whom the weekly local press speculated would be Watford's next big signing. Actually, 'interest' is too mild a word. When I read their names on a Friday morning, I was sent into a frenzy of excitement that made concentration during the first two lessons at school (double maths) somewhat difficult. But can you blame me? During 1974/5 I was regularly teased by such names as Brian Greenhalgh, Ernie Moss, Jack Lewis, John O'Rourke, Alan Gowling, Bobby Shinton, Micky Bullock, John Mitchell, and – tantalizingly – the prodigal son Barry Endean. A veritable galaxy that even in 1993 makes me shiver as I recall their illustrious names: if I tried to open my tin of Oxford Mathematical Instruments right now, I'd probably still noisily spill the protractor, setsquare, and compass under my desk.

But even without recourse to big name signings, Watford started the New Year the way they meant to continue – with a 'shoot on sight' policy that brought another three goals in a home win over Grimsby. Concentration during the following Friday morning's double dose of sums was further disrupted by my preoccupied calculations of the 'mathematics' of promotion.

January 1975. No. 1 for 1 week:
'Down Down' – Status Quo

I was never a fan of Quo, with their morbid songs about relegation. Pathologically optimistic, I preferred instead the evocative optimism of Terry Jacks' 'Seasons in the Sun' and saw an allegorical reference to winning sequences in Ray Stevens' 'The Streak'. In my world there was room only for aspiration.

Consequently when Watford organized a Friday night friendly against the famous and stylish Tottenham Hotspur at the end of January, you could truthfully say that I found the prospect diverting. It was an evening game, yet I think I still arrived at the ground at lunchtime. The previous day.

There were two sides to my excitement. There was my unthinking intoxication at the prospect of meeting seven international players from the top drawer of the Football League, and, more rationally, I realized that here was a chance to assess Watford's true short-term potential — Spurs were in danger of relegation to the very division we were shooting for. It was going to be a big and important night.

The Spurs line-up had me floating somewhere near the ceiling that Friday morning: Jennings, Kinnear, Pratt, Beale, England, Peters, Knowles, Coates, Perryman, Chivers, Conn, Duncan, Neighbour. I knew that I would be chatting to all of these stars. Even Michael Parkinson would have been jealous.

To add to the anticipation, it was announced that Watford would be trying out an experimental new strip for the game: gold and black stripes. The important thing here was that I would have the kudos of being one of the very first to see the new kit before the players took the field — a private showing, as it were. It would be like a glitzy fashion show for the club cognoscenti — among whom we ballboys of course counted ourselves, as we sat round on the horticultural machinery in our torn and misshapen club tracksuits.

In the event, it was a glittering occasion. All the Spurs heroes were there, filling my autograph book with signatures that all seemed to bear a curious resemblance to the logo from 'Vision On'. I was in seventh heaven – especially when we surprised the First Division big boys with a two-goal salvo, and when it was our strikers for the future, Mayes and Mercer, who made the strikes. The game left me in little doubt that we'd go straight through the Second into the top flight.

February 1975. No. 1 for 2 weeks:
'Make Me Smile (Come Up and See Me)'
– Steve Harley and Cockney Rebel

Another home win. Against Huddersfield, a modest 1–0. It was a freezing Friday night fixture. I remember Mum advising two pairs of socks, with my own tracksuit bottoms under my shorts under the club tracksuit bottoms. I took her advice – I decided to brave ridicule from the other ballboys rather than brave the elements with lesser protection.

So if any spectators at that game noticed a ballboy continually haring up and down the Shrodell's touchline, they would probably have put it down to the poor child trying to keep warm. But this wasn't the reason. In fact, I used to run up and down with play at every game. Why? I'm not entirely sure. I guess I felt so much a part of the club, so unswervingly a servant of the cause, that I matched my emotional commitment with physical commitment. It certainly added to the satisfaction of another home win when I came off the field physically as well as emotionally drained.

But then maybe I was just an overkeen little prat.

March 1975. No. 1 for 6 weeks:
'Bye Bye Baby' – Bay City Rollers

Watford went into the final match of the season with all to play for. With a home fixture against mid-table Walsall, the most likely outcome was that we would at last be bidding farewell to Division Three mediocrity. Bye bye baby.

It was another big night. The largest crowd of the season was there to cheer the lads on, and I got there extra early to claim a ballboy berth behind a goal. I wanted to witness this historic night for Watford Football Club at the closest possible quarters.

My memory of the build-up to the game is a little hazy. But as I recall, now that things had come to the crunch, I was at long last experiencing some apprehensiveness and nervousness instead of my usual blind optimism. For once, in the halls of the heroes, some realism.

It was early in the second half before we scored, but the crowd then really got behind us. Although I usually sneered at the fairweather fans at school – the kind who only ever turned up for big games like this – I was pleased that there were nearly 10,000 in the ground to watch the lads and me. And for once I even enjoyed my own personal moment of fame when some boys from school waved and shouted at me from the crowd, trying to be 'in' with me. I'd made it.

I was in a privileged position – among my peers, and geographically. At close hand behind the goal I could see detail of the unfolding historic drama that others couldn't. No one else seems to have seen that, after Walsall had scored, it was Mick Kearns's glovebag, placed in front of his left-hand post, that made a shot rebound at an unexpected angle away from the onrushing Scullion who had looked bound to score. I felt as though I was the chosen one who had been vouchsafed insight into such moments of Fate and Destiny – especially when, with less than a minute to go, an infringement directly in front of me gave us a penalty kick.

Had it really all come to this? Did the final outcome of my season's brush with fame and glamour really all depend on a last-minute spot-kick? Was it truly down to a twelve-yard duel between Stewart Scullion and Mick Kearns ultimately to decide whether 1974/5 would go down in history as the year the Hornets garlanded themselves with glory?

The answer is no. The penalty didn't matter. Scullion actually made it 2–3. Even if he'd missed, Watford would still have been relegated to Division Four.

I'm afraid I may have misled you, much as I deluded myself that year.

March 1975. Highest position No. 13:
'Dreamer' – Supertramp

Everything I've written is true. The truth is that it was

indeed a historic night – that we did indeed wave bye-bye to Division Three. We really had beaten Preston, Southend, Bournemouth and the others, but away from Vicarage Road we had only won one game all season. It's even true that Billy Jennings ended up as club top scorer and Cup Winner (but both of these achievements were for West Ham who signed him in September).

I've written this piece mainly from memory. Yet my memories are happy ones. While writing, I've found that I either don't remember the pain of defeat and relegation, or, more likely, was too much in love with the club to have noticed the pain at the time. (I remember being delighted that we scored four at Chesterfield even though we let in four. I was chuffed that we put two past Spurs even though they put three past us.)

I was young, wide-eyed and oblivious to the truth. Oblivious to the smalltime squalidness of a run-down and declining club. As the song said, I was a dreamer. A crazy little dreamer. Watford were a crap club.

But in one important way – in terms of my feeling part of the club I supported – 1974/5 truly was an unbeatable year. My favourite year. Within another three years, Graham Taylor would lead us back out of the Fourth. And within another six years we would finish runners-up in Division One, would play in an FA Cup Final, and would play in three rounds of the UEFA Cup. The success would be a huge part of my life, and would form a significant part of my identity.

But somehow it all meant more when I was changing in the groundsman's toolshed. When I was hurtling up and down the touchline. When I was wearing an ill-fitting and torn tracksuit that wouldn't zip up. When I belonged.

I've never again achieved that glamour.

D. J. Taylor

Just Accept It, Hansen

NORWICH CITY 1992/3

My father started watching Norwich City in 1929. In
those days they played at the Nest, a precariously
terraced crater of a ground north of the city, with a sheer
wall at one end rising to the teetering private houses
beyond (one resident, according to local folklore, used to
rent out his back bedroom to spectators on match days).
Carrow Road came later, opened on an August afternoon
in 1935 when the visitors were West Ham, defeated by
what commentators of the Wolstenholme generation
used to call the odd goal of seven. My father was a soccer
obsessive, arriving at the ground an hour and a half
before kick-off – these were the old Third Division South
days, but you still got 25,000-plus crowds spilling over
the Wensum bridges or along the road from the station
(the FA closed the Nest due to overcrowding) – and
capable of being sick out of sheer nervous excitement. Six
and a half decades later the flame still burns. He rings me
up every two days or so to talk about the team gossip in
the *Eastern Evening News*, the confidential reports of
Robins' groin strain and Butterworth's hamstring, what

Bowen said to the manager and what the manager said to Bowen, and the burly Norwegian defender (this story turns up every fortnight or so) Norwich are on the point of buying from Trondheim. Two years ago when the club presented him with a long service award they marked the occasion with an invite to the executive box for a home match against Nottingham Forest. City lost 2–6.

Invoking the spirit of my father, who won a Business Houses League Championship medal with the Norwich Union 1st XI in 1946/7 and once applied for the managership of Exeter City, using this as his qualification (he never got a reply), seems the only navigable route into my quarter-century obsession with Norwich City FC. First taken to the ground at the age of six weeks during the course of a reserve team fixture – I lasted a few minutes before my mother, horrified by the spectacle of several cloth-capped elderly men spitting, marched my father and the carrycot away – I made it back for the full ninety minutes at the age of six. Norwich beat Derby County 4–1, an occasion chiefly remarkable for a débuting centre-forward named Laurie Sheffield scoring a hat-trick. But there was more to it than this: the being taught to read out of the *Pink 'Un*, the Norwich football paper; the memory tests based on the league tables (I once gained half a crown – good money for the mid-sixties – by being able to write down the names of all ninety-two league clubs). In a queer way, many of my strongest memories from the 1960s are to do with football, of playing it, watching it and, perhaps most relevant of all, hearing about it at second hand. Watching Weber score West Germany's equalizer in the 1966 World Cup final (I

was five at the time and I can see the parquet floor of the
front room and the veneer of the glass-fronted bookcase
behind which I went off to weep even now); being called
to the telephone late one Saturday afternoon to be told by
my father, from a call-box in Manchester, the stupendous
news that Norwich had beaten United 2–1 (Heath,
Bolland) in the FA Cup 4th Round. To the present
excitement is added the receding glamour of a bygone
age.

My father had seen most of the games in the famous
cup-run of 1958/9 when City, then struggling at the foot
of the Third Division South, made it to an FA Cup semi-
final replay (20,000 people were supposed to have
travelled from Norfolk to White Hart Lane for the fifth
round). He'd seen England lose 6–3 to Hungary at
Wembley in 1953, the first defeat on home territory. Even
more astounding, he knew ex-players: the middle-aged
man in the grey herringbone met outside the ground
would turn out to be Alf Kirchen (Norwich, Arsenal and
England), the track-suited trainer to be the legendary
Billy Furness (Leeds, England, Norwich). And perhaps
most important of all, he remembered. For years the
forward line of the promotion-winning side of the 1930s
– Warnes, Burditt, Vinall, Houghton, Murphy – remained in my head as a kind of litany, and even though I
wasn't there (it happened eighteen months before I was
born) I could tell you about the time the great Ken
Nethercott, one in a long line of superlative Norwich
goalkeepers, dislocated his shoulder in the '59 quarter-
final but carried on until the final whistle, with the
defence massed around him like bodyguards.

If there was an immediate personal context for this obsession – the looming, gargantuan figure of my father – then it was trailed by a broader framework of upbringing, milieu and association. Norwich is a small city: 120,000 inhabitants, a couple of MPs, nothing between it and the sea but the great flat of north Norfolk, the windmills and the wide East Anglian sky. Supporting the local football team, consequently, is an essential part of local patriotism, of identity, definitive proof of Norfolk's superiority to Suffolk, of Norwich's superiority to Ipswich (no cathedral, no university, in fact a sort of extended railway siding in between the Suffolk market towns that you pass through on the way to Thorpe Station). 'We're the pride of Anglia,' the Norwich fans chant, and they *mean it*. I once attended a Boxing Day game at Portman Road in the early eighties when Norwich won 3–2 in the last minute and the atmosphere in the away end was almost tribal. In the 1958/9 cup-run people took this fanaticism to extravagant lengths, dyed their hair yellow and green and dressed up as canaries or Norfolk dumplings. There are photographs in the souvenir book of fat Norfolk matrons pictured in front of prams bearing the legend 'We'll put Busby's babes to sleep.' That sort of fervour is gone now, gone with the huge attendances and the Barclay terraces, but even today, walking back through the Norwich suburbs on a Saturday afternoon in October wearing your yellow and green scarf, you can count on being stopped by the old woman emerging from the shadows with her dog to enquire, 'How'd City git on?' In these circumstances the players come to be regarded as local boys, sons of a sprawling, heterodox family whose doings are treated with a routine if slightly exasperated indulgence. Of course, the last *bona fide* local to play for Norwich was Dale Gordon, who might have come from Great Yarmouth, but Norwich is a small enough place to allow them to blend effortlessly into the local fabric: Bryan Gunn shopping in Jarrold's department store, the late Robert Fleck patronizing the Timberhill nightspots (the less said about which the better). The family club idea is borne out by the tendency of players to stay in the area after they retire, to open sports shops (Kevin Keelan) or join the administrative or coaching staff (Duncan Forbes, captain of the '71/2 promotion side). Most famous of all was Dave Stringer, who really was a local boy – he came from Gorleston on the coast – and ended up as manager. This fierce interest in the players works both ways, of course, and the eager young hopeful who makes it clear that his two or three seasons at Norwich are merely a slightly irksome interlude before the Big Time (or as Tim Sherwood, now of Blackburn Rovers, once guilelessly put it, 'I don't absolutely hate being at Norwich, but . . . ') can be sure of a hot reception on the first occasion he returns with his new paymasters.

Norwich is a modest, gentlemanly club with a playing style to match. I don't think I can remember seeing a Norwich player sent off except on the occasions when Keelan, who had a notoriously hot temper, would register his disapproval of an over-inquisitive centre-forward by banging the ball in his face. In the pitched fan battles of the late seventies and early eighties the Norwich supporters were puzzled onlookers. Even 'On the Ball, City', the club anthem with its evocations of 'splendid rushes' and 'little scrimmages', has a quaint, prelapsarian air:

> On the ball, City
> Never mind the danger
> Steady on – now's your chance
> Hurrah, we've scored a goal!

Norwich City's history over the past quarter-century reflects this feeling of modest aspiration and quiet achievement; a long slow journey towards respectability and, eventually, success. When I started watching them in the mid-1960s they were your standard Division Two makeweights, not bad enough to be relegated, not good enough to be promoted, but with the chance of a decent cup-run to keep the attendances and the public interest alive. Even this, though, was an improvement on the old Third Division South days of the fifties when the club had to apply for re-election several times and on one occasion nearly went out of business altogether. Things started to improve around the turn of the decade. They won the Second Division title in 1971/2 in a nail-biting finish that required two points from the penultimate game at Charlton and a point from the final match at Watford. In 1973 and 1975 they made the League Cup final, losing both times by a single goal (they'd actually won the competition back in 1962, beating Rochdale, but that was in the days before the big clubs condescended to enter). Their league form, however, was variable.

A couple of seasons at home to the likes of Liverpool and Arsenal would be followed by a couple of seasons away to Wrexham and Huddersfield. They went down in

'73/4, up again in '74/5, down again a few years later.
The managers came and went. By the time I started taking
up a position behind the River End goal, or in a rackety
commentary box where my father presided – and con-
tinues to preside – over the Norwich Hospital Sports
Commentary Service, Archie McAulay, who had been in
charge during the cup-run and subsequently guided them
into the Second Division, was a figure of faded legend.
The first manager I remember properly was Lol Morgan,
whose son David was the year below me at primary
school, and who was actually persuaded to referee a
Buckingham Rovers game one Saturday morning on
Eaton Park. ('Who's ref on Saturday then?' 'Oh, Lol
Morgan you know.' '*Cor!*') Next came Ron Saunders,
who even in those days had the reputation of being a hard
bastard: there were rumours of players collapsing after
the training runs on Mousehold Heath, and any local
sports journalist he didn't like got turfed off the coach to
away matches. After that there was John Bond with his
extraordinary suits, his South-Coast numskull's burr and
his garrulous TV interview responses about 'my boy
Kevin', who played left-back and, it was unkindly
suggested, wouldn't have seen first-team football in
normal circumstances. A college friend of mine did a
memorable impression of Bond, only with four-letter
words: 'So I says to my boy Kev, you was f*****' s***,
Kev, you want my f*****' boot up your . . . ' etc., etc. If
Saunders and Bond represented, in varying degrees, professional expertise and glamour, then by the end of the
seventies the Norwich board had plainly decided that you
could go too far with professional expertise and glamour.

Later managers belonged to an older, less obtrusive tradition: Kenny Brown, famous for walking his dog on occasions when Norwich's end-of-season fate lay in the hands of third parties (1985 when Coventry implausibly thrashed the league champions Everton in their final game to send us down – 'We'll be treating this as an ordinary match,' Howard Kendall is supposed to have said beforehand); Dave Stringer, who had the sort of nondescript appearance you associate with the reserve team manager; and his successor, the present incumbent, Mike Walker, who actually was the reserve team manager.

Much of this information, the majority of these details, I absorbed through a kind of osmosis. I lost touch with Norwich City, I suppose, in the early eighties. University was a hundred and sixty miles away: it took half a day to get back. But the data filtered through in my father's letters, which sometimes brought copies of the *Pink 'Un* with their flaring headlines ('CITY GO DOWN TO GUNNERS' FIRE') and their warnings about Justin Fashanu's knee, in the dull Saturday afternoons spent listening to the radio as the fog rolled up from the river to settle over the north Oxford backroads. In London, a year or so later, surveillance grew easier. There were evening games at West Ham, and dogged excursions through the North London streets to White Hart Lane, then as now barely accessible by public transport. As the eighties wore on, though, it became clear that something was happening at Carrow Road, something vague and only narrowly explicable, which had less to do with the steadily improving performances – they won the Milk

Cup in 1985 (a fluke own goal, but as my father sapiently remarked, they all count), got relegated but then won the Second Division championship at a canter and came fifth in their first season back in the top flight – than with deliberate attempts to change the focus and direction of the club. In some ways – not all, but some – what happened at Norwich between 1986–8 was a paradigm of the wider struggles gripping the game, struggles that on the surface had little connection with football and everything to do with business, style and politics. Inertia versus dynamism, city versus county, tradition versus progress – each of these conflicts contributed something to the great boardroom tourney that left Sir Arthur South battered and bleeding in the porch and a relatively unknown businessman and Conservative County Councillor named Robert Chase installed in the chairman's lounge. Sir Arthur, sole proprietor of the Norwich Fur Company, a former Labour mayor and kingpin of the Norwich Trades Council, seemed a figure from a vanished age when set against his challenger, the epitome of the old-style soccer chairman who runs the club as a personal fief. Several managers were more or less thrown out into the street after incurring Sir Arthur's wrath ('I've never seen Dad so upset,' Kevin reported, as John Bond packed his wardrobe of suits and departed). He hung on for a while, like some aged bird of prey, while the newspapers murmured and Mr Chase marshalled his resources. Then, a third of the way into the '87/8 season, with the club nestling at the bottom of the table, the tanks rolled in. Sir Arthur went, and so did the manager, Kenny Brown. They held a hastily convened emergency general meeting at St

Andrew's Hall, with the skinheads outside chanting 'Robert Chase is a homosexual' – its proceedings rendered irrelevant in advance by the fact that Mr Chase already owned most of the voting shares. Highlight of the gathering was an impassioned speech from the floor by an elderly woman decked out in yellow and green favours. 'What I want to know,' she demanded, fixing her gaze on the Chase satrapy, 'is *who are yer*?' It was a good question. Nobody, eyeing Mr Chase and his line of sheepish cohorts, seemed to know the answer. Mr Chase remained impassive, like some trade union baron in the old, or perhaps not so old, Tammany Hall days, happily aware that he will get his way despite the squeakings from the gallery.

It should all have gone badly wrong. Precedent suggested a five-act sporting tragedy involving relegation, the departure of the forward line and the manager insisting that at the end of the day it was just eleven players against eleven players. Implausibly the team recovered to mid-table. There followed in 1988/9 one of the most astonishing seasons in the club's history. It involved extraordinary things – leading the league for over three months, away wins at Old Trafford and Anfield and a cup-run that ended only in a semi-final defeat against Everton, on the same day as the Hillsborough disaster. They finished up fourth, having run out of steam in mid-March, and suffered the indignity of a televised 5–0 thrashing at Highbury. But it was an ominous season, not simply in its demonstration of how well a collection of other clubs' cast-offs (the '88/9 side was assembled at famously nugatory expense) could play when effectively supervised, but in showing what happens when a club like Norwich miraculously performs to advantage on the national stage. It is not a piece of punditry but merely a statement of fact to say that Association Football in this country is run by and for the benefit of about half a dozen clubs (anyone who reads this will know who they are) and who between them exercise what amounts to a stranglehold on public perceptions of the game. One of the fanzines sold outside Carrow Road is called *Liverpool are on the telly again*, and the point is a perfectly fair one. Liverpool *are* always on the telly again, with their thug of a manager screaming from the touchline and then whingeing away at the post-match inquest. When Liverpool do well they get in the newspapers. When Liverpool do badly they get in the newspapers again – *because* they are doing badly. It is also a fact that any club which manages, however pro-temporaneously, to storm these citadels of seven-figure transfer fees and TV revenue is regarded with a sort of fascinated disgust, like a dustman arriving in the Ascot enclosure. The reaction to Norwich's run in 1988/9 began as amused condescension and ended up as outright contempt. Quite early on in the season a journalist from one of the scandal sheets volunteered to eat a piece of the Carrow Road playing surface should they end up winning the league. After the thrashing at Arsenal – painstakingly anatomized by the TV gurus – you could almost hear the sigh of relief echo around the sporting press. Thank God somebody we'd heard of was going to make it and not this band of cut-price upstarts from . . . where is the place anyway?

Naturally this sort of attitude – you sometimes feel that the newspapers keep the CANARIES KNOCKED OFF THEIR PERCH headline permanently on screen – has an insidious long-term effect: if you tell a club that it isn't fashionable often enough, then the players will start believing it. After which they leave, for London or the North-West and telephone-number salaries. Chris Woods. Dave Watson. Steve Bruce. Andy Linighan. Mike Phelan. Andy Townsend. Dale Gordon. Robert Fleck. Tim Sherwood . . . You could compile a very decent Home Countries XI from the players who have camped out at Norwich for a season or three and left after the big money, and who can blame them? Norwich can't afford the four thousand a week and the moated granges. Besides, who wants to live in *Norfolk*, with only the wide sky and the rumble of the sugar-beet lorries for company? There is also the existence of Robson's Law, a long-standing ukase which prevents any Norwich player from playing for England. You can play for England after you leave Norwich, and you can play for England before you arrive, but while you're there, well, we'd sooner have someone from a club we've heard of, thank you very much.

Inevitably, the 1988/9 side started to break up a whisker into the close season. Phelan, the captain, went to Manchester United for three-quarters of a million, Putney to Middlesbrough. There followed a mild yet perceptible slackening of resolve: mid-table in '89/90, a bit less than mid-table in '90/91, nearly relegated in '91/2. They got to the FA Cup quarter-final in 1991, though, and to the semi-final a year later – a dreadful performance against Sunderland at Hillsborough, where Sutton missed a goal my infant son could have scored, Fleck, his ribs strapped after an encounter with the gentlemanly Southampton defence in the previous round, could hardly move, and Byrne, streaming forward unmarked to head the Sunderland winner, seemed transfixed for ever in silent, billowing space. By August the omens for 1992/3 looked unpromising. You could get 150–1 on Norwich for the first Premier League title a week before the opening game. The usual tribe of defectors had shambled off north and west – Sherwood to Blackburn Rovers, Fleck to Chelsea for a reported £2.3 million and the heartening post-Norwich career blight (other victims include Phelan, now scuffling around in the Manchester United reserve team) which produced exactly three goals in forty-two league games. Stringer had resigned the managership, to be replaced by Mike Walker (a handful of more lustrous names reputedly declined), an unknown quantity. Until two days before kick-off they barely had a recognized striker, unless one counted the season before's record signing, Darren Beckford (£925,000 from Port Vale) which, regrettably, most supporters were disinclined to do. In the end they clinched a deal with Manchester United for Mark Robins – £800,000, the second most expensive Norwich purchase ever. The opening game was away at Arsenal, and no one seemed very sanguine. That morning a character in the *Independent* gave his predictions for the following nine months: I can't remember whether he had Norwich down as twenty-first or twenty-second, but he certainly forecast Arsenal to win the title. At a quarter to four that afternoon, in a rented holiday cottage somewhere in darkest Suffolk, I switched on the television: 0–2 down. Half an hour later I switched on again: 2–2. They ran out 4–2 winners, all four goals coming in the space of seventeen minutes, two of them from Robins, eventually let on as sub. Four days later I quit the Suffolk fastness for Carrow Road to watch them beat Chelsea 2–1 (a prudent Chelsea management had decided that perhaps Fleck's debut could wait, but the Norwich fans consoled themselves by catcalling Townsend, another émigré) to go top of the first Premier League table.

Accounts of a successful season invariably have a slightly predictable ring to them ('And then we beat Ipswich . . . And then we beat Ipswich again . . . '). For some reason homespun mundanity always seems preferable to goal-strewn pageantry. I used to enjoy the 'Captain's Notes' column feature in the Fulham programme ('Chester (A) 0–0. One of the worst displays I remember in my time here'). Any such cavalcade usually contains a game in which several outrageous slices of luck conspire to demonstrate that, yes, this is the one; that, yes, this time it's all going to work out. In Norwich's case the occasion was the return match against Chelsea, staged, owing to some quirk of the fixtures computer, at the end of September. Sitting quietly in the main stand amongst the south London scrap-metal dealers and the raucous gentlemen who shout 'Kill the c＊＊＊' whenever an opposition player tumbles over (you get a lovely crowd at Chelsea), I became aware, even before the game kicked off, of an unprecedented level of fervour. It turned out that this had to do with the arrival of David Mellor, then reaching the end of his hopeless struggle against tabloid exposés of his private life. This curious, otherwordly atmosphere persisted when the teams came out, Norwich looking slightly bewildered, as if they feared they might have come to the wrong ground or that somebody had forgotten to issue them with bootlaces. We found out later that the coach had been caught in traffic on the way up from Croydon, where for some reason they'd spent the night, allowing the team ten minutes to change and make it on to the pitch. They were 2–0 down after half an hour. Happily any short-term deficiencies were cancelled out by the decision of Beasant, the Chelsea goalkeeper, to go into autodestruct. Three minutes into the second half Robins essayed an innocuous-looking tap with about the momentum of a friendly back-pass. Beasant swept it up with one of those stylish follow-through flourishes, with the result that the ball spun over his left shoulder into the back of the net. From the stand at least the Norwich equalizer looked about 50–50. ('You f*****' c***, Beasant,' bawled the south London scrap-metal dealers. 'Why don't you f*** off,' etc., etc.) The winner, though, was simply unforgivable. A few minutes from time David Phillips stroked the ball gently forwards from the edge of the Chelsea area. There was no power in the shot, which trickled lazily on, bouncing a little on the uneven surface, and you could see Beasant covering it as he went down. Then the ball gave a sort of spirited hop, flicked over his outstretched hands and came to an exhausted halt somewhere in the side-netting.

Poor Beasant. He was denounced by the manager that same night, shipped out somewhere on loan and didn't play for Chelsea again until the New Year. Predictably, the next day's newspapers were full of Chelsea's short-comings rather than Norvicensian purpose. A week or so later, as the Norwich juggernaut showed no sign of decelerating, the press began to roll out some sadly familiar adjectives – these 'unlikely' contenders with their 'improbable' ambitions. Walker by this stage had already perfected the dead-pan reply to reporters' questions which in early December – when Norwich were eight points clear – allowed him to remark that at least it looked as if we might avoid relegation.

If East Anglian resentment of this habitual condescension found a single point of focus, it lay in the swivel-eyed, nervously cheerful figure of Alan Hansen. Presumably there exists a high-ranking executive somewhere in BBC sports television who is paid large sums of money to select soccer pundits for their qualities of articulacy, lack of bias, personality and so on, and then throw the list away and engage people such as Alan Hansen, who, with his anxious leer, his meagre repository of stock phrases and his pathological obsession with Liverpool, makes Ian St John look like Kenneth Wolstenholme. Each Saturday night during the autumn of 1992 found thousands of Norwich supporters squirming in front of 'Match of the Day' as the man with the glassy stare extended a few perfunctory compliments to players whose names he couldn't remember, and then reminded us all that Liverpool – abject, insipid Liverpool – had a lot of injuries this season. The Norwich fanzines didn't lose any time in exploiting the possibilities of the Hansen phenomenon (there was another one by this stage called *Ferry*

Across the Wensum). Early in the New Year, instead of
the usual caricatures of Mr Chase – still, inevitably, a key
figure in the fan demonology – one of them simply
printed on its cover a picture of Phillips turning away
after scoring against Villa (they won 3–2 and should have
had six – even Beckford scored) above which was the
caption 'JUST ACCEPT IT, HANSEN'.

The slight drawback was that Hansen had a point.
Norwich have always been a schizophrenic side, the away
win at Old Trafford followed by the home defeat by
Wimbledon, the cup glory running parallel with the
league disaster, the majestic first-half display trailed by
the dismal second-half collapse. Nineteen ninety-two/
three saw this tendency magnified to the point of
absurdity. In between beating Villa and Sheffield
Wednesday they went down *seven–one* at Blackburn in
October. Then there is the traditional mid-season collapse, so ingrained a habit that you could set a clock by it.
Graceful exponents of the penetrative, short-passing
game, Norwich customarily play their best football on
the billiard table surfaces of early autumn. Come January, when the pitches clag up and the ball sticks in the
mud, they start to fall apart. December '92 until late
January '93 encompassed defeats by Ipswich and Manchester United, some inglorious nil–nil draws with fodder
from the lower half of the table and the longest goal
drought (Robins was out injured) in the club's history.
Subsequently their progress took the form of a be-
wildering switchback ride of narrow victories against
quite good clubs, followed by heavy defeats against bad
ones. The goal difference had in any case been a thing of

horror since the Blackburn game. In early March they lost at QPR and were definitively written off. Three weeks later, after a typical four-day period in which they lost at Wimbledon and then beat Villa at Carrow Road, they were heading the table for the ninth and, as it turned out, final time.

The crunch came against Manchester United on 5 April. I couldn't go, as it had been shifted to the Monday night (thanks, BSkyB – I lost count of how many times you did this to me this season) and it's a 240-mile round trip from SW6, but Radio Five were doing live commentary and my father had promised telephone communication from the ground. I switched on after twenty minutes and heard somebody like Alan Green mention that 'all' United's goals had come from springing the offside trap. They were already 3–0 up. At half-time the phone rang. 'Well, they pissed that one up against the wall,' my father reported. In the background the tumult of voices blared wordlessly on. I saw the goals next morning on Breakfast TV – the play locked in the United half, a through-ball and a sudden flurry of red shirts, a terrified Norwich defender scuttling back and putting everyone onside, defeat. My father said he hadn't seen anything like it since the England–Hungary game in 1953. I couldn't bear to read the sports pages the next morning: 'CANARIES PLUCKED', 'CANARIES ROASTED', 'CANARIES FALL FROM THEIR PERCH'. Each unfurled tabloid looming up from the crush of the District Line screamed its joyful reproach.

And that was that, the final humiliation following four days later when they let in five at White Hart Lane. We never did get to see the handing over of the trophy at the final home game against Liverpool – I had it all planned – never did follow the open-top bus round the city centre as the yellow and green balloons flew up like butterflies above Mousehold Heath, never did stand on the Guildhall steps and cheer as Mike Walker was awarded the freedom of the city by a kindly mayor.

Carrow Road has changed now, altered irrevocably from the vast, tiered terraces I remember as a child. The Barclay Stand, from which twenty years ago the Norwich skinheads would inform visiting supporters that they were the Barclay Boot Boys, is all-seater, the toilets – always a good sign of a club's intentions – are palatial, and you couldn't fit more than 20,000 people in the ground if you sat them on each other's shoulders. Why, they had 43,000 packed in there for an FA Cup quarter-final against Leicester in the 1960s. Freeman, Hardy and Willis, the three legendary geese named after a local shoe-shop who used to fly in formation over the stand, are gone. Sometimes, walking up from the station on a Saturday afternoon, loitering past the programme sellers and boys holding piles of fanzines, catching sight of my father in his comical checked cap waiting impatiently near the car-park, I wonder what Warnes, Burditt, Vinall, Houghton and Murphy would have made of it all, what they would have thought of Mr Chase, four-million-pound transfer fees and ordinary supporters unable to see the game because of the whim of some bloody TV executive. Perhaps, on reflection, Warnes, Burditt, Vinall, Houghton and Murphy do make something of it all. They would be in their mid-eighties now, gnarled veterans vanished into the thin post-career world of the old-style professional footballer, before the days of testimonials and index-linked pensions, living with their children in grimy northern cities or frowsting in south-coast retirement homes, but possibly – after the away win at Villa, or the Chelsea game – Warnes rang Burditt, or Vinall looked out his address book and wrote to Houghton, to marvel at what time had done to football and Norwich City and to themselves. At any rate, I like to think so.

Huw Richards

The Gospel According to St John the Alchemist

SWANSEA CITY 1978/9

The winter of discontent it may have been in public
memory, but if you were a Swansea City supporter in
1978/9 your poet was Wordsworth rather than Shake-
speare — 'Bliss was it in that dawn to be alive, But to be
young was very heaven'.

A part of me still suspects that Swansea's career
between 1977 and 1986 never really happened but was
the consequence of mass experimentation in some
hallucinogenic drug. This would also explain some of the
away strips. The experience was reproduced years later
on my first visit to New York, where the World Trade
Centre has an express lift offering two options — ground
and 102. From the end of 1977/8 Swansea would climb
sixty-five league places in four seasons. I prefer not to
think about the return journey.

Some of my best friends are Liverpool fans and I
sometimes wonder what it would be like to have their
(until recently) unquestioning certainty of success. They
say I wouldn't understand. What they can't comprehend

is the great paradox of lower division life. At the same time as praying for higher status, we know that lower division football is more fun. Premier League fans become entangled in the deadly seriousness of it all, but lower league football takes itself less seriously, has more sense of enjoyment and relaxation and fewer expectations.

Expectation matters. Promotion in 1977/8 had been joyful, but not unexpected. And by the time the Swans finished high in the First Division in 1982 my concept of possibility was so subverted that I would have believed John Toshack if he had announced that the Swans intended to win the European Cup, the next General Election and the County Cricket Championship. They could hardly have done worse than Glamorgan, anyway.

But this was the year that was unbelievable at the time, the second consecutive promotion that took the Swans back to the division we believed was our natural home — the Second. Toshack was infuriated by this belief and argued that the First must be the aim. He was right. But after a decade in which a place in the Third had seemed wildly ambitious our forty-year mid-century run in the Second, even if more often than not a struggle to stay up, looked like a golden age.

Nineteen seventy-eight/nine was Toshack's first full season in charge, the year that gave birth to the legend summed up in Swindon Town's programme by the omnipresent Tony Pullein (does this guy exist, or is he a codename for some database?): 'Over the past fifteen months or so the Vetch Field has been taken over by the Red Army from Liverpool and, as a result, the club has

been transformed from a struggling Fourth Division
outfit into a throbbing, exciting unit that is now poised to
win promotion for the second season in succession.'

Anyone capable of dreaming up 'throbbing, exciting
unit' should have been writing advertising copy for MFI
rather than soccer profiles. The reality was a little more
complex. Watford had Elton John, we had Toshack's Red
Army and that was how Fleet Street wanted it. Like all
Welsh clubs we were alleged to play in the Valleys. The
last league club from the Valleys – Merthyr – were thrown
out in 1930. I suppose it is better than being ignored.

This was the season Wales won a fourth consecutive
triple crown to go with the Five Nations Championship.
If we'd known it was the last of the line we'd have been
more impressed. It was also a great year for the Midlands
clubs who had provided most of my live football. I
followed Shrewsbury Town on their epic run to the FA
Cup quarter-finals, being carried bodily five yards down
the terraces in the fifth round at Aldershot when David
Tong's weird curling, dipping shot equalized in injury
time moments after Aldershot had gone ahead for the
second time. West Brom came third in the First Division
and Stoke City were promoted from the Second. Even the
team we'd watched on summer holidays, Berwick
Rangers, were promoted for the first time ever.

Seventy-eight/nine also produced the most complicated
terrace chant ever. It may have been the hallucinogens
again, but I am certain I heard Worcester City supporters
perform a fifteen-minute Gregorian chant during an FA
Cup tie against Newport County. Much good it did them
– they were leading 1–0 when a suitably fazed defender

crashed the ball into a team-mate's skull from about three yards and saw it rocket into his own net. Newport won 2–1.

There had been occasions when I half wished I had opted for something more conventional within the narrow terms defined by Bridgnorth schoolboys. At any time supporting the Swans would have been seen as deviant behaviour: in the sixties and seventies it was an open invitation to derision. The chemistry master's comparison between my third-year performance in his subject and the Swans' position in the Third Division was intended as a compliment to neither.

But in my family supporting the Swans is an incurable genetic disorder contracted by my grandfather in the 1920s and passed through the male line. (My brother John was briefly resistant – citing his Bristol birthplace and declaring equal affection for Rovers and City.)

The inheritance included a grounding in myth and legend stretching back to 1920s hero Jack Fowler. Grandpa was a skilled leg-puller and I suspected he was at it again when he said that they used to sing 'Fow, Fow, Fow, Fow, Fowler, score a little goal for me.' But it was later confirmed in a club history.

From Dad came stories of Trevor Ford, the Allchurch and Charles brothers and of Roy Paul, lured to Bogota in 1950. When I met a Colombian last year, the first thing Dad asked was, 'Have you told her about Roy Paul?' (I had.) I heard how Tom Kiley's broken leg cost promotion to the First in 1955/6 and of the 1964 Cup semi-final, an injustice of Guildford Four proportions; the better days, might-have-beens and near-misses cherished by all

supporters of middle-ranking clubs. My first season as a
supporter was perfect preparation for the next decade – we
were relegated to the Fourth Division for the first time.

Distance made us absentee supporters, treasuring occasional trips to the Vetch and the Swans' perennially
unsuccessful visits to the Midlands. I can't tell you
whether it was luck or judgement that the only year of my
life spent less than 100 miles from the Vetch was the one
we spent in the top six of the First Division, but I'm not
complaining about it.

Whether or not absence makes the heart grow fonder,
it certainly makes it more anxious. The true horror of
supporting from a distance is the Saturday afternoon
wait, cursing radio reporters wittering about irrelevancies
like Liverpool v Manchester United. Little equals the
exasperation of entering a tunnel just as the radio was
announcing 'Scunthorpe United one, Swansea Ci — '. A
forty-minute wait for confirmation of another away
defeat – as if we couldn't have guessed.

Distance doesn't make you care any less. Players we
saw only once or twice could inspire fierce debate. Names
like Glen Davies, Alan Beer, Terry Cotton and Clive
Slattery are as evocative of my childhood as any pension-
able teddy bear. 'Slattery will get you nowhere', it was
said, rather unfairly. He wasn't a bad player – and Zico
couldn't have got very far in some Swans teams. I
remember my mother's horror in the spring of 1977 when
I told her that the Swans promotion race was more
important than my A-levels, but I still think my logic was
quite reasonable – I already knew where I was going next
autumn, but they didn't.

Becoming a student meant eligibility for a railcard and more matches. Nothing drastic like an awayday to Workington, but three or four matches a season became twelve or fourteen. Whether this was good news is uncertain – if players gave fans nicknames, mine would have been Jonah.

My first match at Easter 1966 was a 2–0 home defeat by Millwall. I estimate that they won twice in the first twenty-five games I saw them play, and they didn't draw a lot. Vulnerable at home, they defied belief away. I was six years old at the Millwall match. My first away win, in the League Cup at Chester, was in the week before I entered the Upper Sixth. The low-point was that day of wrath, 26 April 1975 – a date I can recall eighteen years on without checking, but with shuddering. Defeat at Rochdale forced us to apply for re-election. We knew we'd be in the same division next season, but psychologically it was much worse than relegation, removing that last illusion of respectability expressed as 'Well, at least we haven't . . . ' Norwich, QPR and Cardiff had all had to plead for renewed status. We hadn't – not till then.

The first league away win had to wait for my first term at university. Travelling down from Oxford to Ealing Broadway and thence by bus to Brentford, Alan Curtis and Mickey Conway – a lively winger whose career was shortly to be ended by a car crash – scored first-half goals and the Swans held on to win 2–0. Wyndham Evans, who had got there as soon as he could, was sent off for a series of late tackles on Steve Phillips.

Student life was full of surprises. Strange place, Oxford. It took me a year to discover that what I thought

was history, they called politics. I had never before been
in a community where football was a minority interest
rather than a major preoccupation of the bulk of the male
population, a discovery that seriously disorientated my
opening conversational gambits. Meeting Steve Ford
from Stoke, my best mate over the next three years, I
informed him that I had been to the theatre there and
took about twenty minutes to realize that his natural
habitat was Victoria Ground rather than Victoria
Theatre.

Football often serves as a refuge from disliked external
reality. By the start of the 1978/9 season and my second
year I realized that Oxford's external reality didn't suit
me at all and strongly suspected that the feeling was
mutual. Unaccustomed success made the refuge all the
more effective.

I struck a bet with Steve Ford about the relative
positions of Swansea in the Third Division and Stoke in
the Second, more bravado than faith. I knew chairman
Malcolm Struel said we were going up again, but newly
promoted chairmen were nearly always over-optimistic. I
remembered the last promotion to the Third — down
again in three seasons, re-election in five.

Doubts had remained to the end in the previous season.
Knowing we were good enough to go up, I had still
turned to Dad as we fell behind at Reading on Easter
Monday and said 'Perhaps Glamorgan will be good this
year.' (They weren't.) This may have had something to do
with our first technicolour nightmare strip, a red and
green striped outfit that revolted even Leighton James,
who was sitting behind us. We won 4–1, and it could

have been more. Two away wins in one season — the times they were a changing beyond belief.

If I had known that John Toshack would be revealed over the next four seasons as a soccer alchemist I might have shown greater faith. But I wasn't convinced when he was hired as player-manager in early 1978. We'd experienced returning Welsh soccer heroes before. Barry Hole (£20,000) and Ronnie Rees (£28,000) were overpriced at 1993 prices, never mind those of the early 1970s. Toshack admittedly came on a free, but against that he was originally from Cardiff. One thing I do understand about Liverpool supporters is how they feel about Manchester United. It's what we think of Cardiff City, with a different accent. Being a published poet was certainly different, even if the title of *Gosh It's Tosh* served equally well as a review. (His subsequent autobiography, titled with equal chutzpah but greater terseness *Tosh*, was altogether classier.)

He was also replacing a local hero. If you believe the authorized version Toshack took us from re-election to near-champions. But this ignores Harry Griffiths, who was resuscitating the Swans (there were a lot of Dying Swan headlines in the mid-1970s) when Tosh was still performing his impersonation of a berserk red-shirted electricity pylon. Harry's appointment, just before re-election, obeyed an ancient football rule: when in extremis appoint the honest and valued retainer. Some boards soon regret this — ours wondered why they'd not thought of it before.

Harry had one great asset, a group of talented youngsters. Alan Curtis, nephew of the lamented Roy

Paul, and Robbie James were the best and most enduring
of them. Otherwise it was the odd free transfer and the
remnants of the fumbling, neurotic team who had
finished ninetieth in the league. The transformation
prefigured Joe Mercer's post-Revie effect on the England
team – results improved as enjoyment and purpose were
restored.

They attacked with a recklessness that might have been
considered excessive in the Light Brigade – a tendency
that peaked in 1976/7 with a league-topping 92 goals but
with the logical by-product of 68 conceded, including
four in the home defeat by Watford that cost promotion.
It had been worth it, but chairman Struel's fears of
another near-miss the following season prompted
Toshack's appointment. Harry stayed on as assistant, and
died suddenly at the Vetch four days before promotion.
Toshack's achievement is extraordinary enough without
exaggeration, but Harry started the rise and made what
followed possible. Five of his players would appear for
the Swans in the First Division.

But he couldn't get vital goals. Tosh could and did,
culminating in the prototypical wicked deflection (has
anyone ever seen a morally equivocal deflection?) off the
left ear of a Halifax Town defender to seal promotion on
the last day of the season. So far, so good.

The close season introduced a fresh novelty – new
players who weren't free transfers; Crewe keeper Geoff
Crudgington had looked like a human octopus, single-
handedly defying our forwards who had scored more
goals than anyone else (87) for a second year; then there
was Alan Waddle. After scoring 179 times in two seasons

it seemed a bit odd to recruit a striker from Leicester City, who had apparently given up goals for religious reasons. But he had, at some time in the early Jurassic period, scored the last goal anyone remembered in the Liverpool –Everton match, then in its Eton Wall Game period.

The first hint of the extraordinary came a week into the league programme at Oxford. I knew that United were ordinary but troublesome opposition. Not so for the Swans, who simply flowed over them. Robbie James, finishing with thunderous finality, scored in each half as palpable excitement grew among the massive Swansea following. 'They've not even won the match yet, but you'd think they'd won promotion again,' one said half-prophetically as they came off to a half-time standing ovation.

A new Pope was elected that day. Whether he issued a statement condemning our next signing I couldn't tell you, but in the next fortnight just about everyone else did. Tommy Smith, he of the gin-trap tackling and the decisive goal in the 1977 European Cup Final, came on a free to firmly implant the press view of the Vetch as a rest home for decrepit Liverpool players. He also arrived in time to face Spurs and their newly acquired Argentinian World Cup winners in the League Cup.

Tommy declared his intention of testing them out. Had he taken on Ricky Villa (winner of the coveted Most Terrifying Foul competition in the X-certificate Argentina–Brazil match that summer), it might have been better than most World Heavyweight Title fights. But in the first few minutes there was a 50–50 ball. Tommy challenged with typical delicacy and Ossie Ardiles went down and off. Tommy might have gone as well, but had to settle for a condemnatory leader in the *Guardian*.

Too bad it diverted attention from the well deserved 2–0 lead that was soon delighting the radio audience in Shropshire. Then Alan Waddle took a hand. Unfortunately he took it in our penalty area. Spurs scored and went on to force a 2–2 draw. And we all know what is supposed to happen to Third Division clubs who blow that sort of chance at home.

Thoughts of going to the replay were dashed by being 1200 miles away railcarding around Europe, the only football fan in a group of six. Irrelevant in France, this became useful in Italy. My Italian was no less non-existent than the others', but communication was aided on occasion by knowing who Paolo Rossi and Romeo Bennetti were, while the average Italian's English vocabulary seemed to consist largely of terms such as 'Liverpool' and 'Dalglish'.

I took much derision for insistence on hunting for British newspapers, pleading the likelihood of a General Election. Jim Callaghan would shortly sell the country a Stan Bowles-quality dummy by inserting the word 'not' into the sentence in which he was assumed to be calling the election – but in reality the football news, and particularly the Spurs replay, was my priority.

It was played on a Wednesday. On Friday morning I ran to the news-stand at Napoli Mergellina station, expecting to buy Thursday's papers. No papers. The Italian railway workers were staging a one-day strike. 'You should be pleased – you're all for workers' solidarity,' said one of my travelling colleagues. My reply was neither printable nor politically correct. 'What if we never get Thursday's papers? It'll be days before I find out.' I brooded as we sat on the ferry to Capri. That is why my main memory of the island is not its famed tranquillity or the Blue Grotto, but of dancing round the main square with a bottle of dubious Italian beer in one hand and Thursday's *Daily Mirror* in the other, acclaiming Alan Curtis's devastation of the Spurs defence in our 3–1 win.

Unseemly? Not when compared to another reaction – the first Swans record. The imaginatively titled 'Swansea City' was perpetrated by someone called Roger Evans (probably not the Tory MP, although clearly capable of almost any outrage) and the players (the ragged cheer in the middle). Elvis Costello it wasn't. Not even in 1978 was popular taste debased enough to allow a lyric incorporating the immortal line 'Therefore for the replay, we went to White Hart Lane,' anywhere near the Top Thirty.

Every day something new and improbable was reported. I began to wonder if the early editions of the British press were an elaborate hoax. Could we really have signed Ian Callaghan and Phil Boersma and staged two three-goal Vetch comebacks (1–4 to 4–4 against Rotherham and 1–3 to 4–3 versus Tranmere) in the space of my four days in Venice and Vienna? Strange as it now seems, Boersma looked the most significant newcomer yet – a player of the quality needed for promotion to the Second, but far from a veteran.

It was a great trip, including seeing Wiener Sportklub dismantle Casino Salzburg 6–1. But the feeling of making up for lost time set me pursuing live Swans action on my return. I should have known better. There was no Lazarus Act at Chester but a 2–0 defeat and Tommy sent off for dissent. Then London, the League Cup and a 2–0 exit at QPR in spite of Robbie's finest hour – dominating a midfield contested by Gerry Francis and John Hollins.

Even in this season, I would see them lose as often as win. But the sense of gathering momentum was not to be broken. They became a fixture at the top end of the Third – Watford, also up from the Fourth, and Shrewsbury were also there from the start. By early November Swindon and Gillingham had completed the quintet who would dominate the season.

Would you rather see your team playing attractively and losing or dully and winning? Be honest . . . Me too . . . But nothing matches the times when your team gets results with style and flair. The 'attack from any-where and if the opposition scores, make sure you score twice' philosophy had been successfully transplanted into a higher division, producing football of a flowing, sophis-ticated *élan* rarely seen in the Third. It might have been easier on the nerves to follow a team that preferred to start victories by going two up rather than two down, and our keepers might have lasted more than a season. But it would not have been half as exhilarating.

The possibilities seemed infinite, and while the press banged on about the Superannuated Scousers we regarded our young stars with pride, anticipation and some anxiety. Of course we knew that Alan Curtis was the finest attacking talent outside the First Division, Jeremy Charles would be better than Dad Mel or even Uncle John and that Robbie James would play 800 league games. But simultaneously we feared that they would be damaged by defenders of limited talent and infinite malevolence, lured away by bigger clubs who wouldn't appreciate them, or simply turn out not as good as we hoped.

Those conflicting emotions bit most sharply whenever Alan Curtis took possession; setting up a buzz of anticipation acknowledging his extraordinary tight control, ability to feint, turn, create space and torment defenders who lacked the contortionist flexibility needed to keep him in check.

Different apprehensions surrounded Jeremy Charles (Charlot), who had reached the stage in his late teens when you outgrow your strength and are liable to lay waste anything within a radius of twenty-five yards. You never knew whether he was going to accidentally flatten a team-mate, swerve an inch-perfect fifty-yard pass off the outside of his boot or do both in the space of thirty seconds. With Robbie your fears were more for opposing goalkeepers. He'd had an indestructible quality since announcing himself as a sixteen-year-old with his first league goal, a thirty-yard screamer on New Year's Day 1974, and had carried on in the same manner, although the rockets did not always go quite where intended. Swans wingers became accustomed to passes that were well directed but hit with a power that suggested he had mistaken them for Linford Christie.

He was a streak player, who scored goals in bursts. Twenty-one this season included eight in the first four matches, then six in eight on the run-in — most hit with alarming power. Robust and barrel-chested, Robbie looked cumbersome until he had to cover ten yards to the by-line or a loose ball. Then he was quick, adept and competitive.

It wasn't all elegant ball play. Style was complemented by physical power — Tommy Smith was probably the hardest tackler in the team, but with little crunch factor to spare over Robbie and full-back Wyndham Evans. Wyndham had played in the re-election team, came from Llanelli, and was good at convincing nervous wingers that he was an escaped Scarlets second row. There were offdays when 'scything' replaced 'crunching' in match reports, but he was a tough, competent, resilient survivor habitually recalled in crises.

The other full-back was another survivor, Danny Bartley, aptly termed 'the admirable Bartley' by one reporter. A neat, precise, resourceful player with the attacking talents of a converted winger, his forays up the left, sidestepping in the manner of rugby player Phil Bennett, were a vital supplement to formidable attacking options. Between Danny and Wyndham were a variety of centre-backs, Leighton Phillips, a languidly elegant Welsh international centre-half (displaced at Aston Villa by the non-languid, inelegant and unWelsh Alan Evans) provided at a club record £70,000 the strongest proof yet of genuine ambition. His regular partner was Nigel Stevenson, a young local anglepoise lamp impersonator known with some irony as 'Speedy', whose reliable power in the air displaced the more obviously gifted Steve Morris.

Tosh had a few goes in the back four, aiding in the destruction of Spurs as sweeper. He would probably have gone in goal if Crudgington hadn't been so reliable, and this year it would have come off. Whether as player or manager he had a touch that made Midas look like a dry-stone-wall mason. Recalled to play alongside James and Curtis for Wales against Scotland, he scored a hat-trick in a 3–0 win. Nobody, however, was going to commit the heresy of regarding him as God; that was Gareth Edwards (which was reassuring as he was known to be a Swans supporter), but John the Baptist looked about right.

Even so the unmatched idol of the crowd was Alan Waddle – a selfless Stakhanovite targetman whose battles with opposing centre-backs and his own limitations struck an immediate chord of identification in the man on the North Bank. Opposing defenders were inclined to dispute the crowd's favourite chanted proposition, 'There's only one Alan Waddle' – his chasing and harassing left the distinct impression that there were two or three.

His contribution was recognized graphically if unsubtly by a vast banner at the Swindon game proclaiming, 'Alan Waddle lays on more balls than Fiona Richmond.' Deft flicks to supporting attackers assisted a high proportion of the eighty-three league goals – nineteen of which he claimed himself, none in a losing cause. His finest goal was yet to come on Boxing Day 1979; a stunning diving header whose minor defect was that it counted for Bristol Rovers.

But Boxing Day and after were never our favourite time. Without knowing the club's view on a continental-style mid-season break I would surmise that it was in favour on the grounds that the team always took one anyway, starting as a rule by displaying their morbid fear of the Third Round of the Cup.

The win at Spurs was something of an aberration –

embarrassment rather than triumph was the leitmotif of
Cup displays in the Toshack years. Three years later, top
of the First Division, they would struggle desperately to
overcome Colwyn Bay in a Welsh Cup tie that went to a
replay. This season had already brought near-disaster at
the hands of Woking and a previously and subsequently
obscure forward named Eggie James, seen off by an
uneasy 5–3 in a second round replay. Our third round
visitors were Bristol Rovers, from a low-lying region of
the Second Division with a young Welsh keeper named
Martin Thomas who had just perfected his Horatius
impersonation. Rovers scored on the break and we went
out muttering: 'We never win much in January anyway.'

So nobody much minded when the weather ruled out
any league games that month. We were terrible in February instead. The most unwelcome of five winless outings
was at Exeter – it was a long way for an even worse
display than the defeat two weeks earlier at Brentford.
Alan Curtis equalized mid-way through the second half,
so we promptly conceded another.

Returning to Oxford I found my door decorated by a
six-foot tombstone representing our promotion hopes,
complete with my name, Toshack's and the rest of the
squad, drawn by Steve Ford's artistically gifted fiancée,
Karen. A Liverpool fan, she had been highly diverted when
we signed Alan Waddle, warning me with more relish than
accuracy 'He's useless.' This time it looked as though she
might be right, but Exeter proved to be the lowpoint.

By now I had settled into promotion-chasing routine
for a third consecutive season, feverishly calculating the
implications of rivals' results and thinking unchristian

thoughts. Nothing changes. An ill-timed foreign trip last
season meant that I became the first person ever to visit
Prague while wishing that they were in West Bromwich
instead. An entire Czech Telecom card was spent in trying
to find the results of the play-off second leg and
twenty-five years of affection for Albion ended the moment I knew. Hence my delight in 1979 when Peter Foley
snatched a fortunate last-minute equalizer for Oxford
United against our rivals Watford on a snowbound
Manor Ground. While denying me a plea in extenuation,
the mid-table finish the following year at least allowed me
to work for finals in peace.

The Easter trip to Swindon, looming ominously with
games in hand, was vital. There were nearly 17,000 there,
including the Swindon fan behind us who, having ingested
Tony Pullein's words of wisdom about the Red Army,
declared, 'There's no future for them – they're an old team.'

Leaving aside our youngsters, this was a bit rich from
someone whose team still had John Trollope, believed to
have a younger brother who had written *Barchester
Towers*, pushing his zimmer frame at right-back. Robbie
James, veteran only in league appearances, thumped a
first-half goal, Boersma, previously inconsistent, played a
blinder before suffering a career-ending shattered leg. And
Swindon won about 146 corners, but failed to convert any
of them, leaving us two points closer to the Second.

But Toshack's Swans were always programmed pre-
season: Off to a good start. Top three at Christmas.
Then out of the Cup and no wins in January (February if
it snows). Let them think you've had it, then it's into the
blinding finish. But whatever you do keep the buggers

sweating to the last possible moment. Why waste effort settling it early? Just as well there were no play-offs in those days – or they would certainly have anticipated their successors of 1988 in getting promoted by the scenic route rather than going directly.

The twelve-match unbeaten run-in was no untroubled triumphant procession. Tommy Smith lacked something in credibility as a serial film heroine, but the team strapped themselves to the rails on a weekly basis. There were six matches after Swindon – we trailed in five.

The last had been scheduled at Plymouth. With the mid-season backlog still working through, it became the last but one, but Home Park was still submerged by several thousand crazed Welshmen who rapidly learnt to disregard theories that ideal opponents on these occasions are mid-table with nothing to play for. Plymouth didn't believe it either. Gary Megson ran amok in midfield, Fred Binney put them ahead before half-time and they led twice. It took the lethal combination of Curtis's ability to make space and strike in busy penalty areas and Toshack's talent for being in the right place – unmarked about three feet from the Plymouth line – to squeeze a 2–2 draw. Having failed narrowly in my attempt on the standing high jump record when Tosh got the second, the next task was to get back to Plymouth station in about twenty minutes for the train east. BBC vans had been spotted lurking en masse next to the ground and we'd never been on 'Match of the Day' before. I made it to Oxford in time, just, and was strangely reassured by Jimmy Hill's belief that we were going to make it.

Forty-five down, 58 points gained, Chesterfield at the Vetch the following Friday night to go. Six days' long wait. Swindon, curse them, won at Brentford. Two more wins would give them 61 points – more than we could manage. Shrewsbury, no longer differentiated from any other enemy, drew at Mansfield then beat Rotherham to move to 59 from 45. Watford, with better goal difference, shared our 58 from 45. Fourteen years on I can sympathize with Gillingham, who seemed fated never to play in the Second. But at the time their dropped point at Colchester after leading 2–0 looked the best news of the week.

There were 25,000 crammed into the Vetch that night, but it was asking for trouble for the public address announcer to joke about Chesterfield fainting when they saw the size of the crowd. We knew all about alleged soft touches from last week and felt no great faith in Sheffield Wednesday, who had kicked off fifteen minutes earlier against Swindon.

After a quarter of an hour Chesterfield had the effrontery to force a corner. Phil Walker swung in a routine cross. It swung on, and on, and on, without interruption – then it hit the back of the net simultaneously with someone turning the sound off.

Now Alan Waddle showed himself a true hero – restoring the decibel level within a minute by steering a header with tantalizing slowness but perfect accuracy inside Chesterfield's far post. Now the demolition, we thought. Chesterfield thought differently. They dug in for the ensuing siege with a bloody-minded tenacity that did them credit – although we didn't see it quite that way.

Near-miss followed shaved woodwork and desperate goal-line clearance as the tension mounted to improbable levels. Cometh the hour, cometh the man. Toshack replaced ex-Cardiff utility man Brian 'Clem' Attley mid-way through the second half to rapturous, trusting acclaim.

The last fifteen minutes brought two discoveries – first that Swindon had lost and a win would promote us, and second, in direct consequence, that fresh levels of tension were attainable. Eight minutes from time we attacked down the left and won a free-kick level with the penalty spot. Bartley, calm and controlled as ever, chipped the kick in and Toshack rose to thunder an unstoppable header into the top left-hand corner.

The image of Tosh jumping for a header that travelled as quickly as any shot, but still seemed to take five minutes to reach the net, is still as vivid as the moment it happened. So too are memories of the next eight minutes. No more tension – just outright terror that, having grasped promotion, a single slip might lose it. Apart from the corner, Chesterfield had barely threatened. Now each time they crossed halfway they looked like the Mongol horde, only much more menacing. Eight minutes? It felt more like eight weeks as I stood on my seat in the back row of the old Double Decker stand, an instant convert from agnosticism to any and every form of prayer that might persuade the referee to blow up.

At last he did. We were back in the Second Division. Mrs Thatcher had been elected Prime Minister for the first time eight days earlier and at the time it seemed like a fair exchange.

Nick Hornby

The Abbey Habit

CAMBRIDGE UNITED 1983/4

I have been watching football for a quarter of a century, and only a few seasons have a life, a heart and a personality of their own. There is Arsenal's double year, obviously; the two recent Championship triumphs; the season I started going; the year they played nearly seventy games, reached two Cup Finals and won nothing; and Cambridge United's record-breaking, mind-boggling '83/4 season, when they went an astonishing thirty-one games without a Second Division victory. (I was working in Cambridge at the time, and split my passions schizophrenically between palatial Highbury and the ruined Abbey Stadium, Cambridge's home.) In some ways I enjoyed Cambridge's catastrophe as much as I enjoyed Arsenal's run of twenty-three league games without defeat at the beginning of the '90/91 season: both sequences had a momentum, a tension and an atmosphere fans will remember for ever.

Of course, it was irritating to begin with – one does not enjoy seeing one's team lose. And it was to some extent inexplicable. The same back four had, just months before, set a new record of a different kind: for the longest time spent without conceding a home league goal. (This run, incidentally, ended memorably. Malcolm Webster, Cambridge's goalkeeper, was invited on to the Abbey pitch at half-time – a fate-tempting piece of timing that the club probably regretted – to receive an award commemorating the feat; in the second half, the inevitable happened. He conceded four goals in less than twenty minutes.)

However, as it became clear that there might be a little history to be made, each 5–0 away defeat, each 2–2 draw snatched from the jaws of victory, became perversely satisfying. Hartlepool recently set a record for the longest period without scoring. How many Hartlepool fans, even in the midst of their temporary jubilation, did not feel a little pang, a sense of something gone, when the net finally did bulge after Lord knows how many goalless hours? Their impressive failure even to convert a penalty captured the imagination of the national sporting media; once the record had gone, they became just another terrible team.

Cambridge United were a terrible team that year. They won four games (two of them after they had already been relegated) and lost twenty-four. They used thirty-two different players, fourteen of whom played in the number seven shirt at some stage during the season, and four of whom were goalkeepers. And they got through the requisite three managers (one sacked, one caretaker, one who saw out the rest of the season). It was brilliant.

*

Andy Sinton

Cambridge United v Brighton, 29.10.83

At the time of writing, Andy Sinton is to play for England, in the World Cup against Turkey. Ten years ago, he was playing for England's worst team, in the Second Division against Brighton. He was just seventeen then, but astonishingly strong and exceptionally mature: even at that age he volunteered to take the penalties (at thirty-five, I still avoid them in our five-a-side games whenever possible) and he scored them, too. He got one in this game, one of those muddy, gloriously stupid afternoons that stick in the mind, right at the beginning of the not-winning streak: seven goals, Eric Young sent off, an injury-time Brighton winner after Cambridge had fought back to 3–3 after being 3–1 down.

I told everyone to watch out for Sinton. I knew that he would go on to greater things – Division One certainly, an international cap maybe. Apart from his strength, he had pace, and he could pass and finish. (He was joint top scorer that season. OK, he only managed six goals, and, OK, four of those were pens, but still . . .) He went to Brentford, and then to QPR, and if the papers are to be believed, George Graham wants to buy him for Arsenal. I don't want to be smug, but if George had asked for my advice ten years ago I could have saved him a couple of million pounds.

Before I am asked to throw in the day-job and take up scouting full-time, however, here are some other players I told people to watch out for, players you are unlikely to have heard of unless you were among the two and a half

thousand who watched Cambridge that year: Graham
Daniels, Keith Lockhart, Steve Pyle, Andy Beattie, Kevin
Smith. Daniels, then a vegetarian philosophy student with
a ferocious shot (and the ferocious shot alone set him
apart from his teammates), is now the Reverend Graham
Daniels, a non-league player-manager (I heard him being
interviewed on 'Sport on Five' recently, after his team had
been thumped in an FA Cup qualifying round) and for all
I know a carnivore; I don't know what became of the
rest.

An amazing fact: five years after the record-breaking
relegation season, only eight of the thirty-two players
Cambridge used were still registered as professionals. (A
quarter of those eight, interestingly, were goalkeepers –
presumably playing behind Cambridge's defence that
year gave them experience unavailable elsewhere.) Twenty-
four drop-outs! Three-quarters of a large Second Division
squad gone! Some of these players were old, and therefore
must have retired; the majority of them were teenagers,
thrown in at the deep end by increasingly desperate
managers. (At least half of the thirty-two players made
their debuts for Cambridge *that season*.) One of these
teenagers, Ray Nicholls, packed up the game soon after he
had made his debut for United; perhaps understandably,
he decided that anything was better than getting beaten out
of sight week after week. The others just seem to have
disappeared.

It could well be that they were all hopeless, and had no
future in the game anyway, but I doubt it. These are some
of the players I saw at the Abbey Stadium that year: Steve
Ogrizovic, Ray Houghton, Asa Hartford, Pat Nevin,

David Speedie, Kerry Dixon, Mark Hately, Neil Webb, Vince Hilaire, Kevin Keegan, Chris Waddle, Peter Beardsley, Peter Lorimer (it is hard to imagine Sinton and Lorimer on the same pitch – Take That never played on the same bill as the Beatles – but they were), Peter Barnes, Mel Sterland, Archie Gemmill, John Robertson, Jimmy Case, Joe Corrigan. It was a tough Second Division, and though one could hardly argue that these young lads held their own – they patently didn't – there were enough storming performances and narrow one-goal defeats to suggest that in a better, fairer, less traumatic world they might be able to cope.

There were the draws against Manchester City and Leeds, two narrow defeats against Chelsea, and the epic triumph against Newcastle that finally ended the run . . . If the teenagers had been introduced singly, and not mob-handed, into a winning, rather than doomed, team, they might still be around today. We can all name players who, once removed from the cosy, protective, winning environment of a good Premier League club, sank through the divisions like a stone; if Andy Beattie had made his debut at centre-half alongside Alan Hansen or Kevin Moran, he might still be playing today. Alex Ferguson, when asked to explain why he coddles Ryan Giggs, has expressed his regret that he blooded too many youngsters too soon when he was with Aberdeen – youngsters who consequently never made it all the way. And Aberdeen have never had the terrible problems that beset Cambridge that year.

All this is by way of saying that I have an intense and possibly cranky admiration for Andy Sinton, who survived the slaughter of the innocents, the cull. There is a sentence that all football fans have used about one of their team, and it begins, 'He was never the same...': 'Peter Osgood was never the same after he broke his leg'; 'Rix was never the same after he missed that penalty in the Cup Winners' Cup Final'; 'Justin Fashanu was never the same after he scored that goal against Liverpool'; 'Peter Bonetti was never the same after that West Germany quarter-final'. Well, Andy Sinton's first full season in the Football League, all of it, was horrific, and he *was* the same afterwards – the same, but better. I have the same misgivings about Graham Taylor's robots as everybody else, but Sinton is different: I don't know how tough you have to be to play in a losing team for seven months and go on to become an international, but that's how tough he is. Respect, as they say on Kiss FM, is due.

Addiction
Cambridge v Grimsby, 28.12.83

Is there such a thing as an addictive personality? Right now, I am trying, once again, to give up smoking. I am wearing a little nicotine patch; I have a packet of nicotine chewing gum by my side, and a packet of last night's cigarettes in my pocket. It's not going that well, really.

In his book *The Easy Way to Give Up Smoking*, Allen Carr likens the smoker to someone who wears tight shoes just for the pleasure of taking them off, and it is a good analogy. Smokers smoke for the pleasure of relieving nicotine withdrawal symptoms – symptoms that only smoking gives them. In other words, we spend a fortune, and take terrible health risks, just to achieve the state that non-smokers maintain effortlessly.

Football addiction works in much the same way, and in some senses my addiction to Cambridge United that season was the purest I have ever experienced. Smoking gives me nicotine, and with it some stimulation and relaxation; my addiction to Arsenal is, occasionally, rewarded by cups and championships and Ian Wright solo goals and Merson chips. My addiction to the appalling Cambridge side of '83/4 brought me nothing at all. It's just that if I hadn't been there to watch, I would have felt uncomfortable: I had to watch Cambridge just to feel the way that the vast majority of the apathetic Cambridge public felt all the time.

It was a grim Christmas. On Boxing Day I went to Highbury to see Arsenal draw with Birmingham City (Charlie Nicholas scored his first goal at Highbury, a penalty); two days later I went to Cambridge to see the Grimsby clash. I was back especially to see the game. There was nobody at my stupendously unheated Cambridge flat, and I had flu; I could have stayed slumped in front of the TV at the cosy parental home for another few days if it had not been for the Second Division fixture list.

I had a feeling that the Grimsby game was going to be The One. I was wrong, of course — by exactly four months, as it turned out — but having already witnessed three months of failure (four defeats and three draws at home) I was in no position to take a risk. Strangely enough, the people of Cambridge had obviously been getting similar vibes. Unless the opposition brought huge numbers of fans with them (the London clubs, for example, or the big Northern teams), United usually got crowds of 2500; for no apparent reason, 4500 turned out to see Grimsby, who brought almost nobody with them at all.

The team responded to the San Siro atmosphere, and went one up through Robbie Cooke in the first half. Even a Grimsby equalizer didn't trouble them unduly, and Andy Sinton put away one of his penalties to give them a 2–1 lead, the score after ninety minutes – Grimsby didn't get their inevitable second goal until deep into injury time. It was the closest United came to a win in the entire seven months.

On the way back to the flat, I experienced what I would later understand as a classic addiction reaction: I felt daft. Why had I travelled all the way back from my mum's to watch that? What was I going to do now? Nobody I knew would be around until the New Year; surely I could have forgone a game against Grimsby for the sake of a few companionable days in the warm. I experience similar regrets after I have lit a cigarette, only weeks or days or hours after swearing abstinence: is this all it is? How come I can't give these up? They're *nothing*. The problem, of course, is that addicts can recognize the triviality, the irrelevance, of their dependence only after they have satisfied their need. On my way home, I could see very clearly that Cambridge v Grimsby had not been much to get worked up about; on my way there, all I could see were the floodlights, the manager's programme notes, and the three precious league points coming our way.

*

Randall Butt
Cambridge United v Cardiff, 10.3.84

Every other week, it seemed, a terrible team came to the Abbey, a team so poor that it looked as though the losing run could not survive their visit. Despite Cambridge's form, Swansea were unable to haul themselves off the bottom until nearly Christmas, but they got a draw. Fulham weren't much better – another draw. Carlisle won away without taxing themselves unduly; even Cardiff scored two second-half goals and walked away with three points. Randall Butt was not pleased.

Randall Butt – great name – was, and I believe still is, the football correspondent on the *Cambridge Evening News*. He cared passionately about what happened to the team, or at least gave every impression of caring: I remember a match report of an away win at Exeter in the late 1970s in which he not only took the referee to task for awarding the home team a penalty, but also expressed doubt that the kick had actually gone into the goal. (Randall thought it hit the post; everyone else in the ground, as he was big enough to admit, saw that it hit the stanchion and came out again.)

That season, Randall Butt played an even more vital role than usual. I was Trying To Be A Writer, a Herculean struggle which invariably involved hanging around outside the newsagents' at lunchtime, waiting for the paper to come in; if there was no word from Butt in the first edition, I was sometimes forced to buy the last one in the evening as well, just in case.

But beyond my self-induced idle fascination, United

fans had to buy the paper just to understand what was going on. Of the thirty-two players that Cambridge used that season, only fifteen or so were familiar even to regular fans. Several were signed on loan, and then hastily returned when the loan period was up; others were rashly purchased outright and lobbed straight into the first team. Frequently the programme, printed too early in the week to accommodate new arrivals, would be unable to assist one in identifying the mysterious figure in the number seven shirt. Watching Cambridge United without the benefit of Randall Butt's briefings would have been like watching a Kurosawa film without subtitles. You could always spot non-Buttists: they would walk into the ground, glance at the players warming up, do a double-take, and ask of their neighbour, 'Who the fuck's that?'

Rereading his match reports of that season now, one is struck by how forthright they are. This Cardiff game, which I remember as being particularly dire even by these new and astonishingly low standards, found Butt in unforgiving mood. He is drily rude about Cardiff's ex-Cambridge number eleven ('Goldsmith . . . proved that United's loss is not necessarily Cardiff's gain'); and he is rightly fierce about the home team's ineptitude – 'a dreary defeat', 'a dreadful display . . . devoid of skill or spirit', 'they sleepwalked their way through a grim game'.

And yet nobody was more generous-spirited when the team had achieved something reasonably close to parity with the opposition. 'Top v bottom – but only one goal in it', is the cheery headline that accompanies his report of the Chelsea game. 'Pride but no points from a battling display', is his mystifying version of a 3–0 drubbing at

Brighton. When the run finally ended, nobody could have been more jubilant: 'Smith shoots United to an epic success'.

Despite the praise heaped on the heads of such excellent football writers as David Lacey and Patrick Barclay, most fans find quality football journalism enjoyable but irrelevant. For supporters of the big clubs, tabloid newspapers are far more pertinent. Only the tabloids carry extensive transfer gossip; only the tabloids reveal the behind-the-scenes tantrums. (An Arsenal fan who reads only, say, the *Independent* would probably wonder why Paul Davis spent a year mouldering in Arsenal's reserves.) Most of the time, of course, they make it all up, but never mind. Even fictitious news becomes a part of football culture.

Further down the league, local papers are the only source of news and sensible, informed views. Cambridge matter as much to Cambridge fans as Liverpool to Liverpool fans; in fact, it could be argued that Cambridge matter more to a *higher percentage* of their fans, because it is impossible to maintain a vague interest in a terrible lower division team. Yet supporters of smaller clubs only rarely get to read about their team in the nationals. Lower league fans have to rely completely on Randall Butt and his peers.

So Andy Sinton was not the only hero that season — he must share that honour with the football correspondent of the *Cambridge Evening News*, who bore every midweek defeat at Barnsley, every 0–0 drawn against Grimsby, with fortitude, good humour and an unquenchable enthusiasim. Why he wasn't made manager some time around Christmas is a question that only the Cambridge board can answer.

'We all agree: Kevin Smith's better than Keegan'
Cambridge United v Newcastle United, 28.4.84

The final whistle blows on the final home game of a long season, the home fans erupt, the players, some of them near to tears, wave, and you are slapped on the back by your friends and neighbours, all of them jubilant. This is the scenario you dreamed of back in August, when it all began; the circumstances hardly matter. Of course, I would rather have been celebrating promotion to the First Division than the end of the most spectacular losing run the English League has ever seen, but never mind. A celebration is a celebration is a celebration.

Did they do it deliberately? Probably not. But the facts are peculiar. The previous all-time losers record, held by Crewe, was for a thirty-game patch – Cambridge cracked that one with a 0–0 draw at Grimsby. How peculiar, then, that they should return to apparently forgotten winning ways *just five days later*, against Newcastle, the third-best team in the division, the team with Beardsley and Waddle and Keegan. Perhaps it's like those stories you always read about childless couples: they give up, they sign the adoption papers, and nine months later they have a child of their own. Maybe once Cambridge had edged Crewe out of the record books they relaxed, and remembered what it was like to win. With the record safe (and one has to say that at thirty-one games, about seven months of football, it looks safe for some time to come), they could just lie back and enjoy it all again; the bun in the oven, the 1–0 win, was an incidental, accidental by-product.

Distance always lends enchantment to the humblest of football triumphs, but even at the time Cambridge's win seemed unbelievable. There is something about football, of course, that lends itself to shocks. Only quantum theorists could believe that the London Monarchs could match the Washington Redskins, or that Kingston could thump the LA Lakers at basketball, or that Bruno could ever have defeated Tyson. So what is it about soccer that allows Sutton to beat Cup-holders Coventry, Colchester to beat Revie's Leeds, Algeria to beat perennial World Champions West Germany? On paper, Cambridge were inferior to Newcastle in every department; and if confidence is a function of performance, as it surely must be, then by definition the home side's confidence was the lowest in football league history. Is it true that, as every non-league manager says on the eve of an impossible-looking Cup tie, it's 'on the day only eleven against eleven', a question of 'Who wants it more?' Desperation certainly has its place, but Newcastle were the desperate team – they were the ones who needed to win to go up. Cambridge were already down. And as for the eleven against eleven theory: why, then, is giant-killing such a rarity? Why do those Icelandic and Finnish teams get beaten by fifteen or twenty goals in European cup ties?

I still have no idea whether football is a much simpler or much more complicated game than I believe it to be. All I know is that I haven't got it right yet. Does one team lose to another simply because two or three players don't perform particularly well? And if so, then why don't they?

when Alan Hansen tells you that Liverpool's two central defenders are playing too far apart, or the back four are playing far too square, that seems a perfectly adequate explanation for why Liverpool are conceding goals. But *why* are the two central defenders playing too far apart? Is it just because they can't be bothered? Don't they like each other? Has their manager told them to play like this? Why? Why do the back four play square some days and not others? When Arsenal beat Sheffield Wednesday in the Coca-Cola Cup Final, the accepted wisdom is that when Morrow man-marked Sheridan, that cut off Waddle's supply-line. So why doesn't every team do that?

Most 'analysis' of football in the media is a simple observation of failure or success, and yet there are so many mysteries to explain. Cambridge's win over Newcastle is one of the most puzzling mysteries of them all: why didn't Waddle make either of the Cambridge full-backs, neither of whom were to have much future in the game, weep with frustration and the shame of their own ineptitude? A few years later, Waddle beat AC Milan almost on his own. Why didn't Keegan and Beardsley score several goals each, before half-time? Why was Kevin Smith's first-half penalty enough to win the game? Questions, questions; answers on a postcard, please.

On the way home, a Newcastle fan tried to push me off my bike, but I didn't mind, really. I understood the impulse, and I was happy enough, anyway. The pleasure of football, in a nutshell: Cambridge had been beating my head against the wall for the previous seven months, and that afternoon, they stopped.

Thanks to John Donaldson

Chris Pierson

The Golden Year

ST ALBANS CITY 1971/2

For some fans, choosing a golden year may be easy. Perhaps for the follower of Colchester United or of Berwick Rangers it was the year in which some mighty Goliath was humbled in the Cup. For others, it might have been a sweet but solitary moment of league success, as it was for Chelsea in 1955 or for Dundee United in 1983. But supporters of Arsenal or Liverpool face a difficulty. Which of those many league titles felt best? And for the spoilt-for-choice partisans of Celtic or Rangers, picking just one golden year may be even harder. But for those who owe their allegiance to clubs like St Albans City FC there is a different and more familiar problem. The Saints have never won a major cup competition. Their last great feat of giant killing came with the 5–3 defeat of Brentford in 1923. They have not won a league title for more than sixty years. So what makes any one year stand out from the rest?

*

After the Goal Rush

Those with very long memories and impressive constitutions might be able to delve back into the golden *decade* of St Albans football, the 1920s. At the end of 1920, City sat at the very bottom of the Athenian League. In the New Year, they did not lose a single game and took the league title at their first attempt. In season 1922/3, they 'moved up' to the Isthmian League, and once again captured the championship at the first attempt. They repeated the treatment in 1927 and 1928. There were FA Cup outings against Gillingham and Hartlepools United and semi-final appearances in the Amateur Cup in three out of four seasons. The team's roll of honour reads like a string of music hall turns – Bertie Butcher, Peter Pierce, Harry Hankey, Fred Hellicar and the improbable Syd Duller. But none was more impressive than the wonderful Billy Minter, scorer of 422 goals in just twelve seasons, including all seven in the famous FA Cup tie at Dulwich Hamlet which the Saints still contrived to lose, 7–8. In season 1927/8, his golden boots helped the Championship-winning City side to net no fewer than 160 goals.

For those who like their football a little less archival, there is a good case for saying that the season 1992/3 marks the pinnacle of City's achievements. In the late 1970s and the early 1980s, City plumbed the depths. (You think I exaggerate, but doesn't the Second Division of the Servowarm Isthmian League sound pretty deep to you.) In 1984, they hauled themselves out of the Second Division. In 1986, they won the first division of what had briefly become the Vauxhall Opel League and found themselves back playing with the big boys in the Premier Division. All this was achieved, romantically enough, under the management of the youthful John Mitchell. Mitchell was the local boy made good and come home. He had shone briefly for the City as a teenager before turning professional in 1972. He played alongside Bobby Moore and George Best in the celebrity Fulham side of the early 1970s and scored the semi-final goal that took the Londoners to the Cup Final of 1975. (I think it was Brian Moore who tried to christen it the 'friendly Final', but we all know 'f' is for forgettable, at best.) Having guided St Albans to the Premier Division, Mitchell was forced to stand down 'for business reasons'. He resumed the reins of managerial office in 1991 and in season 1992/3 the Saints progressed to the first round 'proper' of the FA Cup, disputed the Premier League Championship and were carried to the very threshold of admission to the Conference League.

When the Saints Came Marching in

Given all this, it might seem perverse for me to choose 1971/2 as City's golden year. But, in reality, it is a choice which has much more to do with me than it has to do with them. If there was a time when I could claim to be a 'real' football fan, this was it. I still love the game. I still pay good money to watch bad football, and yet go back for more. But it was only for a time during the early 1970s, when I first watched live football, that I was driven by that compulsive devotion which is the real

hallmark of the fan possessed. Like many of my generation, I was first drawn to football by England's success in
the World Cup Final of 1966. The tournament's earlier
stages – the 'plucky' North Koreans, the excesses of the
Argentinians, the elegance of Eusebio – all passed me by.
I do remember the decision to sideline Jimmy Greaves,
controversial then but surely an idea whose time has now
come. (Might Sir Alf Ramsey be coaxed out of retirement
to become Chairman of London Weekend Television?) I
know as well that, whatever nostalgia dictates, the nation
was not uniformly held in the grip of World Cup fever. I
was the only person in my household who bothered to
watch the final and extra time was greeted as an especially unreasonable imposition, delaying by fully thirty
minutes a family outing to the local putting green.

In the late 1960s, I had seen a handful of professional
games, quaintly enough at Brentford and Hull, and in the
early 1970s I occasionally joined my more worldly
friends on their trips to see Watford or Luton Town.
There were (sometimes) things here that I could enjoy,
but nothing that could compare with the grasp the City
took of my youthful imagination. I moved to St Albans in
the summer of 1970 and began to watch the City
regularly in that autumn. I went to the sole stockists of
City kit (Wren's of St Albans) and bought myself a blue
and yellow scarf. Now I was fully equipped to follow the
Saints. (These were the days of innocence, when it was
not mandatory to wear the new season's away strip to be
a true fan.) And follow them I did, to the sepulchral
Dulwich Hamlet (built for 25,000 and home to 250), to
the dogtracks of Walthamstow Avenue and Slough

Town, to the far distant Harwich & Parkeston and to the
(late) Maidstone United. Home and away, Saturday and
Tuesday, the rhythm of my week was set by the fixtures
secretary of the Isthmian League. When the Saints were at
home, I would sometimes while away the morning
scouring the local market for cheap shirts and naff
records. But more often I simply stayed in bed. I would
madden my mother by lying apparently lifeless beneath
the sheets (this being a pre-duvet era) until we reached the
very threshold of 'On the Ball'. Given this stimulus, I
would bestir myself and slouch downstairs to take up my
accustomed place in front of the TV. When the City were
away, one quick call to Mr Hornet, local barber and
supporters' club Mr Fixit, and I was booked on a mystery
trip to some ramshackle ground in one of the more
unfashionable quarters of outer London. I was always
delighted when Saturday came. But best of all was
Tuesday night, under the floodlights at Clarence Park,
watching the City strike force in full and irresistible flood.
On a Saturday it was easy to imagine that you were
watching a (not very) upgraded sort of park football. On
a Tuesday, with the pitch bathed in light (except in the
dimly illuminated corners), with the orange nets
glistening and the whiteness of the goals picked out
against the dark surrounds, you knew that this was
football for real. A gate of 600 on a grey Saturday
afternoon made the ground look empty. On a Tuesday
night, with 600 in, it felt like a real crowd.

*

Twilight of the Gods

My new-found commitment to the Saints was sealed by the
remarkable events of Saturday 21 November, 1970, and a
game which brought a moment of footballing drama and
ecstasy which, for me, has never quite been equalled. (Less
than fourteen months later I was to experience a game of
comparable drama, but one which dragged me into 'the
slough of despond'). The visitors to Clarence Park on that
autumn afternoon were the mighty and high-flying Sutton
United (recent FA Cup challengers of the *really* mighty
Leeds United). From the kick-off City were systematically
outplayed and Sutton scored in the fortieth and forty-fifth
minutes to go in at half-time with a 2–0 lead. The second
half opened with little prospect of the situation being
retrieved and it was not until the eightieth minute that the
redoubtable Les Burgess managed to pull one goal back.
The next ten minutes have become a part of club mytho-
logy. Within two minutes renewed expectation turned to
delirium amongst loyal supporters in the 'Tree End' as
Bobby Childs snatched an improbable equalizer. Within a
further sixty seconds, delirium turned to rapturous disbelief as leading scorer Johnny Butterfield crashed home a
third goal, to put the Saints in front. Momentarily, it
seemed as if the sceptics were wrong and that God was
indeed appropriately located in His heaven. After this
things fell quiet for the best part of three minutes before
Bobby Childs stepped up to seal the rout with a nose-
rubbing fourth goal. Four goals in seven minutes against
the leading side in the League. This I imagined was why
they called it 'the beautiful game'.

Although I did not know it at the time, I was witnessing, in the autumn of 1970, the last days of the great St Albans City side of the late 1960s. This was the side which had come within forty-five minutes of an FA Cup third round tie with Spurs, losing their second round replay in front of a crowd of 10,000 at Fellows Park, Walsall. In 1970, they had reached the semi-finals of the Amateur Cup for the first time in forty years, only to lose out 1–0 to Dagenham in a replay at Kenilworth Road. In 1970/71, they put on some dazzling performances, scoring in the league ten times against both Clapton and Tooting, with an overall tally of 87 goals in 38 games. They beat Biggleswade 9–0, Ruislip 17–0 over two legs, and secured the Wycombe Floodlit Cup (wow!) by beating Marlow 9–3, again over two legs. But sadly, within less than a year of the stunning win over Sutton, the gifted forward line of Bobby Childs, John Butterfield and Tony Turley had all gone, soon to be followed by manager Sid Prosser. I don't think I was ever wholly reconciled to the loss of Butterfield and Childs. Butterfield was one of the most accomplished players ever to lead the line for the Saints and certainly the more prolific goal scorer. But it was Bobby Childs who earned my schoolboy admiration. In an age which was already nudging itself towards the anti-hero, Bobby Childs was, for me, still the real thing. He wasn't especially tall or graceful or athletic. Indeed, he was most frequently described as 'stocky'. I remember him in a characteristic pose, shielding the ball, suggesting that at any moment he might lean forward and trip over it. But he never did. Blessed with defence-turning close control, he was deft, intelligent, and a master of the dead ball. There was a (well-grounded) air of expectation every time he stood ready to curl another teasing crossed ball on to the edge of the six-yard box. Above all, Childs was cheeky to players, to officials and, when the chance arose, to the crowd. It was with genuine shock that I learnt that he had died in the latter half of the 1980s, when still a comparatively young man.

Strange But True

At first sight (and even somewhat later) it seems strange that what I knew to be a rather humble footballing form should generate such devotion. Of course, watching the Saints was cheap, it was safe and it was easy (unless you were travelling to an away game with Walton and Hersham by public transport). On a Tuesday night, I could finish my homework by 7.20 and be in the ground, programme scanned, for kick-off at half-past seven. But (I like to pretend) there is more to it than this. There are clearly some 'bad' reasons for choosing the parochial and the mundane: idleness, fear, narrow-mindedness, lack of adventure. But the claims made for the spectacular and the exceptional are rarely justified and, by contrast, the everyday and the unspectacular can be rather charming. After all, the commonplace is where we are most of the time. The pursuit of excellence is all very well, but frailty, error and second-rateness are a natural part of the human condition, to be embraced with humour rather than despised. Like everything else, the football I watched at St Albans was often predictable and sometimes grindingly dull. But it was punctuated by flashes of extraordinary brilliance. Across the globe, we are told, at any one moment just so many people are being born, or dying, or procreating or staring down the barrel of a gun. I like to think that at any one moment somewhere in the world one of football's ordinary punters is scoring an extraordinary goal. It has happened to everyone who has played the game. On some (perhaps lone) occasion you have sent the ball thundering past the helpless keeper from 25 yards, or else you have met the ball with your head (eyes closed, of course) and sent it like a bullet into the top corner of the net. Not every sport can offer such a thrill. However often you go to your municipal swimming baths you will not chance upon someone establishing a new world record. Yet, by the law of averages, every Sunday, some bepaunched and breathless punter from publand will strike home the ball in a way that the peerless Pelé or the mighty Bobby Charlton could not have bettered. It can happen anywhere and, if you wait long enough, will happen almost everywhere. This is the beauty of football: a little bit of the sublime, rather more of the ridiculous and quite a lot of everything in between.

There They Go, There They Go, There They Go

For City, the 1970/71 season had been something of a disappointment. The high point came on May Day, when a Bobby Childs goal five minutes from the end of extra-time secured a London Senior Cup Final win over arch-rivals Enfield. The local paper graphically described it as 'a trophy of consolation for a season of shattered dreams'. But, in fact, it was to be City's most successful season for some twenty years to come. They finished third in the league, won two cup competitions and scored well over a hundred goals. None the less, when August came I was looking for 1971/2 to be the season that compensated for the disappointments of the previous year. A 3–0 win over the professionals of Fulham in a pre-season friendly seemed to bode well for the new campaign, and City triumphed 3–1 in their first league match of the year away at Woking. But they managed to win only one of their next five league encounters and this was to set a pattern of inconsistency that characterized the whole season. There were some outstanding wins, including 4–1 away and 8–0 at home to Oxford City, but twice during September the defence leaked four goals in losing at home to Hendon and Bishop's Stortford. At one stage, manager Sid Prosser seemed to have the makings of a really strong squad, with the striking power of Butterfield, Childs, Mitchell and Ratty strengthened by the signing of Welsh international Geoff Anthony and the defence buttressed by the transfer of England defender David Hogwood from Hendon. But October was a shocking month with the departure of John Butterfield (along with defenders Brian Baigent and Mickey Pardey) being closely followed by the loss of Bobby Childs. On the pitch, City were boosted by the goal-scoring prowess of Anthony, Mitchell and club captain and midfielder Dave Neville. But poor form away from Clarence Park meant that by the turn of the year City were effectively out of league title contention.

*

Fame, Shame and Warhol's Trees

The departure of so many of City's leading players to the League's bigger clubs (Enfield, Hendon) and thence to international honours rekindled animated discussion in the local press about City's seemingly eternal status as an *unfashionable* club. The aggrieved sense that in winning representative honours or the plaudits of the critics there is a charmed circle from which the Saints are always excluded is a part of the birthright of every St Albans fan. Manifest in the autumn of 1971, it was to be revived, and with the customary good reason, in the spring of 1992. City finished the season in second place in the Diadora Premier League. Under the non-league pyramid system, when champions Chesham declined to take up the place to which they were entitled in the GM Vauxhall Conference League, this place should have passed on to the Saints. But the Conference refused City access to the senior league on account of the unsuitability of their (charming, safe, accessible and attractive) ground. More particularly, they objected to two fine and ancient oak trees, one of which graces the terracing behind the goal at the aptly named Tree End. Negotiations rumbled on for some time, but the essence of the committee men's ultimatum was that into their League these trees would not come. And so the 1993/4 season began with the trees, but not the City, in their rightful place.

The saga of the trees brought the Saints a brief moment of national fame. Like the man who didn't start the National or the hotel that fell into the sea or the security company that liberated its prisoners, City's trees became a nine-day, space-filling *cause célèbre*. It was a story that was much funnier for the casual reader than for those who had something at stake. In the end it did three things: it pumped up the fans' paranoia that the footballing powers-that-be would do *anything* to deny the Saints their place in the big time; it provided just one more example of the maldistribution of power in the national game, which sees antediluvian administrators dictating terms to long-suffering and disempowered fans; and, third, it may have helped clinch City's decision to quit Clarence Park for a new purpose-built (presumably treeless and perhaps soulless) ground on the outskirts of town. Perhaps given the way they have been treated, a *new* sod is just what the City need.

You Want Cups. We Got Cups.

Although for City the league was out of reach by Christmas 1971, there was still the Cup or, more properly, there were still the Cups! Indeed, City's trophy room had been unlocked as early as 18 August to allow in the first of the season's silverware, the Herts Charity Cup. We might style this 'the Atkins Final', both in tribute to eighteen-year-old debutant and ex-Tottenham schoolboy Stewart Atkins who won the game for City and to distinguish it from the final rather later in the season in which City won the same trophy for the second time. The remarkable feat of winning the same cup competition *twice* in one season might seem in itself to justify choosing 1971/2 as the golden year. But it did not seem quite like this at the time. Following a hiccup in his travel arrangements (Atkins' lift to the game never arrived) the teenager had to hitch to the ground with a passing Sunday League official. Within ten minutes of the start, he had headed the lone goal that won the Cup for the Saints (the 1970/71 Final having been deferred from the previous season). However, success was not so very sweet for Atkins. It was his only goal, indeed his only appearance, for the Saints and within a couple of weeks he had been transferred to near neighbours Hertford. Nor did it bring a broad smile to the face of Sid Prosser. In the local paper he 'fumed': 'Terrible – it was terrible.' (Tragically, the combative Prosser was denied the normal facility of human speech and, according to the local press, all of his verbal utterances had either to be 'groaned' or 'fumed'.)

In 1971/2, City were engaged in a further six cup competitions, seven if you allow for the second running of the Herts Charity Cup. In fact, having a wealth of meaningless cup competitions was just one of the ways in which the amateur game of the early 1970s was way ahead of its time. Of course, it was no accident that the tactical device of 'the aimless long punt up the park' was brought to the professional game by Wimbledon who knew it long to have been the centrepiece of the non-league game. Twice-a-week (eighty games a season) football is a stroll for non-league players. Three points for a win was introduced in 1973, the year in which the league was first sponsored, initially by Rothman's of Pall Mall. And the tradition of cup overkill lives on. The City side of 1992/3 was entered for no fewer than *ten* cup competitions. The Herts Charity Cup had its annual dusting down and was duly restored to the trophy cabinet (for the twenty-fifth time) following a narrow win (1–0, pen) over local rivals Boreham Wood. Their chances in the Billy Minter invitation Trophy were particularly good, since there was only one other team involved, and that was Aldershot. Even fortysomething John Mitchell had to be pressed into service for the Eastern Floodlight Cup tie at Royston Town, which was lost 3–0 in front of just forty frenzied fans.

How to Identify a 'Real' Cup

Back in the 1970s there was a recognized pecking order amongst these cup competitions. A good rule of thumb was that the more meaningless the competition, the greater the chance that it would be contested over two legs. (Can you conjure up the excitement with which we awaited the second leg of the Mithras Cup tie with Ruislip, knowing that City were just 7–0 up from the first leg?) A second clue was to look for the words 'Floodlit' or 'Centenary', as in 'Wycombe Floodlit Cup' or 'Hitchin Centenary Cup'. The day must surely come (though hopefully well into the next millennium) when we shall have a string of competitions that offer the magical combination of 'Centenary Floodlit Cups'. No need to call a seance to beam me up the results: I can wait. The third and clinching criterion for identifying an inconsequential competition was to see if the City had ever won it.

Despite this wealth of lesser competitions, the Cups that really *did* count were probably more important than the league. Without a pyramid to provide at least the formal possibility of advancement, winning the Isthmian

League brought precious few rewards. Indeed, in line with the League's motto *honor sufficit*, there was not even a trophy. From time to time teams made it out of the Southern League into the Fourth Division bigtime, but not from the ranks of the Isthmians. Of course, the FA Cup was unwinnable, but it did provide the promise of a little brief glory and a place in the footballing history books. You could be the chirpy postman who delivered the knock-out punch to mighty United or the part-time chef who roasted the Rovers' defence. It could be *your* roped-off mudpatch on the nine o'clock news. The FA Cup road is peculiarly long and hard for non-leaguers. There is a qualifying competition for the qualifying competition, and two rounds 'proper' before your name goes into the hat with the might of the Premier League. Some sides have lost their competitive interest in the competition before August is out. City have had their moments in the FA Cup. In 1980 they took Torquay United to a replay in the second round. In 1992 they again reached the competition 'proper', only to lose 2–1 to Cheltenham Town in front of 3000 supporters at Clarence Park. But they have yet to establish their credentials by giving some big city side a bloody nose.

Night of Shame (I think)

In 1970 City's FA Cup campaign had come to an abrupt and acrimonious end on a foggy November night at Clarence Park. The Saints had progressed to the threshold of the competition proper, but found themselves drawn away to much-fancied Hendon in the fourth qualifying round. Having secured a draw at Claremont Road, there was a crowd in excess of 2000 at Clarence Park for the Tuesday night replay. The game went disastrously wrong. Having gone two down, City pulled one goal back, but they just could not find their way past the Hendon and England keeper Johnny Swanell a second time, and ended up losing 2–1. The infamy that followed is a terrible blur to me. I'm only thirtysomething but already history can play terrible tricks with the memory. I know for a fact (because it's in the record books) that I really did see City goalkeeper Trevor Howard score a magnificent equalizer with his head in the dying minutes of a league game at Maidstone United. The short-handed City played two goalkeepers, the eponymous Ray Bloxham between the sticks, and Trevor Howard on the left wing. But were Maidstone's floodlights really mounted, as I recall, upon wooden pylons? Again, I remember the super Aston Villa side of 1981 (of which inexplicably little is ever said) as being full of slim good-looking young men with pageboy haircuts. But then I think of Peter Withe and Dennis Mortimer and Jimmy Rimmer, and I begin to wonder if *my* Aston Villa side hasn't actually been strengthened by the inclusion of the entire cast of the simultaneously successful 'Brideshead Revisited'. And *then* I begin to wonder if Des Bremner was *really* in the engine room of the Villa midfield, or was he the man who collected teddy bears, or perhaps even the other one from Abba.

All this is, of course, a digression designed to draw your attention away from the infamous events that followed City's FA Cup exit in 1970. As I recall, it was like this: When the final whistle blew, the pitch was invaded and someone attacked Mr Swanell. There were one or two policemen looking rather bemused. There must certainly have been at least one large and germanic dog. As I wandered around the invaded pitch I remember thinking how large the goal looked and how inexplicable it was that City should have struggled so long without managing to deposit the ball in it. (What I did not comprehend at the time was that this was to be the closest I would ever come to realizing my lifelong ambition of playing under floodlights.) That's all I can remember. But it still adds up to rather more than my recollections of the entire FA Cup campaign of 1971/2. I did not make it to Romford for City's first (and only) FA Cup match. They were 2–0 down in twenty minutes, and three down at half-time. They lost the tie 3–0, and that was that.

'We're (nearly) on the March with Prosser's Army'

In the 1970s, even more important than a good run in the FA Cup was success in the FA Amateur Cup. In the end, the FA Cup always had to finish in glorious defeat. But the Amateur Cup was truly 'The Road to Wembley' and a real chance to win a trophy of substance. The club's Jubilee historian, writing in 1958, saw it as St Albans' 'greatest unrealized ambition' and, by the start of 1972, everything in City's season turned upon realizing this dream. In the first round, on 8 January 1972, they travelled to Dovercourt, home of Harwich & Parkeston of the Athenian League. (The amateur game was replete with references to classical antiquity. You could not move for Corinthians, Spartans, Athenians and Isthmians, not to mention the Mithras Cup. In my more suspicious moments, I detected a conspiracy of ex-public school-boys, conjuring up leagues and cup competitions to keep the *oiks* off the streets. But even more recent sponsors such as Berger and Diadora have a faintly Arcadian ring. No wonder Servowarm's sponsorship was so short-lived!) The game at Dovercourt was a one-sided affair, in which a hatful of chances for City yielded a solitary first-half goal for Bill Ratty. City's only defensive lapse of the game let in John Hurren for an equalizer, and it finished 1–1. In the replay, City were set on their way by a cracking thirty-five-yard drive from Dave Neville, and ran out easy 4–0 winners.

By the time of the replay win over Harwich & Parkeston, City already knew that their next opponents would be Slough Town. 'We are just not getting any breaks,' groaned Prosser, as City's name came out of the hat away to the powerful Athenian leaguers. Slough had a formidable side, which included five internationals, had scored nearly 100 goals by the end of December and had been unbeaten for more than three months. In the days leading up to the tie at the end of January there were doubts about the fitness of keeper Ray Bloxham and the playability of Slough's rain-soaked mudpatch (appropriately and aquarially known as the Dolphin Stadium). The pitch was declared fit to play, but Bloxham wasn't.

Nightmare at the Dolphin Stadium

The epithets 'titanic' and 'tragic' cling to this tie, as if they were newly minted. City had made a lively start when the first blow came in the eighteenth minute. In this case, it was a powerfully delivered upper cut. City attacker Bill Ratty was remonstrating with Slough defender Ray Eaton following a late tackle, when he was felled by the mighty fist of ex-England captain Roger Day. Ratty received a double-fracture of the jaw and was hospitalized for a week. The referee was looking the other way. Within six minutes the Saints had fallen behind. Kevin O'Brien, deputizing for the injured Bloxham, was only able to parry a shot from John Ritchie and the loose ball was driven home. An acrimonious half ended with Slough 1–0 in front. In the second half, full-back Roger Grant was pushed forward to replace Ratty in the front line and it was his corner in the sixty-ninth minute which led to Saints' equalizer. Once again the ball was parried in the mud and Dave Neville was on hand to knock it in. One–one. City's relief was to be shortlived. Within three minutes, Day added insult to considerable injury by beating O'Brien with a diving header at the near post that put Slough 2–1 ahead. But the depleted City side simply refused to surrender and with just eight minutes left John Mitchell's cross was met with a superb twenty-yard drive from midfielder John Oxley. It seemed certain that we would be taking Slough back to Clarence Park where vengeance might be ours. But then came the apocalypse. With just two minutes remaining, Slough forward Ray Hill fell in the box and the referee pointed (inexplicably, as you may imagine) to the penalty spot. In the protests that followed, three City players were booked. But it made no difference and it was that man Day who stepped up to send the ball just beyond the fingertips of the despairing O'Brien and into the corner of the net. Slough

Town 3 St Albans City 2. It had all the qualities of high
melodrama. Injustice heaped upon injustice. The law that
favoured the wrongdoer. The irrepressible spirit of the
weakened underdog. The promise of retribution dashed
at the very last. The crowning moment of glory stolen by
the arch-villain of the piece. I don't know if Prosser
groaned or fumed. I was choked. I can only compare it to
that awful moment on 9 April 1992 when the result came
in from Basildon with its gruesome affirmation of the
timeless truth that it's not often the nice guys who win.

After the Lord Mayor's Elephant

The rest of the season had its minor consolations. Phil
Wood, the elegant and undemonstrative City defender,
deservedly became the local sports personality of the year
(this is not, of course, to take anything away from second-
placed Tommie Atkinson, the London and Southern
Counties Bowls Champion of 1972). In part, Phil's award
was in recognition of the record 550 appearances he had
made since joining the club in 1962. But, in fact, this was to
be something of a halfway house as Phil went on to complete
one thousand first team appearances for the club in 1984.
He is one of the club's classiest players and surely its greatest
servant. Admirers can still find him on the terraces at
Clarence Park. Nor was City's romance with the Cup quite
at an end. The deferred Hitchin Centenary Cup was soon to
be theirs and in one thrilling week in May they laid their
hands upon the golden Mithras Cup and extended their lien
on the Herts Charity Cup. But the first two of these, being
two-legged affairs, were rather unglamorously claimed

following a goalless draw at Baldock Town and 2–0 defeat at Tilbury. A little less than magical. The 2–1 Herts Charity Cup victory did at least mean a win over arch local rivals Boreham Wood. But somehow it was scant consolation for having been dumped out of the previous season's Amateur Cup by the then unfancied Athenian league side. Certainly no one was to be found poring through the *Yellow Pages* looking to hire an open-topped bus.

In the seasons that followed things got worse, a lot worse. In the very next season (1972/3) City's league goal tally was more than halved to just 34 in 42 games. In '73/4, they managed just 30 goals and four wins, and were relegated. By the end of the 1970s, financial difficulties and problems over the use of their council-owned ground left them facing foreclosure. At the end of season 1982/3 they faced the further humiliation of relegation into Division Two. How they made it back from the brink of extinction, under the twin inspiration of John Mitchell and Roy Race is another story, a story whose twists and turns escape me. Living (very happily) in Scotland, I am now an occasional visitor to Clarence Park. I know that all over the south of England there are exiled Scots who turn dewy-eyed at the very mention of the Old Firm or at the thought of happy Saturdays spent at Boghead or Cappielow. I am part of a much smaller band of Anglo-exiles who have to make do with trips to Ibrox or Celtic Park. Yet even here there are echoes of those earlier days. Through the madness of the pool's caption, results from the Scottish Premier League are frequently *preceded* by City's clashes in the Diadora Premier League. And outside of the top half-dozen clubs, Scotland has plenty of the little madnesses and peculiarities that make the non-league scene so appealing. (Indeed, many a Scottish Second Division side would let the English keep Alex Ferguson in exchange for the weekly gate of a Woking or a Wycombe.)

But even were I still living just around the corner, I doubt that I could be the City fan I was in 1971. The pool of human psychical resources is not so deep that we can feed more than one insensible obsession. Even twenty years ago I began to find my attention drifting from the back to the front pages of the newspapers. I had that sense (fatal to the integrity of the real fan) that there were other contests which were still more important. Sure enough, I began to crave success for my political causes more than my sporting ones. Even now I feel that if only the devil were a reasonable man, we could come to some arrangement. I should be happy enough to find myself strapped into my seat in the Purgatory Stadium every Saturday at five to three. Every week, I would gladly relive that terrible afternoon at Slough and see the Cup dashed away by an outrageous 88th-minute penalty. If only it were this easy to be rid of the Tories!

But in August 1971 it looked a little different. There was the League to be won, the skills of Butterfield and Childs to be savoured, a potful of goals to be enjoyed and this, after all, was the year that we were going to Wembley. All this, and the Revolution too. Who could ask for anything more?

Thanks to David Tavener

Matt Nation

Thighs of an Elephant

BRISTOL CITY 1989/90

Maybe I was doing things wrongly, but, in the case of my liaison with Bristol City, the thrill was not in the chase but in the consummation. Having missed out on the euphoria of promotion to the First Division in 1976, on account of being too young to appreciate the fervour which allegedly gripped the city, I spent fifteen years waiting for it to happen again. (Promotion from the Fourth doesn't count because they shouldn't have been there anyway.) Unfortunately, this meant being with the team which, possessing the charisma and playing standards of a broken deckchair, was neither loved nor hated, noticed during nor missed after four seasons in the First Division; three successive relegations, during which most of the players used were not fit to tie Gerry Gow's wellingtons; being in a lower division than Bristol Rovers, which is the equivalent of being runner-up to John Sillett in a Miss World contest; and, most disgraceful of all, losing a play-off final to Walsall, a team so execrable that during the following season they allowed Chelsea to put seven past them on their own ground.

During this time, growing pains, spots, athleticism and libido came into the romantic part of my life, stayed for a while and went away again. Bristol City's success just seemed to go away.

Until 1989/90 and promotion from the Third. Local sports reporters, galvanized into writing something other than 'mediocre', 'slumbering Bristol giant' and 'Fred Ford would have kicked over cups of tea if he'd been in that dressing room at half-time,' began losing their load about the peripheral qualities of the team. Bob Taylor's tendency to put the ball into the opponents' goal thirty-four times, Dave Smith's speed off the mark down the left side ('Like shit off a shovel,' was the general consensus in the enclosure), Mark Gavin's knack of making all left-backs look as elegant as Larry Lloyd in a bunny-girl outfit and David Rennie's unerring ability to pull his shorts up far too high, put his hands on his hips and be hailed a hero filled the sports pages of the *Bristol Evening Post*. But the motor of the team's successes remained unremarked upon.

It was clear to anybody who watched the game from outside a press box full of perspicacious scribes reminiscing about how John Atyeo used to do it that promotion was attributable to three things: Robbie Turner's upper body, Bob Taylor's lower body and the fondness of both of them (although, to be fair, of Robbie more than Bob) for sweatbands.

Turner should have been surrounded by bearded men equipped with tents, crampons and mintcake. Arms and legs like a pillar box and a chest that gave the impression that he never breathed out, he ran as though he were on a military yomp laden with a thirty-pound rucksack. He must have scared the shit out of *himself*, let alone all of those Third Division defenders with a penchant for birdshit haircuts and solariums. And even the hard cases would have felt their anal nerve twitch when he embarked upon his pre-match warm-up routine. Not for 'Carnage' the pointlessness of five-yard sprints, arm waving and all the other tomfoolery. All he wanted to practise was heading.

At 2.30 p.m. before each home game, he would lumber on to the pitch, station himself on the six-yard line before the East End and lovingly attack crosses fed to him by a member of the club whom nobody appeared to know. His mellifluousness when doing so never failed to give rise to thoughts of what Robbie could have achieved alongside Margot Fonteyn had there ever been a suitable pair of tights to accommodate him. He would soar, feet at a quarter to three, elbows jerking symmetrically backwards, thrusting his head forward to meet the ball at the moment he considered to be optimum. The fact that this moment usually coincided with the ball either still being on the instep of the unknown member or trickling out of play on the far side of the pitch was of secondary importance. Just as many an adolescent football match is won or lost before it begins, due to the opponents looking bigger, better or more stylish (or threatening to lamp you the next time they see you in the shopping centre), so Bristol City nicked victories they otherwise mightn't have through Turner straining, grunting, jerking and thrusting immediately before kick-off.

Had it not been for the ability to kick footballs better

than anybody else seen at Ashton Gate in the previous fifteen years, Bob Taylor, on the other hand, would have earned his money in commercials, peeling off expensive jeans in launderettes. Taylor was the first Bristol City forward I had ever seen who actually looked – and played – like somebody I wanted to be.

When I first went to Ashton Gate in the mid-1970s, there was a distinct dearth of role models. The team were playing decent enough football, borne out by promotion to the First in 1976, but the problem was that the players were too vapid. Clive Whitehead was one notable exception, in that he ran as if attempting the Charleston atop a rolling barrel. Gerry Gow kicked people now and again and Paul Cheesely was very good at headers, but the rest of the team were the footballing (and political) equivalent of John Major. And their aspect, barnets of this epoch notwithstanding, was, to a man, appalling. Most of them had moustaches and, even those who didn't, were either too thin (Tom Richie, Gary Collier), too short (Trevor Tainton, Jimmy Mann) or else were Gerry Sweeney.

The following decade was, for the most part, equally dismal, except this time the football was abhorrent too. Bob changed all that. Arriving at the fag end of the eighties, he looked like Dirk Bogarde, ran properly and gave everybody a decent reason to get up in the morning. He was all the adjectives you read about forwards under six feet tall but the most striking and most neglected aspect was his thighs.

It wasn't just that they were big. Anyone can have big thighs. Willie Young had big thighs. It was that they were *footballer's* thighs. They struck that perfect balance between bigger-than-average and Welsh prop forward. They had contours usually only found on a physical map of Nepal, they jiggled visibly when he ran, not extremely enough to warrant accusations of cellulite growth, but delicately, subtly, Dirk Bogardely. Thighs like Bob's gave us hope, strength, somebody to want to show off about. Bob should have had to hold an HGV licence for his lower body. Bob was awesome.

Fearsome physiques and good looks were not the only attributes shared by Taylor and Turner. Same age, same forename, same initials, both living proof of the success of Bristol City's home-grown youth policy (both came from north-east England and arrived at City via a total of half a dozen clubs). These two were simply *destined* to belong together, more so than any other predatory pair I had witnessed at the Gate. (Joe Royle and Tom Richie in the 1970s weren't bad, but Richie ran around far too much to be taken seriously as a goalscorer.) This eternal bonding was attributable to four easily forgettable yet significant pieces of towelling: both were purveyors of the sweatband, the anachronistic fashion accessory perfectly acceptable on the wrists of any midfield stalwart worth his place in *Shoot!*'s Focus pages a decade beforehand but, in the 1990s, exclusive to overweight racquet sport players with a heightened sense of the ridiculous. Any other self-respecting modern-day footballer would have commissioned his agent to baulk at the very idea of sporting such an item, bricking it at the thought of supporters smirking behind their hands, dressing room ribbing and the ensuing nickname of 'Sweatbandy', or something equally imaginative. Now, I am not claiming that such ruminations never fleetingly passed through the minds of Robbie and Bob. Terrace gossips even spoke of lucrative advertising contracts with sportswear companies, of prescriptive methods from the Board trying desperately to re-create the promotion season of 1975/6, and of them looking like a pair of tossers. But I know why these sweatbands were dusted off, ammunition provided to terrace wags of opposing teams, and why both risked being ostracized by their friends and family. For just as one spends all morning at primary school praying that one won't have to be Philip Hibbs's partner in the games lesson because he talks about waggling his dinky, and just as one gives an exceptionally wide berth to people in the street with megaphones and clipboards, or eyes with a mixture of suspicion and pity anybody who voluntarily admits to sacrificing a considerable part of his/her wage to follow a team which plays on a peat bog, wears blue and white quartered shirts and boasts 'Goodnight Irene' as a club song; so two over-sized young men in under-sized kit wearing sweatbands are treated with a greater than usual amount of hesitancy by their opponents.

Robbie and Bob may well have been basket cases, but even if they weren't, they frightened defenders into performances reminiscent in their fluidity of Gordon McQueen tap-dancing in a broom cupboard, by merely *pretending* that they were. The flowing football propagated by Joe Jordan may have been the *apparent* reason for a successful 1989/90, but this was made possible only by the fear factor instigated by Robbie and Bob.

The golden year was marred, however, by a skeleton in

the closet: I began following another team. This didn't mean 'Oh, Yeovil got a point at Wealdstone, I like a bit of Yeovil,' or 'Darlington can't go down, it wouldn't be the same without Darlington.' This meant Stamford Bridge. Hard cash. Once or twice a month I fell victim to the pulling power of Chelsea.

Quite why I chose Chelsea, I don't really know. Admittedly, I was resident in London for a large chunk of the year, but *Chelsea*! The ground was a tip. Pat Nevin was no longer there. Kerry Dixon had slowed up enough to resemble a constipated sloth with bunions. Mr Chairman was as generally attractive as John Wark in a gas mask and Stamford the Lion was a wanker. There weren't even any sweatbands. Maybe I was overcome by the glamour of Fulham Broadway station; maybe I wanted to follow a team with a 'reputation', having never forgotten being 'wedged' from a coat hook at school for being a Bristol City fan ('wedging' was a particularly arduous activity which involved being hung on tall, protruding objects by the back of one's invariably nylon undergarments); maybe because I had read a tabloid article on Ian Hutchinson, a barmaid and a pool table; maybe, although almost definitely not, because Chris Garland was born within 100 yards of Ashton Gate. Maybe I was just a sad case.

Unfathomable. Bristol City, the Babbies from the Gate, were coasting at the top of the Third and playing some palatable football into the bargain. The defence was still only kicking in the direction it was facing, but at least it was facing in the right direction, the midfield was efficiently workmanlike, right down to the over-sized arse of

Rob Newman, and the forwards and wingers were turning it – and ten thousand fans – on every week. What was I doing? Out of sight, out of mind would have been a fitting epigram, had I been in possession of either. It was despicable. Even now, I feel such remorse that I parade up and down main thoroughfares, yelling, 'I paid money to watch Graham Roberts. Mutilate me,' in the hope that such acts of self-flagellation will cleanse my conscience. But they won't. I failed to share the hitherto unattained peaks of ecstasy of promoted City because, albeit temporarily, I preferred watching John Bumstead and Peter Nicholas to shelling out the train fare to watch Robbie Turner and Bob Taylor.

In my defence, it must be said throughout this period of unfaithfulness there was never really any doubt as to which team tugged more strongly at my heartstrings. Many of my acquaintances were perfectly happy in these 'swinging' relationships, openly admitting to supporting two or more teams, usually Liverpool and their home town team, in that order. A friend of my father's, who had never experienced alcoholic excess, mass family bereavement or institutionalization, freely confessed that the torch he held for Bristol City was of equal length to the one he held for Bristol Rovers. He probably wets the bed as well.

I couldn't come to terms with it. I went to the Bridge, I enjoyed myself, but I felt dirty afterwards. There wasn't even the clandestine fear of being caught. I talked openly about 'The Chels', referred to the players by their nicknames, even went to a couple of away games in London. The sordidness of it all was so exciting.

The process of purification began one wet Sunday afternoon in January 1990. The Babbies had just stitched up Swindon in the third round of the FA Cup and I was idly dozing in front of the television, watching the nubiles at the FA toying with the bag full of little balls. The City's name was drawn fairly early for a home tie and, in keeping with the romance of the FA Cup, I breathed a sigh of apathy, fairly indifferent to the fact that, as in most of the years I could remember, the City were maybe going to pull out some of the stops against a mediocre side from the middle two divisions.

The nubile caressed the ball between thumb and forefinger for longer than decency permits. A puckish smile seemed to flicker across his lips, his nostrils flared teasingly and he glanced at the camera so flirtatiously that I am sure he has never been allowed to work on British television since. I was beside myself with anticipation. 'Come on, you old tosser, who is it? Port Vale? Peterborough? Tranmere?' Part of me wanted this game to continue until dawn, part of me wanted it to stop and most of me didn't give a tinker's cuss either way. After what seemed like an eternity, he announced those three little words: ' . . . will play Chelsea'.

My body prickled and glowed all over. I was completely unable to speak. I had experienced a moment like this only twice in my life: once at the funfair after Karen O'Connell had agreed to go on the waltzer with me and again after falling flat on my back, having attempted to demonstrate to the same person how easy it is to walk afterwards. My mouth was open, but nothing came out save an unintelligible, rather obscene croak. My

flatmates, unaware of my predicament, later congratu-
lated me on an apparently flawless impersonation of
Bobby Gould. The moment had arrived. A decision
would be seen to be made. The sordidness was over at
last.

27 January 1990, pissing rain and the City took those
Cockney geezers after five minutes. Graham Roberts was
guilty of a minor infringement on the edge of his own box
(although any minor infringement committed by Graham
Roberts, including merely stepping on to a football pitch,
is usually followed by the sound of wailing sirens), and
the free-kick was masterfully executed by David Rennie
and Andy Llewellyn. Rennie was never on my list of
favourite people, but he contributed significantly to team
results in two ways; he invariably failed to flick on near-
post corners – the only variant the City ever used
(although local scribes always interpreted this ineptitude
as leading to 'pandemonium in the box'), and he special-
ized in rolling free-kicks one yard sideways with his toe in
order to allow the mere artisans to welt the ball into
Sturminster Road. This he did, allowing Llewellyn to
realize the purpose for which he was placed on this
planet, namely to wang the ball forwards as hard as he
could. The ballboy with the shortest straw set off, the
fans began to read the lawnmower advertisements in the
programme and Llewellyn trundled back to the halfway
line to await the retrieval of the orb.

   But we were all wrong. Glancing up from a feature on a
Qualcast 302 grassbox, I noted that Lewie had scuffed his
shot and that Beasant had fumbled. What happened next

made me glad, not for the first time in my life, that I wasn't Dave Beasant. The ball ran loose and the Chelsea defence was nowhere. But Bob and Robbie were there. Robbie jerked, Bob jiggled, they adjusted their sweatbands and the swine went sniffing for truffles. You could see Beasant's life flashing before him as the two bore down on him from two yards and it can't have been pleasant, pegging out immediately after having seen twenty-seven stone of naked Geordie aggression *and* ten seasons at Wimbledon. Robbie got there first, but was disappointed. He made contact with the ball.

As Robbie lumbered away, index finger raised, sweatband throbbing and face contorted as though he were the victim of a non-anaesthetized enema, I had the awful feeling that he had kicked Beasant's head clean away from his body. By the look of glee in Robbie's eyes, so did he. But he hadn't made contact and the ball was in the net. Robbie slowly realized what he had done, Bob smiled modestly, Rennie made matey thumbs-up signs to the press box and Roberts shouted at the St John Ambulance crew about a foul on the keeper. One–nil and, God, did I hate Chelsea.

At some point in the second half, Mark Gavin did his jelly legs act somewhere out on the touchline, sending Steve Clarke the wrong way so many times that he gave the uncanny impression that he was playing blind-man's-buff on a skid pan. Gavin played the ball low into the box and it reached Robbie again. The Chelsea defence, being from London and all that, seemed to have retreated to the dressing room to wait for the rain to stop (apart from Roberts, who was having a go at the groundsman about the pitch markings). Even Beasant was AWOL. Perhaps he was looking for his head. Robbie was alone, with the ball and an empty goal in front of him.

There is a scene from *One Flew Over the Cuckoo's Nest* in which the patients are having a game of basketball and the big American Indian pretends to have no idea of the rules. At one point, he is standing underneath the basket with the ball in his hands, surrounded by screaming team-mates imploring him to slam-dunk the ball into the basket. Yes, Robbie appeared to want to ham it up a bit. He had received the ball to feet for the second time in one hour, possibly in his life, and wanted to tease us a little. None of this lashing of the ball into the roof of the net, none of this 'Well-I-don't-care-if-it-goes-in-off-my-knee-from-a-yard-they-all-count' balderdash. Robbie wanted to do it properly.

The problem was that he didn't really seem to know what constituted 'it'. His index finger rose to his lower lip. He ran his fingers through his hair. Everyone was gesturing towards the goal, but the flurry of activity merely panicked him. He jumped up and down a couple of times and jerked and thrusted, but the nasty people continued shouting. Desperately, he followed the direction of fifteen thousand pointing fingers. Finally, attracted by the shininess of one of the stanchions, he rushed towards the goal, scuffing the ball with him, which trickled into the net via the bar, both posts and Roberts' arse. Two–nil and I would have felt sick if Chelsea had tried to touch me.

Incredibly, shortly before the end, Robbie received the

ball to feet again, this time with his back to the goal and to Roberts. But Roberts suddenly decided to go and remonstrate with the wheelchair enclosure and Turner decided to do something which caused every over-sized fan in the stadium to start dreaming of a career in professional sport. Hard cases with prison records fell weeping into each other's arms. Fathers glanced down at their sons, ruffled their hair, winked and smiled. The entire City bench looked as bewildered as Bobby Robson at a press conference: Turner turned.

It wasn't really a very good turn. If you had closed your eyes for thirty seconds, you would have missed it. It was like Terry Butcher playing hopscotch on the moon, but a turn is a turn, they all count. He hared down on goal, the ball somehow reached Gavin. Three–one, I couldn't remember their name, but they were loathsome.

After having redeemed myself on the fidelity front, I genuinely believed that the rest of the season would be relatively obstacle-free, culminating in the Third Division championship, the players being granted freedom of the city and an open-topped bus tour and, maybe, a reference in the papers to a West Country soccer hotbed where tousle-haired street urchins kick tin cans around the streets until nightfall, then go to bed still wearing their football shoes. One thing prevented this vision from materializing into fact: Bristol Rovers.

Objectively speaking, Bristol Rovers ruin everything that can possibly be ruined. Gary Mabbutt and Nigel Martyn would now almost certainly be the most-capped players in their respective positions, had they not innocently chosen to ply their trade in their formative years at a club so terribly, terribly wrong. The M32, which sweeps majestically into Bristol from the M4, past new housing estates, a psychiatric hospital and countless pylons and electricity sub-stations, could be a thoroughfare of elegance rivalled only by the Avenue des Champs Elysées or the Kurfürstendamm, were it not for the remains of Eastville Stadium near the centre of the city. My replica City training top was rendered unwearable by a water-filled ditch and four misanthropes who decided: 'Lads! Iss a shithead! (Roverspeak for a more discerning Bristolian football fan.) Less chuck 'un down the railway bank!' And, most significantly, this collection of footballing sparring partners won the Third Division championship.

The rivalry between the two Bristol clubs will never be mentioned in the same breath as the rivalry between clubs in North London, the North West, the North East or even Northampton. It does not revolve around the number of trophies, full internationals or drink-drive scandals, but around the highest mid-table position or the round in which one is knocked out of the League Cup. So when the City managed to combine beautiful players, beautiful football and a Cup win over Chelsea all in the same season, one would have thought that, despite Rovers' better-than-average showing, the superiority question would have been settled once and for all.

If anything, the reverse was true. Many Bristolians were ebullient about the 'success of Bristol football'. Friends and family in both camps were referring to players of both teams by their first names, smiling on hearing that 'Rovers got a point as well' and uttering sentences containing words like 'Rovers', 'outplayed them' and 'brilliantly' without a negative particle. On many occasions I was reprimanded by these self-appointed members of football's ACAS for whingeing about Rovers' success, and gently told that only City's results were important and that it didn't matter if other teams did well too.

Well, it bloody well *did* matter. City were going up anyway, but Rovers simply had to suffer. They had to be bad. They had to have leaking roofs, betting scandals, fights in the dressing room, humiliating home defeats. Like beer without pork scratchings, a City success cannot be properly savoured if it does not occur at the same time as a Rovers failure.

I even went to Twerton Park three times that season, just to see them lose at home. I put money into their coffers, stood on the terraces surrounded by those godforsaken shirts, listened to the inane, irrelevant chants (something like 'Ashton Gate is full of shit/shit, shit and more shit') and willed them to lose. It wasn't much to ask: I didn't want anybody to break a leg, I didn't want to hit anybody and only occasionally did I want to shower Gerry Francis with verbal abuse. I just wanted the home team to get pasted. Short on sweatbands, but long on those silly cycling shorts, they simply had to lose. Geoff Twentyman, who looked like a scoutmaster and played football like a dodgem car with no steering, had to lose. Devon White, who made Robbie Turner look like Olga Korbut, had to lose. David Mehew, the owner of a gait like a chronically incontinent pigeon, had to lose. Christian McClean, who was simply abject, had to lose. They

all had to lose. I took friends along, friends who had no
interest in football, just so they could see Rovers lose at
home. If I had had the choice between a City away win
and a Rovers home defeat, I would have probably
plumped for the latter. In fact, the watershed in my
relationship with my German girlfriend occurred at a
Rovers home game. At the end of the game, having
experienced English football for only the second time in
her life, and completely detached from any kind of
Bristolian rivalry, she declared exotically, erotically and
enigmatically: 'They weren't very interesting and the fans
eat crisps all the time.'

But they never lost at home that season. They even
turned over the City 3–0 in the run-in to promotion. I
was frequently accused of being a bad loser, but the fact
remained that Rovers were not very appealing. Even
though it pains me to do so, I can sympathize with
Liverpool fans after their defeat by Wimbledon in the
1988 Cup Final. Wimbledon were not the better team,
they were simply better on that particular day. Similarly,
Rovers were not the better team in 1989/90, they simply
acquired more points over forty-six games.

Quite how this was possible remains a mystery, but one
is entitled to hypothesize: It was glaringly obvious that all
other teams were envious of the fact that the City were
going to be one of the few teams ever to have played their
way out of the Third Division. Consequently, they raised
their game against the City but let the old boys' act get in
the way when playing against their fellow carthorses at
Twerton. In short, the City were robbed of the Third
Division championship by other teams' spite. Borne out

of nothing more than an immense distaste for Bristol Rovers FC, this theory will always make me feel better. And if I live to be 150, I shall never forget City's championship season of 1989/90.

During the games that I attended in the promotion season, my eyes rarely strayed from my loved ones and I spent an awful lot of time eagerly anticipating the thrill at the end or praying that it would never arrive, depending on whether the City were leading or not. Nowadays, irrespective of the score, I find my eyes wandering towards the advertising boards, stewards and other items of comparable interest during the ninety-minute session and I spend a lot of awful time eagerly anticipating carpet slippers and mugs of steaming beverage and fantasizing about the thrill of the viddyprinter. The City yielded to me in 1989/90 and now I've lost interest, let myself go a bit.

Mind you, so have they. Robbie's acuteness in front of goal was matched by the acuteness of a Plymouth Argyle talent scout, who paid a six-figure sum to lure him away. (I still have giggling fits, normally stoppable only with the help of a blood-thinning agent, when imagining a talent scout, commissioned to find a handy new forward, sitting in the Dolman Stand, jabbing a decisive finger at Robbie and declaring: 'That's the answer to our goal-drought!') Bob was deemed by Jimmy Lumsden to be sub-standard and was flogged to West Brom for £300,000. He then showed why nobody will ever employ Lumsden again, except perhaps as a sandbag, by scoring like an over-sexed rabbit on Clembuterol. Dave Smith decided to get opposing full-backs sent off at Plymouth, not with the City. Joe Jordan, smouldering, sinewy, shrewd, knew he could do no more and took off to Hearts under the guise of bettering his CV. The power, the speed, the brains and the jiggly thighs, all gone for under half a million.

After Jimmy 'Foresight' Lumsden had been sent packing, Denis Smith arrived, complete with reputation for having broken lots of his own bones and being as aesthetically pleasing to watch as Luton against Sheffield United without the goal posts. Having 'saved City from the drop' — always and inexplicably considered a praiseworthy feat among managers — he attempted to achieve promotion the following year by buying and not playing Jacki Dziekanowski and then filling the team with centre-halves who excel in getting booked or sent off for bloody stupid offences. And then Russell Osman, no-nonsense, international-calibre centre-half. International calibre of a dum-dum bullet, nonsensical enough to sell an Under-21 international centre-forward — some say the new Bob Taylor — when the City are not only in the black, but also in the relegation zone.

The City trundle on. They're nice enough, probably do right by their families, roll up their sleeves (when it's warm), go in where it hurts now and again and do nothing to make anyone temporarily forget about John Atyeo. They won't go up and they won't go down. They are neither dazzling nor atrocious. They are neither as beautiful as Bob Taylor, nor will they ever be mistaken for Eric Gates in a toffee-eating competition. I am neither happy nor sad, just certain that they will always be afloat, mainly because they seem to sell all their best players at a profit, albeit with incorrigibly bad timing. And I am none the less extremely fond of them, although only in the same way that certain stand-up comics are fond of their mother-in-law.

But I witnessed 1989/90 and that was enough for my three-score years and ten. And one day I will bribe my grandchild to put down his/her hand-held computer game, haul him/her screaming with boredom on to my knee and say: 'Robbie/Roberta, see this sweatband? Well, behind every sweatband there is a promotion story . . . '

Graham Brack

Où Sont les Neiges d'Antan?

SUNDERLAND AND
CHARLTON ATHLETIC 1962/3

I have become a less fastidious eater with the passing of the years, but I still recall the texture of my first Shredded Wheat with a *frisson* of horror. It was stringy and became lodged between my milk teeth, so that mouthfuls were separated by an undignified oral housekeeping procedure. I was trying to eat it because I wanted the pack-tops, and my mother refused to buy the boxes and throw the cereal away. A small number of pack-tops, conjoined with a postal order for 15s 11d and despatched to some magical wonderland, equalled an England replica football kit.

It was the summer of '62. I was nearly seven and football was the most important thing in my life. I played it in all weathers, against anyone who would turn up or – if necessary – against inanimate objects such as the coal bunker. Saturdays were too far apart for my liking, and the close season was unutterably long. This is not a view I currently hold.

I realized that in some place called Chile, England were taking part in the World Cup. I saw no television pictures, because the action took place after my bedtime. Once I got the hang of time zones I became accustomed to waking to fresh disappointments. Nations of whom I had never heard walked the world stage, and many of them looked capable of giving our brave lads a stuffing.

I cannot tell how I discovered that the Football League season was about to disrupt the school holidays, but on 18 August I bounded out of bed shortly after seven o'clock wishing away the next eight hours of my life, until the glorious moment when we stood on the raking slopes of the Valley to watch Charlton Athletic murder Swansea Town. I genuinely believed this (you must make allowances for my tender years).

Charlton were one of the great fifteen-minute teams. From the first whistle they ravaged the opposition like trainee Vikings gaining some work experience. If this rampage bore fruit in the form of a goal, they might scale the heights; I once saw them fillet Don Revie's Leeds on a day when Mike Bailey decided to walk on water. If, however, they had nothing to show for it all after quarter of an hour, they breathed a collective sigh and took to shambling around the pitch like prisoners in an exercise yard, oppressed by the pointlessness of it all. And pointless was how they often finished.

According to my match programme, carefully annotated in blue ballpoint, the 1962/3 season began as an exception. With barely two minutes gone, Charlton were two up. Two minutes from the end, it was still 2–0. They drew 2–2.

At the other end of the country, my first loves were in action at home to Middlesbrough. Sunderland had come third in Division Two the previous season, and I had high hopes that they could go at least one place better this time. They now had Brian Clough and George Herd, each of whom had dented the bank balance to good effect. Clough, direct, boisterous and determined; Herd, twinkling, deft and sly; but the greatest of them all was Charlie Hurley.

An encomium on Hurley could fill this book. Carved from the finest mahogany, gifted on the ground and supreme in the air, handsome enough to make girls think there might be something in football, and blessed with supreme intelligence, his presence could paralyze the opposition before he touched the ball.

When Sunderland won a corner, Hurley would commence his rumble towards the penalty area. If he felt like intimidating the opponents, he might stroll rather than jog. When he arrived, we could begin. Indicating with an upraised arm the point to which he wished the ball delivered, he bounced on the balls of both feet like a gymnast contemplating a vault, and the crowd chanted 'Charlie, Charlie!' in ecstasy. The demented defence looked first at Clough, then at Hurley, and wondered which required more attention. Some surrendered without a fight.

The ball came over, and all too often we groaned at its inadequacy; but once or twice a game we felt the electric thrill along our spines as it headed unerringly for the designated yard of air-space. With the leap of an athletic dolphin, a red and white striped blur surged into view. There would be an apocalyptic crack as ball met polished hardwood brow. Charlie would smile as the net bulged, wave to the crowd in acknowledgement, and trot sedately back to his place at the heart of Sunderland's defence.

I adored him.

A lot of the pre-season interest focused on two novelties. Ipswich Town had won the League Championship in a performance that was to earn Alf Ramsey the England manager's job just a few months later. Opinion differed on the likelihood that they could repeat the feat, and when Tottenham Hotspur clouted seven bells out of them in the Charity Shield match the hiss of incipient bubble-bursting became deafening. Having bought a copy of *Training for Soccer* with my Christmas money, an admittedly unusual purchase for a six-year-old, I could appreciate the Spurs' manager's crafty tactics. Ipswich's success had depended on a curious forward formation with a balding, gaunt former inside-left, Jimmy Leadbetter, playing on the left wing in a withdrawn position. Nicholson simply told the full-back to leave him to the wing-half, and Ipswich folded. Once the other clubs knew how it was done, they took turns to humiliate the champions, who struggled against relegation for most of the season.

The other source of anticipation was the arrival of Oxford United to fill the vacancy left by Accrington Stanley. I still recall the thrill of opening my *Playfair Football Annual* and reading the club details for the first time. They sported a stocky right-half with a receding hairline and a loud voice. He was called Ron Atkinson.

On Wednesday 22 August, 1962, Oxford recorded their first league victory, 2–1 over Lincoln City. That same evening Sunderland were sneaking a win over Charlton at Roker Park. In those days the first midweek fixtures (the second and fourth games of the season) were home and away matches between the same clubs, and by careful planning my father had arranged our holidays in Sunderland so that I was at the wrong end of the country for both, because on the Friday night we clambered into our Austin A40 and set off up the Great North Road to my grandparents' house.

It was there, at twenty to five on Saturday morning, that my grandfather broke the news to me that Sunderland had switched to white shorts so that they could be seen more easily under floodlights. Had anyone else told me, I should not have believed him; as it was, I dug out the *Playfair*, which failed to record this momentous change. That evening brought further profound disillusionment with the discovery that Sunderland had lost 1–0 at Leeds whilst Charlton had held Chelsea to a mere five goals at Stamford Bridge.

On Tuesday night I was ordered to bed, despite the fact that Sunderland were in action at the Valley, and I had to scour the Stop Press next morning to find the result, a 2–2 draw. With five points from four games, Sunderland were a little behind my schedule, which called for them to win at least thirty-eight games that season; Charlton, with two points, already had the look of footballing dodos. The best that one could hope for would be that two teams with even less ability would beat them into the relegation places, but this was doubtful.

At the weekend I was not allowed to watch Sunderland play Swansea; my protestations that, having seen them a fortnight before, I might be able to offer useful advice to the Sunderland players, were swept aside. It was the following Wednesday before I was taken to see my first Football League match at Roker Park, when my heroes entertained Rotherham United, a team with the distinction of being at the outer limit of my reading ability.

The kick-off was at a quarter past six, and around forty thousand people filled the ground. Both my grandfathers bought me a programme, so I read each carefully before concluding that there was no difference between them. Refusing to sit on the barrier, I stood beside my father near the corner-flag where the Fulwell End meets the main stand, a place which was to be my preferred spot for two decades. From this vantage point I was able to see almost nothing at all, and I am thus unable to give an account of the game other than to describe in detail the back of Lol Morgan, the Rotherham left-back, who was given a rough time by whichever Sunderland player it was who was running towards me at speed. However, I did not let a small thing like seeing no action spoil my enjoyment of the evening. The crucial point was that the lads won 2–0, and they were inching up the table.

The following Saturday there were two major events taking place. We were going home, and Sunderland were playing at Chelsea. My father was strangely reluctant to return a day early so we could go to Stamford Bridge, and since cars with radios were rarer than hen's teeth in those days, I passed Saturday afternoon agog with excitement, wondering if I could receive wireless broadcasts without a receiver if I concentrated very hard. I failed, and so did Sunderland, losers by a single goal. When Rotherham beat them in midweek, it was beginning to look like a mid-table year.

No such stability for Charlton. Fresh from a magnificent one–nil drubbing of Luton, they had been on the receiving end of the same scoreline at Southampton, and then found themselves hit for six by Stoke, for whom one Stanley Matthews was making a name for himself. Saturday was my seventh birthday, and I was taken to see Charlton surprisingly defeat Scunthorpe by the only goal. It requires an effort of will to recall that Scunthorpe had finished the previous season in fourth place and might have made it to the First Division with a little more luck. Since Sunderland were at home to Luton, I was fairly sanguine about their prospects and they duly obliged with a 3–1 win. I had found one of the two teams worse than Charlton who might save them from relegation.

The League Cup was limping into view over the horizon. Several top clubs were still giving it the cold shoulder, but nearly half the First Division were there. One of them, Leicester City, were drawn at home to Charlton, and were lucky to escape with a 4–4 draw. I was certain that this was a misprint for 4–0, and refused to believe otherwise until the replay, when Charlton won a famous victory by two goals to one. Meanwhile, Sunderland were giving Oldham Athletic a seven-goal hiding. I would have settled for seven goals every week; after all, if you score seven, you should win more than you lose. Unless you're Charlton Athletic, I suppose.

On 6 October, a second candidate for the relegation zone journeyed to the Valley. Walsall were going through a rough patch, and had given a tryout to a young goalkeeper called Alan Boswell. Charlton had injury problems, and gave a game to Brian Ord, who was one of the last Football League players to be conscripted into National Service. Ord had few opportunities to make his mark, and he was determined to take any that appeared, so when he received the ball just inside the Walsall half and saw Boswell a few yards in front of his line, he unleashed a half-volley that I still judge the hardest shot I have seen in my life. Boswell barely touched it with his fingertips and it grazed the top of the crossbar. Charlton went on to win 3–2, their third victory of the season. The very next week they made it four, crushing Norwich 4–1 at Carrow Road. Sunderland drew one–all at Newcastle, and one of my grandfathers started a delightful habit of posting me a copy of the local *Football Echo* and a match programme.

In my childhood, an essential part of Saturday evening was hurriedly finishing your tea when the six o'clock news came on the wireless, so that you could be outside the newsagent's shop at a quarter past six when the *Echo* van arrived with the *Football Special*. Despite those being the days of hand typesetting and manual illumination of the reports by monks, the paper was ready within ninety minutes of the final whistle, contained entirely fresh material and gave an adequate report of the second half. Now that we have so much technology in the printrooms, the paper takes fifteen minutes longer to print, although most of the inside pages are copied from earlier editions, and may have second-half reports consisting only of goalscorers. Why?

Since Sunderland's next matches were against Walsall and Norwich, I pencilled in the expected four points and concentrated on my own footballing career, in which I had just broken into the junior school second XI for a match against Midfield. My father and uncle came to watch for the only time in my life, we won 11–0 and I scored in the first half-minute. Forgive me, but I had to work that in somewhere. It may be the only printed reference to a goal I scored available to future historians. To cap a great day, I notched up another near the end with a thunderbolt that barely bounced twice before slithering into the net through a crowd of players. It was too late in the game to make the back page of the *Football Echo*.

Sadly, I was too optimistic. Walsall were indeed given the anticipated gubbing to the tune of 5–0, but Norwich beat the lads 4–2. In the League Cup, Sunderland held Portsmouth at Fratton Park and dumped them 2–1 in the replay. Charlton bowed out in the same round, beaten 3–2 by Leyton Orient, then a First Division club. (I know it defies belief, but it is true.)

The England team, or the valiant efforts of Tottenham Hotspur in the European Cup-Winners' Cup, were of the least importance to me.

December dawned, and I was disappointed to learn that a trip to Charlton v Middlesbrough was out of the question because we were paying a visit to my Uncle Jack's house in Essex. I had a particularly magnificent boil on the palm of my right hand that day, which provided some comfort in what was otherwise set fair to be a crushingly boring experience, but the day was transformed by my aunt's simple sentence after lunch.

'Right, off you go to the football, then.'

No wonder they were happily married for nearly fifty years.

'The football' turned out to be West Ham United v West Bromwich Albion, my first Division One game and my first look at Bobby Moore. I was surprised to find that the crowd was smaller than at Sunderland and I could see almost all the game, which ended 2–2. Personally, I was convinced that Sunderland could have given them a goal's start and beaten both in one afternoon; Charlton might have kept it to six, if they had been allowed fifteen men. My uncle never took me to West Ham again; on our next visit I was taken to see Romford play Kettering in the Southern League, and shortly after that he moved to Sutton Coldfield and future visits were to watch West Brom. It wasn't Sunderland, but it was the First Division, which in some way compensated for having to talk to my cousin who was A GIRL.

Christmas was nearly upon us, with all its great traditions; lots of presents, including *The Topical Times Football Annual* and the *FA Book for Boys*. Notwithstanding assiduous research, I have never seen a copy of any publication called 'The Topical Times'. I believe this may also have been the year when I first saw *White Christmas*, but trying to date so regular an occurrence is like attempting to catalogue all your cut knees. Strangely, though I was sent to Sunday School every week – a commandment that caused some friction when 'Star Soccer' began on Sunday afternoons – I do not remember being dispatched at Christmas, and it was some time before I discovered that churches opened for business on Christmas Day, a dénouement which caused me to reconsider an earlier inclination to train for the priesthood.

I woke on Boxing Day, full of anticipation at the thought of Charlton v Newcastle. Bounding to the french windows, I heaved open the curtains, and to my intense joy I saw our back garden coated liberally with fluffy white snow. Pausing only for a brief refuelling stop, now mercifully free of Shredded Wheat, I charged out with my ball for a game in novel conditions, and came in to be rewarded by my mother's admiring comments about the colour in my cheeks. As I remember, balaclava helmets were *de rigueur* in back garden footballing circles that winter, though the grey wool balaclava is a hopelessly impractical garment for sport. When leaping for a high ball the wool is likely to fall over the eyes, and there are few sensations as uncomfortable as having a soggy patch of saliva-impregnated wool rubbing against one's chin. I note that in a long career for Blackpool and England Jimmy Armfield never once took to the field in a balaclava, and if it was good enough for Armfield it was good enough for me.

After lunch I retired to my bedroom to gather together the impedimenta judged essential for an afternoon at the Valley; scarf, gloves, balaclava (dried out on the boiler top) and ballpoint pen. Imagine my surprise when I returned to the lounge to find my father sitting by the fire in his indoor clothes.

'I'm sorry, son,' he said. 'They can't play in this.'

Now, there was ample evidence that Charlton could not play in any conditions, but even my undeveloped brain detected the subtle distinction between the reasoned disparagement of ability stated in relative terms, and the categorical frustration of an otherwise adumbrated intention. Why couldn't they play? I'd demonstrated earlier that snow halfway up the shins was no impediment to a satisfactory game of football. I'd heard my grandfathers graphically describe splendid encounters of the past when

Sunderland had taken to the field in the teeth of North
Sea gales and temperatures beyond the normal experience
of Nanook of the North (reasoning that it might be
difficult for them but it would be a lot worse for the
bunch of southern pansies opposing them).

I passed a grim afternoon in front of the television
watching 'Grandstand', and I can still hear Frank Bough
warning us that the half-time score he was about to give was
not a mistake, before imparting the news that Oldham were
beating Southport 7–0. They settled for eleven in all.
However, the gloom descended as we heard first of Brian
Clough's awful knee injury at Roker Park, and then that
Bury had sneaked a 1–0 win. I think the extent of the injury
escaped me, for I was surprised when Clough was missing
for the return match three days later, which Bury won 3–0.

Still the snow fell. There had been twenty-four Football
League games played on Boxing Day, and it was to be 9
March before a full programme next took place. The third
round of the FA Cup was almost obliterated by the weather;
only three ties survived, including Sunderland's win at
Preston. This deserves a place in the chronicles of sport for
two reasons: it was the first occasion on which I was allowed
to watch Saturday night football on the television (if there is
anywhere nearer Heaven for a seven-year-old than sitting
with a mug of drinking chocolate long after bedtime
watching his favourites win 4–1, I have yet to hear of it), and
it marked the first televised pitch invasion.

When the cold snap prevented the scheduled league
matches on 12 January, Sunderland arranged the home leg
of their League Cup semi-final against Aston Villa for that
date, the first League Cup match to be played on a Saturday

afternoon. By twenty to five they must have wished they had not bothered; losing 3–1, they were unable to exact revenge at Villa Park and had to settle for a goalless draw.

You could list all the league games played in January on one page of this book. If you plot the postponed matches on a map, you are impelled to the conclusion that there was some pretty funny weather going on that month; in general, conditions were apparently worse at First Division grounds than they were at less exalted stadia a few miles away. In Scotland, Montrose's home games were almost unaffected, but their near neighbours Brechin must have welcomed the snow. Having not won since 12 September, they beat Queen's Park on 2 January and notched up a win at Montrose ten days later, subsequently failing to win again all season. Raith Rovers won only twice, and both victories were away matches played during the cold spell.

To general astonishment, the match referee declared the Valley playable on 9 February when Bury were the visitors. The surface was like polished glass, and many of the participants in the pantomime wore basketball boots, inspiring me to allow my mother to buy me a pair. There was no prospect of skill or craft deciding the game, so Charlton managed a comfortable draw. By this stage the newspapers had given up trying to compose meaningful league tables, but it was fairly clear that Charlton were up to their collective armpits in the smelly stuff at the wrong end of the table. Sunderland had not played a league game in 1963, but they were cracking on with the FA Cup, dealing handsomely with the might of Gravesend and Northfleet 5–2 in a replay after a gallant draw at

Gravesend. The non-leaguers borrowed a set of blue shirts from Charlton for the replay, and their performance was brought down to Charlton's level. Charlton's own Cup interest ended at this stage, beaten 0–3 by Chelsea.

The draws for successive rounds were beginning to resemble poorly compiled multiple-choice questions. Teams that were able to complete their ties might find they were obliged to wait a month to discover the identity of their next opponents, and the FA Cup Final was eventually delayed three weeks to 25 May. The FA was having a busy time; planning was under way for the 1966 World Cup, an event which led Dr Andrew Stephen to be photographed playing with a scale model of the new Hillsborough. This was considered the stadium of the future, though the only feature of it remaining in my memory was a weird cable-car suspended from a wire above the halfway line, in which the referee would sit, communicating his decisions by radio to all and sundry. I did not grasp what he would do when the play was directly under his box, nor how he would get up there in the first place. So far as I am aware, no such funicular exists at Hillsborough, but perhaps the builders are running behind schedule.

Alf Ramsey's reign as England manager began with a crunching defeat in Paris on a night when Ron Springett made sure that wherever matches were played in the 1966 World Cup, he would not be involved in them. It strikes me as odd that there was controversy then over the principle of the England manager selecting his team; Walter Winterbottom had only suggested an eleven to the FA International Committee, who might (and did) make alterations, whereas Ramsey insisted upon a free hand.

Looking at the current composition of the FA com-
mittees, I am heartily glad that Graham Taylor is not
obliged to consult them, or Bobby Charlton would still be
a regular choice for his country.

When my clubs resumed league action, it was a surprise
to discover how little difference the prolonged hiatus had
made. Sunderland were still winning and drawing,
whereas Charlton had totally failed to improve. They lost
to Norwich and Grimsby before creaming Plymouth 6–3,
avenging an earlier 6–1 defeat. Sunderland launched into
a sequence of eight undefeated games which incorporated
a draw with Newcastle and a 7–1 thrashing of Norwich.
Over Easter Sunderland suddenly tied up like a tiring
four-hundred-metre runner in the home straight, taking
just one point from Stoke and crashing to a defeat at
Cardiff. When they drew with Huddersfield and
Scunthorpe, they faced the prospect of a tight run-in
against an improving Chelsea. At least they had no cup
distractions; Third Division Coventry had skinned them
2–1 in the fifth round.

On the last day of April the action was thick, and so
was the Charlton defence. Having taken the lead at
Rotherham, they clung on grimly for victory. Since
Walsall were losing at Grimsby, this gave them a little
hope, but Luton's game on the next evening brought
them a win over Swansea. Sunderland scraped a draw at
Scunthorpe, but they had the assurance of knowing that if
they won their last four games, they were up.

On Saturday the foot of the table was turned upside down
again as Luton crashed at Leeds while Walsall won at
Rotherham. A relieved Sunderland trounced Southampton

4–0, and a delighted seven-year-old sat in his bedroom with his times tables out working through the permutations. Charlton, meanwhile, were one point behind the others, with a game in hand, but when they travelled to Scunthorpe in midweek and lost 2–0, the times tables were dragged out again. Even worse, Walsall sprang a surprise by winning at Newcastle. As a Sunderland supporter, I had no doubt that Newcastle had thrown the match just to annoy me. It was the kind of thing Novocastrians did.

Saturday frazzled the nerve-ends. Sunderland edged past Swansea by the odd goal in seven, while Charlton faced Luton away. Now that my brother was ten months old and able to stand if you propped him against something, I rested him against the settee and told him he was the Luton goalkeeper. Charlton won the lounge encounter by something over thirty to nil, but lost the real thing 4–1.

On Monday the victorious Luton side were shoved in front of Sunderland under telepathic orders to do nothing. To my great delight, they did just that, rolling over to the tune of 3–0. Sadly, Walsall thumped Norwich, and it was all back in the melting-pot.

We now come to the climax of the season. In Rotterdam, Spurs gave Atletico Madrid a roasting as they took the Cup Winners' Cup. On Saturday the sums were very simple. At the bottom, Luton had 29 points, and were playing their last game against Stoke, who needed a win to be sure of promotion. Charlton had 28 points with two games left, one of them at home to Southampton. Walsall had 31 points, with only the match the following Friday against Charlton to come. If Charlton lost either match, they were down.

At the top, Sunderland faced the only team who could catch them, Chelsea, at Roker Park. A draw would see them up. Chelsea picked a team of experienced cloggers and planned on scoring a breakaway goal. That is exactly what happened. To my horror, a wild corner-kick cannoned into the Sunderland net off the backside of Tommy Harmer, and Chelsea smuggled a win. The only way Sunderland could go up was if Chelsea failed to beat Portsmouth at home on Tuesday.

I have done some slick praying in my time, but Tuesday night involved two hours of alternating intercession and imprecation. In the event, Chelsea squeezed home 7–0, but it was touch and go for about six minutes. I had to admit that I had not really believed they would fail. Since Black Saturday I had been anticipating the inevitable, so it caused no great heartache. I had done the grieving earlier.

But what of Charlton? On Saturday we had given their game a miss so as to be near a wireless, so we did not see them beat Southampton. Luton's defeat at Stoke meant they were already down. It all hinged — as at the top — with a direct encounter between the two competing sides. Charlton were one point behind, so only a win would do, and the match was at Fellows Park.

I was bundled into bed at the usual time, just as the teams kicked off, and lay awake wondering how I could find out the score. It crossed my mind that there were always policemen at football matches, and if I dialled 999 it was possible that the policeman who answered might be able to tell me the result. Against that, if my father caught me I might die without ever knowing. I had given the telephone a wide berth since my mother had caught me making a call to Singapore at the age of three, and I was not certain that I cared to risk further punishment.

I must have fallen asleep, for the next thing I knew was my father's hand shaking my shoulder shortly after seven the next morning. He had a copy of the *Daily Mirror* in his hand, folded to reveal the inside back pages.

'Thought you'd like to see this,' he said. I focused my eyes gingerly. Small black fairies danced around before crystallizing into print. They spelled a magic message.

Walsall 1 Charlton 2.

Walsall had hit the post and had a shot cleared off the line, but had been unable to equalize. For once that season Charlton had played for more than fifteen minutes, albeit in a line along the edge of their penalty box.

It was Cup Final morning, and in the afternoon I watched Manchester United beat Leicester City 3–1. The game over, I jumped down from the settee, grabbed my ball, and opened the back door. The garden looked as inviting as ever. There was no Royal Box, nor a press gallery; no medals were on offer, nor international caps. The cricket season was in full swing, and my father had told me firmly that football had to stop for the summer months. But at a quarter to five on that May Saturday, there was still the thrill of the game, the joy of sprinting behind a ball, the exuberance of the guaranteed victory that comes of taking on an inanimate opponent such as a rain-barrel. I paused at the top of the steps, waited for the cheers of the crowd inside my head to build to their peak, then strode forth to glory.

And I never wore a balaclava on the pitch again.

Don Watson

Psycho Mike and the Phantom Ice Rink

LEEDS UNITED 1974/5

Arsenal v Leeds, Highbury,
Wednesday 24 February, 1993

We all know the force of thirty thousand voices roaring.
Precisely because of that, it's all the more awesome when
that power is suspended.

I couldn't fail to be moved at the sheer density of the
silence commanded by the announcement of Bobby
Moore's death, as if it formed a frame around the level of
noise we take for granted. But I was conscious that my
memories were different from the one that everyone
around me was holding in common at this moment.

In the silence you could hear it running through the
minds, even of those too young to have experienced it
first hand: The announcer's voice filtered through a
cheap loudspeaker. 'There's people on the pitch, they
think it's all over.' Hurst in dark and light grey. 'It is
now!'

I remember where I was distinctly. It was a housing

estate in the suburbs of Birmingham, where we were living at the time. I was six. It was what my mother would have described as a beautiful sunny day, the sort I usually liked to spend with the curtains drawn watching the television. But today I was outside.

It was almost as silent that night at Highbury, the whine of televisions from behind the windows as distant as the traffic on Finsbury Park Road. Then the boy next door rushed out with the news.

'So what?' I responded, eager to deflate him. 'Scotland will win it next time.'

Scotland v England, Graham Hanson's front room, Harrogate, North Yorkshire, May 1974

Being a Scot living in England, even, or perhaps especially, from an early age is being in a condition of exile. Most English people do not understand this, although they are generally appreciative of the 'outsider' nature of other immigrants – Afro-Caribbeans and Asians have visual demarkation on their side. Even the Irish get recognition because of the sea. But the English don't quite understand that Scotland is a different country with a different culture, sense of humour, history and pattern of voting. How many times have I heard people say that England is an island?

I even know an English girl, whose family have a croquet lawn in the grounds of the one-time crofter's cottage they own as a summer home, who thinks she is Scottish because she was born there and attended Edinburgh Ladies' College. I doubt whether a similarly colonial upbringing in India would have caused her to claim she was Indian.

Football casts exile into the sharp focus of a television screen. In later years I would make friends with another Anglo-Scot and we would make up the quorum of two, necessary to make a satellite of the terrace camaraderie. But, in '74, I was the away fan in hostile territory, watching the Home International clash with an English friend and his dad.

One of the basic facts of football often overlooked by the dull objectivity of commentators is that half the fun of your team scoring is taunting the opposition. Conversely, the worst thing about conceding a goal is that you have to put up with the same treatment. This is one thing in a football ground, it is possibly quite another in your own living room.

I know a Liverpool supporter whose way of celebrating a live televised goal in the presence of a friend with opposition sympathies is to shout, 'YeeeesFuck Off!' I didn't go that far, but I don't think Mr Hanson ever saw me in the same light again after that day. He and Graham hung their heads as Jordan and Lorimer combined with customary deadliness, their feelings of dejection hardly soothed by the figure bouncing up and down on the sofa and singing along with the Hampden faithful.

'And sent them homewards, TAE THINK AGAIN!'

Elland Road, 1972 onwards

Why Leeds United? There were reasons enough. I don't remember Bobby Collins, but I do remember Billy

Bremner, Eddie Gray and Peter Lorimer – the Heart, the Art and the Strike of the classic seventies team, shortly joined by David Harvey, one of the few Scottish goalkeepers not designated as dangerous to the supporter's health, welfare and general happiness; the skilfully adaptable Frankie Gray, and the terrible two-some – Gordon McQueen and Joe Jordan. If Billy Connolly had been a football player, he would have been one or possibly both of these dextrous hard cases. I can think of no higher compliment.

United played in the Scottish style, which was perhaps not surprising since the core of the Scotland team that went to Munich for the 1974 World Cup Finals was Leeds United. There were more Scots in that Leeds side, and fewer English players, than the current first-choice Rangers team. It was tough and competitive, yes, but rarely cynical, at least in the years I saw them. If the tackles occasionally went over the top it was as a result of short tempers and a furious will to win which transmitted to the terraces, not out of premeditated malice. It was also immensely skilful. Perhaps a year or so before there had been a dourer game plan, but there was a delicacy in Leeds' play, in the feinting runs of Eddie Gray, the flighted passes of Celtic soul brother Johnny Giles and the balance of Allan Clarke. Even Norman Hunter I remember as much for his faultless, and occasionally quite breathtaking, distribution, as for his crunching challenges.

As a city, Leeds was the apotheosis of the seventies, after all it was here that the outdoor scenes of *A Clockwork*

Orange, the film whose aesthetic defined the decade, were shot. The concrete stanchions and flyovers of the self-styled Motorway City of the seventies were breaking through the shell of the Victorian textile city like the skeleton of some grotesquely beautiful insect in a futuristic horror movie. It was the perfect setting for a soundtrack of the Sweet's 'Blockbuster' or Elton John's 'Saturday Night's Alright for Fighting', the myopic ironies of which were lost on the packs of Tetley Bittermen who mobbed the arcades as the clubs exhumed their contents.

Music still brings back memories, but the architecture that used to form the backdrop has changed. The Northern Soul stomp in the Gemini club, the Jazz Funk pyrotechnics at the Central, the ominous beat of Joy Division at the Fan Club, the self-conscious Weimar Tanz at the Warehouse, brittle Factory funk at the Up-Zone and the Electro Sleaze at the Phonographique are all dislocated sounds and spaces. But at Elland Road they still stamp out the same beats.

The atmosphere has changed at the home of Leeds United, mostly for the better. All the same, fragments of that (often quite literally) purple decade of the seventies linger on. It still amazes me that Chicory Tip's 'Son of My Father', a ditty otherwise relegated to a bargain basement of the mind inhabited by 'Top of the Pops' cover version LPs and their hot-panted sub-Pan's People cover girls, lives on in terrace chants.

Even now, when I hear 'Jamie, Jamie, Jamie Forrester,' I think of 'Allan, Allan, Allan, Allan Clarke,' and the days when the Kop would fragment and the cry of 'Celtic' would go up. To my great satisfaction, the reply of 'Rangers' was never as loud.

Then came the rival chants of 'Scotland', 'England'. There was a time, around the 1974 World Cup, when the 'Scotland' drowned out the 'England'. I felt at home at Elland Road.

From the first time I stood at the top of the stairs that led out to the Kop and looked up at the hands clapping in unison, my gasps, bays and howls joined with theirs. I merged with the noise.

Scotland v Yugoslavia, my living room, Friday 14 June, 1974

After the opener against Zaïre, the disappointing scoreline mitigated by the fact that it was Jordan and Lorimer who had once again provided the goals, and the agonizing failure to turn an unbelievable superiority over Brazil into goals (Billy stabbing wide from a matter of feet!), the Clydeside Clan, my mother's family, descended for the match against Yugoslavia.

My grandfather on my father's side, who was then still alive, had been a high-ranking civil servant. My Dad (the Prof) is a prominent scientist in his field (microbiology). I have often joked that he tends to have difficulty with things he can see with the naked eye. He did his parental duty by taking me to Elland Road, until I started making the solo trip towards the end of the Championship-winning season of '73/4. But he certainly never watched football with the intensity, and certainly not with the patriotism, that my uncles brought that afternoon. In fact it was not until much later that I discovered he had been a dedicated Stirling Albion supporter in his youth, which had probably been partly responsible for his resigned nature.

My maternal grandfather, whom I never met, had been a tug-boat captain on the Clyde. He was fully bilingual in Gaelic and English. My uncles spoke enough of the old language to be able to discuss people within their hearing on trains, sometimes with embarrassing results. I am often ashamed that I speak none. They all had a streak of the wide-boy, and by the seventies were beginning to reap the dividends of the opportunities of the sixties.

I don't remember whether the Prof was watching that day; if he was he was a silent presence as the rest of us abused the referee, who was a hapless defence against the Slav clogging, and raised the clarion calls for Scotland's charges. Within minutes we were on our feet. My Aunt Reena with her filed tombstone teeth and nicotine stains up to the elbow was raising her shrill above the men: 'C'mon, boyz! Ah wir away, wir away!' as Joe Jordan, the toothless wonder of a centre-forward Leeds had signed halfway through the previous season from the Greenock club Morton, rampaged through the centre of the Yugoslavian defence.

Of course it ended, as it always does for Scotland, in dignified disappointment; Jordan's equalizer immediately neutralized a late Yugoslavian breakaway goal but it was only enough to send Scotland out undefeated.

All the same, for all the dynastic New Year's dinners with three generations sitting around a table, that was the closest I felt to the Clydeside Clan.

Leeds v Luton, Elland Road, Saturday 7 September, 1974 – the Scapegoat

Towards the end of the '73/4 season, I started making the trip to Leeds in the company of Psycho Mike. Psycho Mike wasn't what you'd call a friend, in fact he wasn't even a friendly rival. He used to play in a Sunday football team for which he was the leading scorer. In turn, I was the top scorer for my local team. When we met on the pitch Psycho Mike was a proto-Vinnie Jones, trying to diminish my contribution by a series of on, off and over the ball challenges. But the friends I did have were either Manchester United fans, like Graham, or their interest in football didn't go beyond the token gesture. So Psycho Mike and I would call a truce and take the bus out to Elland Road, where I would study Eddie Gray's feinting runs and Peter Lorimer's shooting, and he would make notes on Joe Jordan's power in the penalty area and no doubt Norman Hunter's challenges, ready for our next soccer war.

We were an uneasy partnership. Much like Brian Clough and Leeds United, neither of us basically liked one another very much. A few years later, when I had exchanged the starry jumper and the Leeds scarf for a spiky haircut and a razor blade necklace, Psycho Mike ambushed me in the town's landscape gardens after an under-age drinking session. The bust-up between Leeds and Clough came sooner.

In the last year of Don Revie's leadership the season before, Leeds had taken the Championship, but the team, many of whom had played together since the late sixties, had reached its peak. Clough had taken over as it had begun to roll down the other side.

Appointing Clough as manager of Leeds United was like Adolf Hitler becoming leader of the Labour Party in 1945. Clough had been one of the team's most prominent critics, propagating the old image of United as the team of efficiency over flair, long after Giles, Cooper and Gray had proved their consummate artistry. I remember feeling physically sick when I heard the news. After all, how could this walking Mike Yarwood sketch take over from the statesmanlike Don?

Leeds had started the season by losing at Wembley to Liverpool in the Charity Shield Match, with Billy Bremner sent off for tussling with Kevin Keegan (both players were suspended for bringing the game into disrepute for stripping their shirts off as they left the field and then squaring up to one another again). Then it got worse. Of the first five matches we managed one scrappy one–nil win against Birmingham at home, one away draw and lost the rest.

What was this big-mouthed git doing to our team?

It was Psycho Mike's idea that we should get to the ground earlier than usual for the Luton game, to stake out a good position on the Geldard Road end for the match. It ended up being one of the poorest-attended games at Leeds for years, and we sat on the concrete steps of the Kop, as the drizzle came down, watching the meagre crowd take their places. By kick-off there were still gaping holes, showing the concrete bone through the flesh of the support.

Clough's big summer signing, Duncan McKenzie, had

been dropped, after missing an open goal in the 3–0 defeat at Stoke and it was left to Allan Clarke, who had scored two of the three goals we'd scraped so far, to slip Leeds into the lead. A damp celebration ensued. Then Luton equalized.

The discontent was almost tangible. Here was the team who had broken the record for an unbeaten run from the start of the season only a few months before. Now we couldn't manage to triumph over a team that everyone thought were a gag from an Eric Morecambe routine. Everyone knew who to blame, but a manager is not a visible figure. A crowd needs a focus for its ire and there was John McGovern. Who did he think he was to be wearing Bremner's shirt? As Billy was the symbol of the successful Leeds, McGovern became the image of our current failing.

The Leeds team under Clough was a heart-transplant patient whose chances of survival were rapidly diminishing.

I remember one point when, under pressure from a striker, McGovern put his foot on the ball and back-heeled, selling the challenger a dummy and clearing himself some space. A begrudging murmur of approval went up. But he'd misjudged, allowing the ball to go too far behind him, unaware of another forward coming up on his blind side. He was ignominiously dispossessed and the Kop were not inclined to be generous in their judgement. The fact that one of the old hands tidied up the mess that the new boy had made only emphasized that Cloughie's boys weren't up to wearing even that uniquely seventies LU logo that had been introduced the previous season.

For the rest of the game, particularly after an unthinkable equalizer, his increasingly nervous touches were greeted with gales of boos, sweeping down from the Geldard End with the drizzle. John McGovern was the transplanted organ, and the host was rejecting.

After the match, Psycho Mike and I hung around.

There wasn't much magic in the air that day, but all the same the ground seemed to deflate as the crowd filed out. There's a strange atmosphere about an empty football ground. Like a disused railway station or a deserted supermarket it seems to be a contradiction in terms. You can walk down and stand on the very edge of the pitch. Touching the grass with your foot is like reaching out to a mirror and finding your hand passing through the surface. Players come out of the tunnel, looking shiny, besuited and polished and walk right past you. It's a bit like sitting in an empty cinema and seeing the cast of the film clambering out from behind the screen. Surely players aren't real?

Then out came Cloughie to do a television interview, and we just stood there and watched. Then he finished, walked right over to us and said, 'All right there, lads?'

We looked around. Who, us? Well, there wasn't anyone else around. So we chatted for ten, maybe fifteen minutes. It seemed like hours. We told him what we thought was wrong with the team. He listened to what we had to say as if it mattered, and took the trouble to reply to us.

What struck me the most was that there was none of the pomposity you occasionally saw on TV.

'Don't listen to all that crap in the papers,' he reassured us about some worrying transfer rumours. 'And don't worry,' he said, at the end, 'it'll all come right.'

We recognized that he cared, and we believed him, implicitly.

'Cheerio then, lads,' he said, adding with a gleeful wink, 'Don't get too pissed over the weekend,' knowing that nothing flatters an adolescent more than being taken for an adult.

'They didn't do too well today, did they?' said the Prof when I got home, half smiling.

I didn't reply.

'I met Brian Clough,' I said instead and stomped upstairs to the sanctity of a Sensational Alex Harvey Band record, leaving him looking bemused.

Huddersfield v Leeds, League Cup 2nd Round, Leeds Road, Wednesday 11 September, 1974 – the Villain

Away games were generally supposed to be dangerous territory, quite rightly in a number of cases, and not the place for an unaccompanied fourteen-year-old. But an exception was made for the League Cup tie at Third Division Huddersfield. It was, after all, only a few miles further down the motorway from Leeds, and scarcely likely to be a hive of hooliganism.

There was an anticipation amongst the thousands who made the short trip. Clough's name was chanted with a certain defiance and Psycho Mike and I joined in with full voice. It was going to be all right.

The Third Division team were cast in the role of sacrificial lambs. Slaughtering them might not appease the gods, but it would certainly make us feel better.

We scented blood as we were awarded a penalty early in the first half. Lorimer calmly sent the keeper the wrong way and the delirium in the crowd was out of all proportion to the importance of the game.

Then for the first time I experienced the feeling of a celebration curdling, as realization swept through. There had been an infringement. The kick had to be retaken.

Lorimer lined up his shot again. The keeper dived the wrong way, but the ball struck his boot and bounced clear. Luck has always played a part in football, but in the history of Leeds United it has tried to hog the limelight. And it's nearly always been bad.

Clough's future was determined by the chance position of a goalkeeper's foot.

Then the unthinkable happened, and Gowling scored for Huddersfield. The sacrificial lambs had turned on us, teeth bared.

In the end, Lorimer's last-minute strike was a cloudburst of relief, which promised at least to diminish the taunts we would face on Thursday morning. But the result meant that Clough had guided Leeds to one win in seven matches (actually the same record as Revie had achieved when he took up the job). The premature drama was already reaching its conclusion.

Burnley v Leeds, Turf Moor, Saturday 14 September, 1974

'Hey, rock and roll,' sang the yellow, white and blue band at Turf Moor to the Showaddywaddy tune, 'Cloughie's on the dole.' Everyone seemed relieved, after all it had never rung true – Clough and Leeds Utd? Nah!

I didn't join in. 'I still think they found the man to replace Revie,' he was quoted as saying in the paper.

Fifteen years later when Howard Wilkinson arrived at Elland Road, the first thing he did was take down the pictorial reminders of the Revie years. That was what Clough had tried to do, and I still believe now that it would have worked. But it was all too soon. He tore the old heart off the sleeve of the lucky suit while it was still beating.

Burnley was my first unofficial away match. Officially I was at the Bradford Ice Rink. The sun shone, Peter Lorimer scored, and it seemed to the crowd like the bad times were over.

Then Fletcher of Burnley equalized. As if that wasn't enough, they were awarded a penalty on the hour and went ahead. A matter of minutes later, Gordon McQueen was sent off and although Ray Hankin went too, we all began to wonder whether the gods had been satisfied with just the one sacrifice. John McGovern began to look even more nervous.

*

**Leeds v FC Zurich, European Cup 1st Round, Elland
Road, Wednesday 18 September, 1974**

The mists started to fall, and the graveyard on the hill
above Elland Road began to take on its Gothic horror set
quality as Swiss champions FC Zurich lined up as Leeds'
first opponents in the European Cup.

Psycho Mike was giving the match a miss. I was there
with Weasel Garrett and his dad. Weasel Garrett was a
would-be bully who never quite had the strength of
personality to pull it off. He had given me a sour
reception when I first arrived at the school, but by the
time of the FC Zurich match we had struck a truce, so
much so that his dad mistook us for friends and paid the
50p for my entrance to the Geldard.

Later he was to compound his original sin by trying to
turn on me again, and urge others to do likewise. But he
made the mistake of breaking a collar bone, enforcing a
long absence from school. The day he came back, insults,
books and apple cores were flying through the air. The
classroom looked like a scene from *Poltergeist*, and in the
middle of it sat a crestfallen Weasel. I stood in the
doorway, looking proudly at my achievement. Football
teaches you a lot about life, and I had already learned
about the art of scapegoating.

But for tonight it was me and Weasel and Mr Garrett
and the great Leeds United revival. Terry Yorath was
playing number four instead of Bremner, who was still
serving out a seemingly endless suspension. Yorath had
suffered the boo-boy treatment from the terraces himself
in the past, and he was to do so again, but for now he was

rehabilitated simply because, if he wasn't Billy, he'd still
been the Don's signing and as far as the crowd were
concerned it was better the Dunce of the Don's Class than
Cloughie's Duffer.

By half-time Clarke had struck again, twice, and
Lorimer had proved his usual infallible self from the spot
kick. But the goal of the game was the fourth, and the
starring performance by another of the old stalwarts,
Terry Cooper, with a weaving run for the by-line leaving
a befuddled defence to watch his precision cross to Joe
Jordan's head and the sweet, silken ripple of the net under
floodlights.

The upstart and his sub-standard players had gone, it
was Yesterday once more. The unlikely name of Maurice
Lindley, Revie's assistant and the caretaker manager, rang
out from the Kop, with only a trace of doubt in the voices.

**Leeds v Arsenal, Elland Road, Saturday 5 October, 1974
– the Hero**

Despite a defeat away at Zurich we were through to the
next round of the European Cup, and the papers were full
of speculation. Who would manage Leeds United? Who
had been responsible for the Guildford pub bombings? If
you wanted to be unkind you could say that they found
someone who at least looked and sounded convincing for
all five vacant positions.

According to some of the accounts, Jimmy Armfield
never really managed Leeds United, he was just the
figurehead for a team that was running itself. But the fans
were eager for a talisman, and for a while it seemed that

this pipe-smoking Lancastrian had exercised his not inconsiderable charm on results. If he was the symbol of the return to order, it was, though, the legacy of Clough that was to bring about the totemic first victory.

Although football fans do not like change to come too quickly, they do desire a sense of dynamic. In order to maintain excitement, a football club must produce new heroes all the time. The importance of the new hero is cast into dramatic light when the club is troubled. Joe Jordan had emerged in the Championship season, but his entrance had been less spectacular because it was set against a background of continual success. In subsequent years much greater importance has been placed on the likes of Frank Worthington, who joined as the team was being pulled towards Division Two, Eric Cantona, who came as we were stuttering on the way to the Championship, and last season, Jamie Forrester, whose pace and conviction have given him the mascot status in a lacklustre post-Cantona side.

Duncan McKenzie made a second entrance to the United side as a substitute early in the first half. This time his impact created a thunder above the tea bars of the Geldard End.

It may not have exactly been his first touch, but he certainly hadn't been on the field long when the ball was played to him, just inside the penalty area, and with his back to goal. There were defenders around him, but his movements were so fast, it was one of those goals where you burst out laughing as your arms go up. Not that it was spectacular, exactly, you just didn't know that anyone could do that, flick the ball up, turn and place the shot so quickly that it was in the corner while you were still wondering what he was going to do.

By the end of the match the fans had burst into an early chorus of 'Noel, Noel' – 'Duncan, Duncan/Born is the King of Elland Road.' (It wasn't until I read Hunter Davies's *The Glory Game* that I realized they hadn't made it up on the spot.)

Cloughie goeth and, all too late, the Shaman cometh. I often wonder what would have happened if he had played (and played like that!) against Luton.

Leeds v Liverpool, Central League, Elland Road, Saturday 26 October, 1974

The following Saturday was Liverpool away, which involved another fictional visit to the ice rink. Although I wonder that my parents didn't guess that something was up when I had to rise at six-thirty in the morning to make the trip to Bradford.

The coach was due to depart at eight, but the bus that took me into town was late, and it was five minutes past by the time I rounded the corner to see Psycho Mike sitting on the bench, and the coach conspicuous by its absence.

'It was already gone when I got here,' claimed Psycho Mike. But I still have my doubts. Perhaps for some peculiar reason Psycho Mike, the apprentice delinquent, was afraid to make the trip on his own.

So instead we weighed up the alternatives. There was the ice rink (we really did go there during the off season). Or there was Elland Road and the reserves game.

It's the only time I have ever seen the second team play and it was an odd experience. The odd thing is that what you are seeing is a game of football, no more no less. A first team game is a spectacular (or less so) piece of drama, an interaction of opposing fans, players and officials, each with one another. In the reserves all that is missing.

Precisely because of that it is, apart from the obvious problem of under-motivation, a good forum to view a player's array of skills. And there was certainly one who stood out on that occasion. He was a midfielder capable of holding up the ball, switching the play, producing the unexpected and controlling the field. In short, he was potentially a perfect replacement for Billy Bremner. His name was John McGovern and within a month he was snapped up by the new manager of Nottingham Forest, Brian Clough.

Coventry v Leeds, Highfield Road, Saturday 9 November, 1974

Another early start for the ice rink.

Although the bus didn't leave until nine, I was there for eight-thirty, experiencing for the first time the slow awakening of thirty-odd sleepy fans, spirits rising as the motorway miles slipped past.

At the service stop we were ambling out of the shop. I was engaged in trying to get the wrapper off a Mars Bar while not spilling the can of Coke, when there was a sudden outbreak of panic. Adrenalin pulsed, the Coke can fell and fizzed its contents over the tiled floor, the Mars Bar fell underfoot.

A Sheffield United coach had pulled into the same service station, and as if it was a matter of routine they piled off the coach and made straight for us. A few of the hard cases exchanged a couple of punches and to my great amusement Psycho Mike got a kick in the leg, but we were outnumbered, so we ended up barricaded inside the shop as the Blades fans celebrated outside. 'Leeds fans stink, Leeds fans smell, Leeds fans run like fuckin' hell, na na nah, na na nah, na na nah-nah, na nah-nah, nah nah.'

So the shop assistants, who were not keen at being locked in the shop with a bunch of hooligans, were trying to chuck us out, and the Sheffield fans were making faces at us through the window. The whole thing seemed hilariously funny. It never really dawned on me that these twisted faces on the other side of the glass were for real, that they wanted to cause me injury and it was only a reinforced plate glass window that was stopping them.

Finally the police arrived and we were escorted back on to the coach, the sleepy hum transformed into a buzz.

The match was what we are still at the time of writing waiting for this season, the first away win. A debut goal from O'Hare (his last before he too went to rejoin Clough at Forest), an own goal and, gloriously, another one from Bremner. Billy was back and we were on our way.

'Did you hear the Leeds score?' the Prof asked me when I got in late that night. He had this funny little smirk about his face, and I thought, 'He knows.' But I said I hadn't. 'Oh,' he said, smirking again, 'they won,' and I smirked too, trying to make it look like a pleased reaction.

*

Carlisle v Leeds, Brunton Park, Saturday 23 November, 1974

The ice rink was in Carlisle this week.

As Leeds had made their stumbling start to the season, the lowly Cumbrians had briefly held the leadership of the First Division after three consecutive wins. But by the middle of November they had begun the inevitable slide back towards the Second Division.

The tiny ground was, almost literally, heaving with Leeds fans, who had taken over one whole side, the length of the pitch. It was one of those times when the crowd's density gave it a life of its own from the moment the teams marched out. It was a constant struggle to keep on your feet, as a ripple ran through the packed bodies and you had to find a space of concrete big enough for a size-five shoe.

The sequence of scores was perfect. The mass weighted down in the first half as the home supporters erupted into the chaos of celebration, followed by the jolts of anger and then determination. Determination that the eleven yellow figures on the pitch would not dare to incur our collective wrath by letting us down like this. The discontented mumbling at half-time and the feeling of an altogether unjust conspiracy of misery. Then the aggressive bray as the teams came out for the second half, followed by the resolve that, by making our presence felt, we could alter the course that events were taking. And slowly our force taking hold as we willed Joe Jordan around the keeper, and those moments as the open goal seemed to expand in time and space, then sweeping down four, five, six steps, the ground falling away from dangling feet as you are sustained by the crowd, gradually slipping down to the ground as the noise subsides. The feeling that our extra sense was connecting with the players on the pitch. The ball falling free to McKenzie in the penalty area and the inevitability of his strike past a wrong-footed keeper. This time the celebration has the opposite effect and a space of a full three-yard radius opens around you. For the first time, you can see the ground and without the surrounding body heat, you remember the air is cool. And the final whistle following so fast you don't have to even think about worrying about an equalizer. Then the crush for the exit sweeping you off your feet again.

Outside the ground Psycho Mike was determined to steal a Carlisle scarf as a souvenir and had his eye out for a suitably soft target, not accompanied by a hard dad. I was plodding along in a happy daze when I realized we had gone past the entrance to the coach park. Psycho Mike turned around as I shouted, then a look of alarm came over his face and he bolted past me. It seemed a bit melodramatic; after all, the post-match traffic was still thick and it was unlikely the coach would be going far, even if they hadn't noticed we were missing.

Then I saw them. A group of Carlisle supporters across the road had spotted us. We were adrift from the rest of the Leeds fans and still decked in scarves. Again that adrenalin rush, but this time it was a real jolt, transforming the movements around me into a juddering sequence of freeze frames.

Fifteen years later I was driving through Carlisle with

my wife when I took a wrong turning. With a pulse of recognition, I realized I was back on the same street. It was narrower than I had remembered, and it seemed all the more difficult to believe that I had managed to run so fast that I'd sped past the main pack before they'd had time to cross.

One of them at the back jumped out in front of me and stood with his legs spread and arms out ready to catch me. As if he were a goalkeeper I gave my McKenzie shuffle and slipped by as he lost balance. He half recovered as I went past but his grasping hand missed the scarf that was trailing in my wake.

Psycho Mike had a ten-yard start on me, with two chasing him. I outran the second and the first was too busy chasing Psycho Mike to realize that I was behind him. Within arm's reach, he made a grab, but Psycho Mike found a last desperate burst of speed and evaded the outstretched fingers. The pursuer lost his footing and spun round. Seeing me he made another lunge, but he had come to a halt and I was still travelling at full tilt.

We arrived back at the coach out of breath, gasping out our stories to anyone who would listen.

At the time it was an all-round great day out. Looking back, it all seems like a disaster that miraculously didn't happen.

*

Leicester v Leeds, BBC News,
my grandmother's house, Loch Lomondside, Scotland,
Saturday 28 December, 1974

I had my ticket booked on the coach for the Leicester match, but I wasn't there.

Graham, Colin and I were just on our way out of the school door, to pick up the bottle of Clan Dew (whisky and wine) we had stashed at Graham's house to celebrate the end of term. The headmaster's secretary stopped us.

The Prof was waiting in the headmaster's office. His father was dying, and we were to start for Scotland straight away.

We got there about seven o'clock on the Friday night. My grandfather had died an hour before we arrived. The next day I watched the goals of our two–nil away win on the television news in my grandmother's house. The celebrations of Psycho Mike and all the others from the Harrogate coach who would be there had an inappropriate ring in this house, which was strangely empty and silent, despite the number of people who were walking and talking softly in its dark wood rooms.

Derby v Leeds, the Baseball Ground, FA Cup 5th Round,
Tuesday 18 February, 1975

That Cup Saturday it was pissing it down. We were all sitting on the coach and ready when the driver came across with the news that the match was off. It would be replayed on Tuesday.

My ice skating prowess was now reaching a crucial

stage. If I was to master fully the complex triple twist, I would need to go into mid-week training.

One of the casualties of the new backpass law, apart from Leeds' defensive record and Lee Chapman's ability to stay onside, is the sort of goal by which Leeds progressed into the next round of the Cup. The ball is played across the goal in an innocuous sort of way, and the defender (in this case David Nish), facing his own goal without a forward in sight, plays the ball back at about chest height to the place he last saw the keeper. But the keeper has come across, expecting the ball to be played towards the outside of the back post, and it just sails on into the net. Cue riotous disbelief from about 10,000 Leeds fans.

For some weeks Psycho Mike and I had had our eye on the flag on the top of the dome of Harrogate Spa Building. It would look just fine with LUFC embroidered on it, draped across the back window of the coach. Arriving back from Derby we decided that tonight was the night.

A Restoration building with a façade that concealed an Escher-like pattern of courtyard roofs, it proved a more challenging climb than we had anticipated. In fact at one point I lost my grip as we clung to the apex of a slated, steep slope and found myself clinging to a guttering, some hundred or so feet from the cobbled ground. Fortunately I managed to scramble my way back up, treating it like the same sort of adventure as the escape from the mob at Carlisle. Looking back I break into a cold sweat at the thought of both of them.

It took us nearly an hour to get up there and about

another half an hour to get down. Once we did, Psycho Mike rolled the flag up and wound it round his body, then put his jacket (a conveniently baggy black Harrington) over the top. We hadn't realized from the ground just how big our prize was. Once it was concealed in this way, Psycho Mike looked like Alan Foggon.

As he toddled across the road, I spotted a police car across the way, parked outside the town hall. Since our route home took us past that way there was nothing to do but, as they say in Glasgow, brass neck it out.

So we walked straight past. The patrol car engine started up. We carried on walking. Perhaps it was heading off in the other direction. But no, we could hear the sound of the engine coming closer. Then the sound we really didn't want, of a gear being shifted downwards as it cruised to a halt beside us.

I was walking on the roadside, so I heard what the constable said clearly, although he was talking to Psycho Mike, who was slightly in front.

'You're out late, son.'

Psycho Mike, it turned out later, had thought he said: 'You're putting on weight, son.'

Fortunately he didn't come back with anything like, 'Too many Creme Eggs,' which might have aroused suspicion, relying instead on the old standby: 'Eh?'

'You're out late.'

'We've been to a football match, Derby away,' I contributed, producing a scarf and praying they weren't Man U fans.

'Oh yeah, what was the score?'

'One–nil.'

I still don't know if that was a test or a genuine enquiry, but whichever, they drove away quite happy.

Leeds v Anderlecht, Elland Road, Wednesday 5 March, 1975

For the European Cup Quarter-final against Anderlecht it wasn't so much a case of the mists of spring as the last fog of winter. From the Geldard End you could occasionally see the centre circle drift into view, only to disappear again.

Since Leeds were kicking away from us we had only the sound of the crowd from the South Stand as a clue to what was happening. Never have I seen anything quite so bizarre as 18,000 people saying 'Shhh' and cocking an ear every time the ball entered the opponents' half. It was like listening to a game on the radio, without the commentary to interpret the sounds of the crowd.

But there was no mistaking the roar that started in the South Stand and travelled around the ground, rippling the length of the West Stand and eventually reaching the Geldard. Leeds had scored, we knew that much but no more.

'South Stand, South Stand, who scored the goal?' came the question.

'Joe, Joe, Joe Jordan,' came the reply.

Within a few minutes the fog had become distinctly denser, we could now see little further than the edge of our own 18-yard line and the players were pulled off the pitch. For nearly twenty minutes there was nothing to do but speculate. Would we lose the goal if the game was called off? The consensus was that we would, so it was some relief when slowly it seemed to be clearing. Finally the South Stand came into view. We waved as if it was the *Titanic* coming in to dock.

We could just make out the second goal, from McQueen's header, but in the second half, attacks came towards us out of nothing. Finally Lorimer fired in a loose ball right in front of us, and we were on the way to the semi-finals.

'United Lift England's Pride,' was the headline in the paper the next day, which no doubt disgusted Messrs Stewart, Gray (F.), Bremner, McQueen, Lorimer, Jordan, Giles and Gray (E.) as much as it did me, particularly the three Scots who had scored the goals.

Leeds v Barcelona, European Cup Semi-Final, 1st Leg, Elland Road, Sunday 9 March, 1975

The FA Cup-shaped Grail had been extinguished at quarter-final stage, after two replays with Ipswich. The League had slipped away by spring, but there was still the European Cup.

I expect it will be a long time before Leeds will feature in it again, but I'm glad they have revived the semi-final stage of the European Cup, the single most important match that a club can host at their own ground. A UEFA Final doesn't even come close.

The combination of fanatical support and a low roof make Elland Road the noisiest venue in England, but that night the decibel level went into hyper-drive. There was still an hour to go before the kick-off when the buzz began to break out into song. By the time the players walked out on to the pitch, the noise seemed to be an entity in itself, like the sound of the blood rushing through some gigantic organism.

Then within five minutes the beast held its breath. The ball was played clear through to Cruyff, and we stood behind Dave Stewart watching the greatest footballer in the world bearing down on him. We could just see it, the elegant shuffle, the body-swerve, the sweep around the keeper and the dreadful inevitability of the unguarded net. All of the fourteen goals United had scored in the competition to date flashed before our eyes. But it didn't happen. Gordon McQueen appeared from nowhere and neatly took the ball off Cruyff's toe, stopped, balanced and played the ball back into attack. Scotland 1 Holland 0.

The opening goal was Bremner's career telescoped into a matter of moments, as Jordan nodded the ball down to him in the penalty area. Expectation held the ball in the air. The beast held its breath once more. Billy's strike was exuberance itself, the sort of triumphant shot that's hammered in twice as hard as necessary, simply for celebratory emphasis.

The beast roared, catching the scent of victory.

The strike from which Barcelona claimed their equalizer was a rare glimpse in that match of the continental striking power we had expected from them, but the free kick from which it was scored was one of those surreal pieces of European refereeing. Bremner's early strike had banished the nerves, but now they were creeping back, in their sickening familiarity.

The beast was wounded.

Yet doubt never really entered into it, we just had that feeling that season that the European Cup was ours, and being all square with one of the best teams in the world, and having conceded an away goal bothered us, yes, but there was still more anticipation than resignation.

The second goal was right in front of me. Jordan, rising high above the defence, someone missed their shot, and it was Clarke it fell to. There was one thing about Clarke, you could criticize his languid ambling, and I did, frequently and loudly (in fact I was once threatened by one of our own fans for doing so). But in a situation like that you trusted him.

The beast had risen, even before the ball touched the net.

Barcelona v Leeds, European Cup Semi-Final, Second Leg, BBC Radio 2, Monday 24 March, 1975

I know the quiet confidence that Barcelona fans felt that spring of '75. I felt it myself after Leeds' creditable 2–1 defeat at Ibrox.

On our part there was certainly trepidation, as Leeds travelled to the Nou Camp Stadium, but despite the slender margin of our lead, there was an underlying confidence that we were destined for the European Cup Final.

There was no full commentary on the radio that night, so for the first half we were reliant on score flashes. And the only one came scarcely more than five minutes after the kick-off. Lorimer had scored from the inevitable

Jordan knockdown. The Scots were on the rampage again!

The second half was a trial of endurance as the late night radio reception howled and squawked, the quality of the commentary voice varying between poor loud-speaker and walkie-talkie in a blizzard, and the Nou Camp beast produced noises that were heart-stoppingly close to the victory roar.

When they did score the commentator was drowned out altogether. Then in a fateful moment Gordon McQueen was sent off. At the time I didn't think of the ramifications of losing our centre-half for the Final, I was just trying to keep in mind the mental picture of the stadium conjured from the commentator's words and extend my will-power towards protecting the area behind David Stewart.

As the final whistle went, the team fell to the Barcelona turf in triumphant exhaustion, and I slumped in similar fashion on my bedroom carpet.

The next day the *Evening Post* ran a feature on the backroom staff at Elland Road. Tomorrow, they promised, the Fans. The next day I scanned the paper eagerly, but, perhaps ominously, the feature never came.

Leeds v Ipswich, Elland Road, Saturday 19 April, 1975

Leeds still currently run a Premier Card system for away matches. Beginning as an FA restriction on travelling Leeds fans, it was kept on by the club voluntarily, a move which is less than popular with the fans. 'Just another way of getting their hands on our money,' they grumble at the ten-pound charge for the membership card which entitles us to buy tickets for away matches.

Personally I never grumble about the Premier Card, because as a way of allotting tickets for popular games it seems like a fairer way than the betrayal we suffered in '75. There were 8000 tickets allotted to Leeds for the European Cup Final in Paris. For a team known to take that many supporters to routine away League games it was a catastrophe waiting to happen.

Most of the tickets went straight to season ticket holders. Nowadays, when season tickets are sold for all areas of the ground, that might be fair enough; after all, the season ticket holders are the financial bedrock of the club. But then a season ticket holder was someone who turned up to the West Stand when it wasn't raining, clapped each goal politely, drank their flask of coffee at half time and left ten minutes from the end, no matter how finely poised the score, to avoid the traffic jams on the way home. When the club talked about 'home advantage' and the intimidating atmosphere posed for teams in away legs, they weren't talking about the West Stand, they were talking about the fans that stood on the Geldard End, admittance to which in those days was by paying your 75p at the turnstile only.

At the last home match of the season, after the awful truth of the ticket arrangements had been announced, there was precious little baiting of the away supporters, there weren't many of them to bait. Instead the Geldard pointed accusing fingers at the West Stand. 'We are the true supporters,' they sang.

The chant of 'If you're all off to Paris clap your

hands' continued, as it had done throughout the season. But I probably wasn't the only one who knew that my clap was just for show. My summer job in a Harrogate hotel was never going to finance a trip to Paris and a ticket from a tout.

All the same, the match was a celebratory affair. They went one up in the first half, but Trevor Cherry equalized and then Carl Harris, the Welsh Under-21 International playing his first team debut, scored the winner (the omen of a hope for the future), avenging the FA Cup defeat earlier in the season.

Psycho Mike and I walked back into Leeds in the sunshine. The rows of terraced houses that lined the road back to the city centre were being knocked down. Next season we would travel to the ground on an inner-city mini motorway. The rag and bone ponies that used to graze on the sparse grass at the roadside would be confined to a traffic island. Times were visibly changing. Looking back, this match, above all the others, seemed like the bubble of an innocent idyll.

Leeds v Bayern Munich, BBC Television, my living room, Wednesday 28 May, 1975

One of our recreations when we weren't at football matches was stealing deposit bottles from the back of off-licences and hotels, and taking them back elsewhere for the deposits. The week before the European Cup Final we made off with a particularly good haul and converted the proceeds to wine, which we knocked back quickly in the sunshine. Too quickly as it turned out. With only a

Curly Wurly in my stomach to soak up the alcohol, I was soon virtually too drunk to walk. In my hapless attempts to get home, I tripped and broke my nose on the rim of a kerbstone.

I was still nursing a hangover by the night of the match, three days later.

It wasn't exactly the atmosphere in which to be watching a final. But I was feeling too fragile to make the trip out to Psycho Mike's (some miles away) to watch it. My mum had acceded rights to the colour television in the living room only under protest. When the Clydeside Clan had been down, she had done her best to join in with the spirit of things. 'Is that good or bad?' she would ask every now and then. But since it was just me, she just sat vaguely disapprovingly as I ooh'ed and ahhh'ed the various near but not really that near misses of the first half, and abused the referee when Beckenbauer tripped Clarke in the area.

But even that didn't prepare her for the second half. There had been nothing much to celebrate in the Scotland match; Jordan's goal, by the time it came, was a consolation, so she had never seen anyone jump out of an armchair, punch the air with both fists and shout 'YEEEEEEEESSSS!!!!!' which was what I did on the hour mark.

Madeley had headed the ball across the area, it had bobbled about a bit, and fallen to Lorimer, and Lorimer had done what he normally did, caught it full on the volley and sent it swerving past Maier. 'YEEEEEEEESSSSS!!!!' It was a moment in which everything, the whole season, had

come right, it had all led up to this. There was just the
formality of the last half-hour to be played out before
Bremner would be presented with the European Cup.
Even the Prof, who had been watching quietly, with a
faint curiosity, looked pleased for me.

And then it all went wrong. 'The German players are
protesting, now what's he given.'

Even now I find it hard to be objective about that
moment. For years I was convinced, from replays and all
the more so from studying the photographs of the event,
that as the defence had played out one player had nudged
into Bremner, another into Hunter, in a deliberate
attempt to push them into an offside position. It seemed
to me one of the great injustices of the game that Leeds
were banned from Europe for the riot the fans went on
that night, while Bayern had been allowed to take the
Cup despite blatant cheating on the pitch.

Now I'm not so sure. On video at least it still looks as if
Bremner was pushed, although it seems possible that it
was as a result of the usual penalty area scuffle for the
ball. But this is still a game in which a player can dive in
the penalty area, and the FA can fine the other team's
manager for protesting about it.

Anyway, it got worse. Whatever happened, the Leeds
players were clearly unsettled, and Bayern broke away to
score. Even at that point, I thought we could get it back.
Then Frank Gray was stripped down the right, Müller
slipped in front of Madeley, who was lacking attention or
fitness, or just the energy that the younger McQueen
might have had, and slipped the ball past Stewart. That
was two. It was over.

'Yesss!' saluted the Prof. I still don't know why he did this. Perhaps he thought it was a good goal. Perhaps the secret resentment of a Stirling Albion supporter just bubbled to the surface. But it seemed like the final indignity.

As the Leeds fans tore up the seats and threw them at Beckenbauer as he and his team-mates paraded the cup, I had to quell the urge to pelt the Prof with cushions.

I felt disgusted and betrayed. All the injustices of being a Leeds fan came to the fore, Lorimer's own disallowed equalizer in the dying moments of the '67 FA Cup Semi-Final against Chelsea, Jeff Astle's ridiculous goal which denied us the Championship in 1971, and now this. I wanted to be in Paris, so that I could go and smash things with the rest of them.

Rationally of course I know you can't defend the behaviour of the Leeds fans that night, but so little of the media made any attempt to understand what had happened, dealing instead with descriptions of 'bloodlusting bullies' seeking to 'crucify the name of sport' and '*les animaux Anglais*'. Quite apart from what happened on the pitch, there was the issue of the tickets.

Before the match there were sympathetic stories of the fans who were taking their life's savings off to Paris in the hope of securing a ticket. Afterwards there was no recognition that being forced to make that sort of investment in a game contributed to their volatility.

One paper even gave sympathetic airing to a ticket tout who had been reduced to the unthinkable measure of selling tickets for their face value. 'I'm too scared to take them [the tickets] out of my pocket,' he whinged. 'Several of us have been beaten up and had tickets taken.'

Well my heart pumps custard for them. Here you have a bunch of petty extortionists out to take a week's wages from the loyal fans who should have had the right to purchase the tickets legitimately in the first place. Like the man says, to live outside the law you must be prepared to risk a punch on the nose.

And so it was over. The television went back to its standard programming as if nothing had happened.

We won nothing that season. But looking back I remember the dramatic swings of '74/5 more vividly than the invincibility of '73/4. Even now in 1993, as we hand over the title to the last team in the land that we would wish to succeed us, when the Leeds fans chant for the last few times, 'We are the Champions', and use the audacious counterpoint of 'Champions of Europe', there is the echo, a tribute to the team who were the moral European Champions of '75, just as Holland were the moral World Champions of 1974.

As a season it was an epic, with the first drama building to a conclusion before September was out. What more could we have asked for?

I still wouldn't have said no to a happy ending.

Giles Smith

In Off the Post

CHELSEA 1973/4

You can search long and hard for a word to describe the
kind of season Chelsea had in 1973/4, but nothing serves quite so well as 'crap'. They got off to their worst
start since the war. They got off to one of their worst
middles, too, picking up just two points in the whole of
December. And their end wasn't up to much either. By
contriving to scrape a couple of dodgy 0–0 draws late
on, the team crawled to seventeenth place, five points off
relegation. There had been unfathomable humiliations
away to Leicester and at home to Ipswich. They had
gone out of the League Cup in the second round and the
FA Cup in the third. Their two biggest stars had walked
out halfway through, the manager was rumoured almost
hourly to be poised for the sack and the ground looked
like war-torn Poland because building work on the new
East Stand was running a year behind schedule – not
bad for a project which was only meant to take ten
months in the first place. The *Chelsea Football Book*,
the annual club publication and normally a source of
unflagging optimism and relentless propaganda, referred

to it as 'the season that lasted for years'. It was that
crap.

But from where I was sitting, things didn't look bad at
all. In fact, I had a great season, the season of my life. I
played a blinder from start to finish. I was Mr 100 per
cent. I look back now at the programmes, removing them
gingerly from my official Chelsea Football Club programme binder – a piece of folded cardboard clad in
white leather-look sticky-back plastic, with a stiff paper
pocket gummed to the inside. The spine is blue and
stamped with duff gold lettering, in the manner of
Reader's Digest condensed books. It says 'Chelsea
Football Club – Official Programmes' and there's a
picture of the club's lion insignia. And below that, where
it says 'Season', I have positioned the printed paper
sticker (supplied) – '1973/4'. You've never seen anything
so cheap in your life – though of course it was hideously
expensive, setting me back 50p in times when you could
buy a complete club strip for £2.70.

Still, because of the binder, these programmes are in
pristine condition, even now. Not a page that's been
creased, not an ear that's been dogged. No fingerprints,
no smudges, no coffee or meat pie stains, all the way from
Sheffield United on Saturday 1 September (lost 1–2) to
Stoke City on Saturday 27 April (lost 0–1). The covers
are still a convincingly bright blue and white, and they're
all here, every first team home fixture – twenty-one league
games, one FA Cup match (our pathetic Cup form played
into my hands there) and two testimonials. Yes,
testimonials! I was in deep. I was committed. I raise these
pages to my nose, but none of the original print odour

remains to spin me back in the approved Proustian
manner. After all this time, they smell faintly of dust and
cardboard box. But the words and pictures are enough.
They bring the whole thing back. And to think I wasn't at
a single one of these games.

In 1973 I was eleven, and where I was sitting was in
fact Colchester, in Essex. I had never been to Stamford
Bridge in my life. Actually, I had never seen Chelsea play
anywhere at all. London was just an hour away on the
train – unless you had parents as strict as mine, in which
case it was an hour and several years. My father used
British Rail to get to work every day, so he knew what
football fans were like. He'd stepped into enough charred
carriages, recently vacated by Manchester United
supporters, to realize that a) there was no way he was
letting me go near this kind of action and b) there was no
way he was risking his own safety by taking me near it.
(Actually, he didn't need much dissuading: with the
exception of the night he came home and proudly
announced he'd said hello to Sir Alf Ramsey on Ipswich
station, my father never expressed a second's interest in
football.) But I wasn't going to let a small matter like the
impossibility of my ever watching the team prevent me
from getting involved. Chelsea and I kept in touch. In
1973/4, we wrote to each other constantly.

I should say the content of my letter barely varied.
'Dear Sir/Madam,' it began. 'Please send one copy of the
following home programme.' Then would come the name
of the opponent, the date and even – with a precision
which was, on reflection, worryingly neurotic – the time
of kick-off. 'I enclose a postal order for 5p and a stamped

addressed envelope.' Then I would sign off with the mildly previous but clearly essential, 'Thanking you in advance, Yours faithfully.' (I'd checked with my father on that crucial faithfully/sincerely distinction because, after all, this was Chelsea I was writing to: etiquette was important.) I must have written this letter twenty times that season. As correspondences go, it wasn't exactly Flaubert to George Sand. But I bet George Sand was never as excited to hear from Flaubert as I was to get a letter from Chelsea.

To be accurate, our correspondence pre-dated the '73/4 season. I had first written to Chelsea during 1971/2, my second full season as a Chelsea fan. Like many of my generation, I had latched on to the team because my period of kicking a ball around a playground and looking for things to have in common with (and hold against) my peers had coincided exactly with Chelsea's period of glory – their 1970 FA Cup win over Leeds and their 1971 European Cup Winners' Cup triumph over Real Madrid. And of course, like everybody else, I was duped. Since then, we've had twenty years of trophy-free despair, excluding periodic Second Division Championships and the occasional lucky streak in no-hoper tournaments named after office equipment. Even so, I still stand by the principle on which I chose my team. I know people who support the teams of the towns in which they grew up. I know people who support Colchester United for this reason (there could hardly be any other). It has always baffled me that one could base this essential life-decision on something as random as the circumstances of one's birth. My method – though destined to backfire horribly

— was at least rigorously scientific. The Chelsea of the early 1970s, the Chelsea of Peter Osgood, Charlie Cooke, Alan Hudson and Peter Bonetti, was magnetically successful.

The first time I sent a letter to Chelsea, it was addressed to Peter Bonetti. Looking back, it was recklessly forward of me to assume I could write directly to the Chelsea goalkeeper without going through a secretary or an assistant, or even through the manager, Dave Sexton. But having acquired, at Christmas 1971, a pair of Bonetti-endorsed goalkeeping gloves — thin and green with a velvet finish — I felt we were already to some extent acquainted. In the light of subsequent events, it strikes me as richly significant that I was forced to say postally what ordinary fans, who could hang around outside the dressing room after games, said in person. 'Dear Peter Bonetti,' I wrote. 'Can I have your autograph, please? I enclose a stamped addressed envelope.' The letter ended, 'Thanking you in advance, Yours sincerely.'

I had figured I should send him something to sign, in case he didn't have a piece of paper handy wherever he was when he opened the letter. (And where exactly was he going to open it? At home, with a sackful of others? On the team coach? In the dressing room before a game? I wondered about this a lot.) I went back to the red folder containing my nascent collection of Chelsea cuttings — arranged chronologically where possible and consisting largely of neat clippings from *Shoot!*, with a sizeable number of match reports from my father's *Times* and my aunt's *Sunday Express*, plus some archive material, retrieved without permission from my elder brother's collection of old *Goal!* magazines. Given that the success of my Bonetti autograph quest was by no means guaranteed, I was naturally reluctant to risk any of my colour material. I settled eventually for a black and white image taken from *Shoot!*. It was about three inches tall and two inches wide and showed 'the Cat' jumping at a striking angle to palm away the ball. Judging by the completely static attitude of the crowd visible behind the goal, the picture had been taken during a pre-match kick-about. It also had a drawing-pin hole in the centre at the top, bearing witness to a period of exposure on the pinboard in my bedroom. (I operated a rotating display policy, rather like the Tate, in which pictures would go on loan to the board for a fortnight before being returned to the main collection in the red folder.) If it all went wrong, the picture would be a loss, but not a desperate one. I put it in the envelope with the letter.

I reckoned on a long wait before I would hear back from Peter, recognizing even in my naïvety that he probably had more pressing things to do than turn his attention immediately to signing tiny, pin-holed pictures of himself warming up. In fact, clearly he didn't, because the stamped addressed envelope came back to me, if not by return of post, then within five days, and inside was the picture, signed 'Peter Bonetti' in biro across the ground beneath his feet. As I writhed with delight on the hall carpet, a great truth came home to me: you could write to Chelsea and Chelsea wrote back.

I pasted the Bonetti picture in an autograph book, which only otherwise contained the signatures of friends and members of my family. My cherishing this item, my

returning to it repeatedly for several years, seems normal
enough in the circumstances; my treasuring the envelope
in which it had arrived — an envelope on which, you will
realize, I had written the address myself — looks a touch
more desperate. But this was contact with a world which,
though it clearly existed, might as well have been Narnia
as far as I was concerned. I was tantalized by anything
which had passed that way.

Writing off for match programmes seemed the obvious
next step. Thanks to my Uncle Frank, I already owned
two Chelsea programmes. Uncle Frank had been, until
the 1970/71 season, a linesman and referee. Even before
my Chelsea obsession caught fire, I was impressed by a
photo on Frank's sitting room wall showing him at some
sort of dinner-dance with Bobby Moore. (I don't think
he'd gone to the dinner-dance with Bobby Moore. I
suspect he went with my aunt. But clearly Bobby Moore
represented the rarer photo opportunity.) Frank had
obviously at some point passed on a pile of old football
programmes to one of my brothers, who had in turn
passed them on to a cardboard box in the attic. When I
raided this, during some idle weekend or other, I uncov-
ered a programme for the Chelsea home League game
against West Bromwich Albion on 30 January 1971 —
'Linesman (Red Flag): Mr E. F. Merchant (Colchester)' —
and one for the 1967 FA Cup Final between Chelsea and
Spurs, which my uncle must have attended in an unofficial capacity. I was faint with excitement. These were
the very objects that people who had actually been to
games guarded jealously, tokens of an experience to shore
up against the passing of time. And for me — who carried

them down from the attic and made them my own – they became an almost unbearably vivid reminder of occasions with which I had had absolutely nothing to do.

'Dear Sir/Madam,' I now wrote. 'Please send one copy of the following home programme. Versus Manchester United, Wednesday 18 August 1971, kick-off 7.30 p.m. I enclose a postal order for 5p and a stamped addressed envelope.' We were by now nearing the spring of 1972, but for my first tentative mail-order programme purchase, I had elected to go back to the beginning of the season and the first home fixture. I say tentative, but I had already conceived some breathtaking scheme to work forwards from there, acquiring each of the back numbers, catching up with myself towards the end of April, and seeing the season out as the jubilant owner of an unbroken home collection. In the event, funds restricted me to a handful (Crystal Palace, Stoke City, Jeunesse Hautcharage of Luxembourg in the Cup Winners' Cup First Round, Second Leg), the incompleteness of which was a source of nervy frustration at the time. What is it about small boys and completion? I could say I was displaying a precocious interest in the aesthetics of wholeness, but the truth is I was just being preposterously anal. Small boys are pushed that way by the makers of bubble gum cards, by the designers of petrol station promotions, by Stanley Gibbons and countless others who encourage us to 'collect the set' and are never made to answer for the psychological implications of what they do.

Needless to say, though, that Manchester United programme was a gripper. I was lucky to be getting involved at a time when clubs were beginning to exploit the publicity possibilities of programmes, turning out miniature magazines rather than the old-style programmes, which were basically nothing grander than a team sheet, a lucky number and an advert for the local Tandoori. The ugly, but not entirely euphemistic phrase 'Matchday Magazine' would not appear on the front of a Chelsea programme until 1976/7, but even in 1971 Chelsea programmes were twenty pocket-sized pages long and entirely without advertising. On page three of the Manchester United one our chairman Brian Mears offered a few words of welcome to the season, making sure to thank 'everybody connected with the club for their valued contribution', an address which seemed to me thrillingly personal and immediate, even though it had been published some seven months previously and not directed at me at all.

In the 1972/3 season, I wrote to Chelsea eleven times asking for programmes (an advance on my '71/2 performance, but still only really a warm-up for my devastating '73/4 form). My twelfth didn't come through the post, though. It came direct from *someone who had actually been to the game.* More than that, it came from *someone who had actually been to the game who was related to me.* One of my brothers was at a teacher-training college in London. At home for a weekend, he casually mentioned to me that the next Tuesday night he and a couple of friends were going to watch Chelsea at home to Wolves, 'just for a laugh'. I knew then the bitterness of the cuckold. It struck me as tragic that my brother was about to fulfil what for me would have been a lifetime's ambition, but what for him was merely the obligation to occupy an evening. Still, he said he'd bring me back a programme.

To be frank, I was rather anxious about this. During the last year or so, the absolutely flawless condition of my programmes had become paramount. I wanted nothing creased or damaged and, while I was waiting for them to arrive in the post, I would endure sustained anxiety attacks at the thought of any GPO-inflicted violence. What if the postman took it into his head to crease the package down the middle, or leave it wedged in the letter box, its contents irretrievably scored? (Luckily, our front door had a capacious and easy horizontal flap: if we'd had one of those small, upright tin-trap models, I would probably have gone through the entire first half of the 1970s without sleep.) For people who go to games, the wear and tear on a programme can tell a heartwarming narrative. Much as people grow attached to the scratches on their records, which indicate a history of use, so a programme virtually papier-mâchéd by rain or wrecked in a shocking turnstile incident might bring back all kinds of memories about the game. But obviously all of that had absolutely no relevance to me at this time. I wanted my programmes undistressed, properly characterless.

Strangely this respect for the programme as a physical entity persisted for some time after I had begun going to games (at Colchester United first, and then much later at Chelsea). It became something of a mission to make it back home with the programme still box-fresh, unscathed by the weather or the terrace crush or the return journey. I remember a Colchester match against Peterborough at which a small fight broke out and the crowd I was part of shifted uneasily to the side, and, in that moment, I experienced fear: but what I feared for most was the safety of my programme. I have to say, I became stunningly skilful at protecting my interest. I still possess the programme from the Colchester v Ipswich pre-season friendly, dated 10 August 1976. It is a cumbersome, single sheet of only slightly stiffened paper. And it is utterly without blemish.

So I was nervous when I went to my brother's bedroom on his next weekend at home, and he dug down into his bag for the programme — Tuesday 6 March, Wolverhampton Wanderers, kick-off 7.45 p.m. But I had to hand it to him — he'd got the thing out of there in mint condition. As my heart expanded, I examined the cover — sharp-edged, clean cut, no foxing or stippling, no distress marks around the staples. Perfect. And then I opened it. On page three, beneath the team lists, my brother had written in black ink the score (Chelsea 0 Wolves 2) and the scorers (Dougan, Richards). I was astounded. You don't *write* in programmes. And to think this person was going to become a teacher.

There are no ink stains on my '73/4 set. I was in complete control. I knew this was going to be my season and I rapidly devised a routine to smooth the path to victory. On Saturday mornings on home match days, I would cycle to the post office and buy the necessary postal order and stamps. If there had been an evening game in the intervening fortnight, I would double up. This way, my order would be on Sir/Madam's desk first thing on Monday morning. I could probably have taken out a subscription and spared myself the effort, but I doubt I would have been able to find the lump sum. As it was, my programme habit would eat deep into my resources, forcing me to supplement my income by washing an aunt's car on a fortnightly basis, even when it wasn't dirty, and, when the weather allowed, hoisting a Flymo over my godmother's handkerchief-sized lawn for an inflated fee.

We kicked off against Sheffield United. Of course, I have no detailed idea of what this game was like. But I do know the programme contained an extraordinary picture of Ian Hutchinson going up for a high ball in the previous weekend's game at Derby, and that chairman Brian Mears devoted a page to asking us for our continued patience with respect to the building work on the East Stand. Take as long as you like, I wanted to say. Against Birmingham City, the programme ran a double-page squad picture – twenty players, and only one of them (Peter Houseman) with a plausible haircut. And David Webb answered '20 Chelsea Questions', revealing that he lived in a detached bungalow in Chigwell and that his business interests included a dress shop and a mini market. It may seem far-fetched to say such details were magically detaining, but it was the case. Later in the season, I devoted hours to thinking about John Hollins – his dachshunds, Sweep and Jack, and his peculiar Sunday lunch habit: 'Yorkshire pudding and gravy first, then the roast beef and veg.' But in the absence of any actual football, what else was there for me to attach myself to?

Against Coventry, Alan Hudson said he'd be spending this year's holiday in Cornwall, and Peter Bonetti was shown 'having the game of his life' against Liverpool at

Anfield. There he was, springing to catch a Kevin Keegan penalty, pushing out a Steve Heighway cross, smacking away an Emlyn Hughes volley. And against Wolves, Bonetti was saving another penalty against Coventry, Chelsea were thumping four goals past Birmingham and Steve Kember was remarking, 'If I ruled the world – I'd bring back hanging.' Nice hearing from you, Steve.

At home to Ipswich there were fabulous rain-drenched pictures from QPR and the Club Shop was advertising 'a new range of Stainless Steel souvenirs'. (I wasn't tempted.) Peter Houseman's Testimonial was played against Fulham, and against Leicester City Ron 'Chopper' Harris maintained that his biggest anxiety was 'getting injured', which was pretty rich coming from him. Versus Leeds, John Hollins was shown actually splitting the net with a penalty at home to Leicester, and against West Ham on Boxing Day, that squad photo was back again, but this time in colour and marked 'Season's Greetings'. It was the most touching Christmas card I had ever received.

At home to Liverpool, I was able to observe the building progress on the new East Stand (embarrassingly slow). But then, this was the year of the three-day week – that desperate government ploy to conserve energy in the face of mining and travel strikes – and it hit football, as well as football stands. Chelsea's home fixture against Burnley took place on a Wednesday afternoon, to comply with power regulations. Of course, the only significant repercussion from my point of view was an enforced reduction in the number of programme pages. A note in the QPR programme on 5 January apologized for the meagre sixteen-page offering. 'We hope to resume a 20-page issue as soon as conditions allow.' But conditions never allowed again for the rest of the season.

By now, things were extremely recessionary on the pitch, too. Or so I read. For the away game at Sheffield United on New Year's Day, Dave Sexton attempted to reverse the team's decline by the bizarre tactic of dropping Bonetti, Osgood, Hudson and Baldwin, and in effect signed the death warrant for the Chelsea we once knew. Both Osgood and Hudson protested by refusing to train with the first team. The club suspended them and put them both on the transfer list. I read with alarm the soggy, cliché-strewn announcement in the Derby County programme: 'There comes a time in everyone's life – at work, within families, in sport – when there is a clash of personalities, and it is evident that for some time such a situation has existed at Stamford Bridge between the manager and one or two players.' Hudson went to Stoke, Osgood to Southampton. I carried on buying the programmes. But I can't pretend my confidence wasn't dented.

We did at least welcome back Charlie Cooke, re-signed from Crystal Palace, in the Manchester City programme on 9 February. But my faith wasn't fully restored until Eddie McCreadie's Testimonial against Manchester United at the season's end. I had to pay 10p for this, the final piece in the jigsaw, but it was worth that alone for the page entitled 'Eddie McCreadie – Poet.' 'For several years Eddie has written poetry for his personal enjoyment and not for other eyes. We asked him whether he might like any of his poems published in his Testimonial Match programme, and he decided he would like to share the following with Chelsea Supporters tonight.' And below were five short poems from the Chelsea and Scotland full back, the last of which — 'It Might Be Cold Tomorrow' — seemed an eerily appropriate note for my season to end on:

> I've never felt so happy
> And yet sad,
> I love you today,
> It might be cold tomorrow.

Now that I live in London, I can go regularly to Chelsea's home games. I get to a few aways, too. I always buy a programme and can still experience an irritating sense of inconclusiveness on the rare occasions when they're sold out or unavailable. And though I no longer store them in an Official Programme Binder, there is something about my reluctance to throw them away and my tendency to leave them mock-casually in prominent places — on the chair in the bathroom where visitors might notice them, or on my desk at work — which suggests they still serve as some sort of psychologically suspect talisman for me. In fact, I have sometimes wondered whether my entire purpose in going to games wasn't simply to acquire a programme to keep afterwards.

But these days, in the words of the poet Eddie McCreadie, 'I tread the cold ice of reality' ('Winter Thoughts'). I go to games with my friend, Ben. We were introduced two seasons ago by someone who knew that we both went miserably alone to Chelsea games and who thought we might enjoy pairing up and going miserably together. Which we do. But Ben and Chelsea really go back. He grew up in London, just across the river from the ground, and he was present at the games that I could only fantasize about and appreciate postally. He has a glorious store of first-hand experiences of which I can only be in awe. He was there on the day Wolves fans built a bonfire on the away terracing. He once went to a game wearing seven Chelsea scarves and came away with none. He was involved in a pitch invasion at the conclusion of a Second Division match against Hull City and was actually knocked to the Stamford Bridge turf by a fleeing member of the victorious Chelsea side.

But that says it all about me and Chelsea in those early days. Some of us were going shoulder-to-shoulder with Graham Wilkins just outside the centre circle: some of us were at home, filling out postal orders.

NOTES ON THE CONTRIBUTORS

Graham Brack is a pharmacist, married with two children, who lives in Cornwall – one of the few counties with no professional football team. He was born in Sunderland and considers that adequate reason to support them, though he draws the line at going to home matches. His ambition is to become a full-time writer, but he is wisely keeping the day job for now.

Roddy Doyle was born in Dublin in 1958. His first novel, *The Commitments*, was published to great acclaim in 1987 and made into a successful film by Alan Parker. *The Snapper*, published in 1990, has also been made into a film by Stephen Frears. *The Van* was shortlisted for the Booker Prize in 1991 and his fourth novel, *Paddy Clarke Ha Ha Ha*, won the 1993 Booker Prize.

Nick Hornby writes regularly for the *Sunday Times* and the *Independent on Sunday*. He is the author of the bestselling *Fever Pitch*, which won the 1992 William Hill Sports Book of the Year Award. For health reasons he has had to destroy the lucky olive that won two cups for Arsenal in 1993.

Ed Horton is twenty-nine. When not obsessed by football he tries to play chess and bring about the overthrow of capitalism, with limited success. His heroes include Dino Zoff and Abbie Hoffman.

Steve James (Matt Nation) was born in 1967 in Bristol. Has worked as a teacher and translator in Hamburg since 1990. Has followed Bristol City since 1972. Emigrated shortly after promotion in 1990, after having realized that the City had gone as far as it is possible for them to go.

Harry Pearson is unemployed and lives alone. When not watching football he fills his time by reading medical textbooks and polishing his collection of artificial limbs. Neighbours describe him as 'A quiet man who keeps himself to himself.' His book about football in the North East, *The Far Corner*, will be published in the autumn.

Chris Pierson now watches football in the West of Scotland and teaches political theory at the University of Stirling. Despite the failure of his political team to snatch even an honourable draw over the last twenty years, he (just about) refuses to be downcast.

Huw Richards is thirty-four, works as a journalist on the *Times Higher Education Supplement* and at weekends writes about Rugby Union for the *Independent on Sunday*. A former inmate of Oxford and Cardiff universities, he reinforces the affinity for success shown by lifelong support of Swansea City by also supporting Welsh rugby, Glamorgan cricket and the Labour Party.

Harry Ritchie was born in Kirkcaldy in 1958. He has written two books, *Success Stories* and *Here We Go: A Summer on the Costa del Sol*, and is the literary editor of the *Sunday Times*. It is his fervent wish that Raith Rovers will revert to wearing a white strip with two blue hoops.

Giles Smith comes from Colchester in Essex. He now lives in London and works at the *Independent*. His season ticket at Chelsea for 1994/5 is in the West Stand, Row 5, Seat 146.

After scoring forty-three goals for the 14th Norwich Cubs XI in their 1970/71 season, **D. J. Taylor** retired from the game at the age of ten. His subsequent strikes include the novel *Real Life* (1992) and *After the War: The Novel and England Since 1945* (1993).

Don Watson was on the staff of the *NME* during the eighties and was the last writer included in the *Penguin Book of Rock & Roll Writing*. He has published one novel. His book about the USA '94 World Cup, *Dancing in the Streets*, will be published by Gollancz in the autumn. He is married to the writer Carole Morin.

Olly Wicken is thirty-one. He read Classics at Cambridge and is Managing Director of a successful market research company. He also owns a pair of Graham Taylor's old boxer shorts. Olly is worried that this says it all, really.

MY FAVOURITE YEAR

was published in association with

When Saturday Comes

The Half Decent Football Magazine

When Saturday Comes is a monthly football magazine that aims to provide a platform for the opinions of intelligent fans, and supporters of Liverpool and Arsenal. We cover a wide range of topics that fans are likely to talk about, from terrace racism to international match fixing scandals, from Ron Atkinson's weird commentaries to the latest trend in team kits.

Six of the contributors to this book, Harry Pearson, Ed Horton, Olly Wicken, Matt Nation, Huw Richards and Graham Brack also write regularly for *When Saturday Comes*.

When Satuday Comes should be available in all half decent newsagents and a one year subscription costs £14 UK, £19 Europe and £24 anywhere else in the world. Please make cheques/PO's payable to *When Saturday Comes* and send to *When Saturday Comes* Subscriptions, 4th Floor, 2 Pear Tree Court, London EC1R 0DS